Degrees for a
New Generation

Degrees for a
New Generation
Making the Melbourne Model

Mary Emison

MELBOURNE
UNIVERSITY
PRESS

MELBOURNE UNIVERSITY PRESS
An imprint of Melbourne University Publishing Limited
11–15 Argyle Place South, Carlton, Victoria 3053, Australia
mup-info@unimelb.edu.au
www.mup.com.au

First published 2013
Text © Mary Emison, 2013
Design and typography © Melbourne University Publishing Limited, 2013

Edited by Ann Standish
Typeset by J&M Typesetting
Cover images: (top) courtesy Fairfax/Craig Abraham; (bottom) courtesy University of Melbourne/Casamento Photography
Printed in Australia by McPherson's Printing Group

National Library of Australia Cataloguing-in-Publication entry:

Emison, Mary, author.
Degrees for a new generation: making the Melbourne model/Mary Emison.

9780522862386 (paperback)
9780522864274 (ebook)

Includes index.

University of Melbourne—Curricula.
Universities and colleges—Curricula—Victoria—Melbourne.
Curriculum planning—Victoria—Melbourne.
Education—Curricula—Victoria—Melbourne.

378.199

Foreword

Universities function within multiple, and not necessarily congruent, contexts: their own history and missions; national political and funding regimes; dynamic, even unpredictable, international developments. Across the world, however, universities that aim to be centres of academic excellence are confronting a range of similar challenges and opportunities. One of the most pressing is curriculum change, as universities increasingly need to respond to shifting expectations of employers and students and to dramatic movements in access to knowledge and its dissemination.

Curriculum change has usually happened by accretion and review; it is far more challenging when general and sweeping. Across the globe, universities are re-examining curriculum structures in the light of changing perceptions of twenty-first-century needs and challenges from other national education systems. They have found that the stakes are high if shared objectives in refreshing the curriculum spill over into internal curriculum 'wars' or if understandable professional conservatism undermines the necessary shifts in university culture.

Across its first 150 years, the University of Melbourne had developed about one hundred undergraduate programs, many of them double degrees, and many hundreds of postgraduate 'professional development' programs alongside research higher degrees. Programs involving professional accreditation were, following the British model, mostly at undergraduate level. The challenge a new vice-chancellor, Glyn Davis, brought to the University in 2005 was whether such an academic structure was the best way to fulfil its stated aim of being one of the finest universities in the world. The exemplary consultation process he oversaw in 2005 was pivotal to the achievements that followed. My task of chairing the subsequent Curriculum Commission in 2006, then overseeing the planning and implementation of its recommendations in 2007 to 2009, was underpinned by the broad support for change to academic structures secured during those consultations in 2005.

This book details the University's response to the challenge of curriculum renewal. Mary Emison is the ideal author, having been closely associated with every step of the process and having had, since her retirement, the opportunity to reflect on what was achieved – and what was not. Her deep knowledge of higher education policies and practices – nationally as well as within the University – made her an invaluable colleague during years of change. So too was my project officer Gioconda di Lorenzo, whose meticulous documentation, courtesy and commitment was integral to the confidence colleagues across the University came to feel in the objectives and process of change.

The magnitude of the change was vast: the undergraduate program was consolidated into six 'new generation' degrees, and professional programs – both for accreditation and career development – shifted to graduate level. All of them needed radical internal rethinking about content and delivery. Research higher degree programs were to be enriched by embedded options of specialist seminars and skills development. The 'Melbourne Model', as it was soon dubbed in the media, required a radical change in the focus of course advising, since the graduate school model could only work if undergraduate course advisers were careful to outline all options: that, for example, a Bachelor of Science student had options ranging from a PhD or a graduate medical degree to law, teaching and engineering.

These curriculum changes were sweeping and ultimately were to require or enable change in every other dimension of the University's life, from space planning and student services to marketing and planning. They could not have been achieved without some of the steps highlighted in this book: the Commonwealth's flexibility on the transfer of HECS places to graduate programs; pivotal internal moments when particular deans provided persuasive leadership for their colleagues in trying circumstances; and the University Council's substantial underwriting of the costs through a 'Growing Esteem Transition Fund'. The latter enabled faculties to support the sweeping curriculum review and redrafting under the leadership of the chairs of course standing committees, who demonstrated remarkable leadership. The establishment of the fund was only one of numerous occasions when the bold thinking of Senior Vice-Principal Ian Marshman proved crucially important.

The emphases of the model were on discipline depth in undergraduate courses but with adequate breadth through electives, and with multiple options built in for as long as possible for pathways to future study and career choices. The wider goals of the Growing Esteem strategy were to be met through an emphasis on research encounters and community engagement. Graduate schools were to offer state-of-the-art professional programs in distinctive, attractive physical spaces. Research students were to have enriched possibilities for broader academic and career development.

Other necessary changes were less obvious at the outset, but no less important. The development of graduate schools, with a goal of offering a distinctive student experience, generated debate and rich outcomes where once postgraduate coursework programs had been the poor relation in terms of curriculum structure and the wider student experience. A corollary was that exciting options were generated for teaching and learning spaces, led by Peter Jamieson, our adviser on space design. If the University was now to offer 'new generation' degrees and real graduate schools, what would twenty-first-century classrooms, social areas and study spaces look like? What new spaces should the library provide? The answers are everywhere to be seen across the University.

Other major elements of the model were resolved in unforeseen ways, and not always to the satisfaction of their proponents. The sharp reduction in undergraduate options – generating the principle that these were now 'university' rather than 'faculty' courses – led to a highly useful but short-lived Board of Undergraduate Studies. Ultimately, faculties argued successfully that they should retain 'ownership' of courses in the interests of securing the requisite 'buy-in' of staff. The same argument held against the proposition that, as it was more important than ever that students experienced 'seamless' and consistent advice and policies, there should be only a few, large student centres. Instead, faculties have developed their own centres, characterised though they are by a far greater consistency than before in student-related policies and procedures.

Mary Emison's detailed, insightful account of the making of the Melbourne Model highlights the processes and achievements; to her credit, she also reflects on lessons to be learnt from mistakes made in terms of some over-elaborate structures and shortcomings in internal communication. The changes were vast and required attention to external communities of alumni, prospective students and employers. The changes were also controversial and generated public debate, not always favourable or well informed. In the end, however, the most important lesson of this extraordinary story is the importance of creating a whole-of-university approach to fundamental change. From the consultative beginnings led by the Vice-Chancellor to the assiduous work of course planning and implementation, those who take the greatest credit are the thousands of academic and professional staff who made generous commitments of time, energy and reflection to ensuring that radical change in their university would also ensure, in the words of the University's motto, that it would earn the esteem of future generations.

Peter McPhee AM
Professorial Fellow
University of Melbourne

Contents

Introduction

Transforming Academic Structures in the University of Melbourne

What triggers change in a large, long-established university? How are reforms decided upon and how are they put in place? How does transformation happen and how is it managed? Often, it is the appointment of a new vice-chancellor that heralds a revised or new direction for a university, within the context of its existing objectives. In the selection process, the body responsible for appointing a new vice-chancellor – the university council – will have identified the directions in which applicants may wish to lead the university. It is most likely that the successful candidate will favour directions that are consistent with the overall objectives and profile of the institution, in learning and teaching, research and interaction with the community – even if they differ in style and appearance. This is the situation that prevailed when Glyn Davis was appointed Vice-Chancellor of the University of Melbourne.

In July of 2005, Professor Davis' first year as Vice-Chancellor, he released a discussion paper to the University community, which set out the strategic options available to the University for the next three to five years. In the paper, Davis argued that higher education was changing; that all universities now had to contend with diminishing government funding, the expanded relevance of international rankings and increasing global competition. As one of Australia's leading universities, Melbourne was in a strong and sound position, but it could not ignore events at the national and international levels. The proposals put forward in the discussion paper were discussed, debated and refined throughout the rest of 2005, through a number of committees and working groups. The end product was the Growing Esteem strategy, a plan that encompassed objectives and directions for learning and teaching, research, and knowledge transfer (later referred to as 'engagement').[1] University Council approved the Growing Esteem strategy in December 2005. The plan set out objectives for the three major areas, with further review and development to be undertaken by a series of taskforces. In recognition of the close interconnectedness of these main activities of learning and teaching, research and community engagement (or knowledge transfer), they were referred to in the strategy as a 'triple helix'.[2] The *Growing Esteem: The University of Melbourne Strategic Plan 2006* (hereafter *Growing Esteem: Strategic Plan 2006*), which set out how the new objectives were to be achieved, was approved by University Council early in 2006.

The central objective of the learning and teaching component of the triple helix was a curriculum review, to be held in the context of the University moving to a graduate school model. This is what led to what was soon dubbed the 'Melbourne Model' (see Chapter 2). *How* the Melbourne Model was conceived, designed and built – and the processes, committees and people involved – is detailed this book.

What is the Melbourne Model?

Driving the change to the University's strategy was a recognition that if Melbourne was to be seen as one of the finest universities in the world, it would need to consider global competition and international movements in higher education more closely than it had previously. Because of this, three higher education models from around the world were considered as templates. These were:

- the European Union 'Bologna Process' (a 3+2+3 model of three years undergraduate, two years masters and three years professional or doctoral level studies)
- the US graduate school model (with a four-year Bachelor of Arts and Bachelor of Science and all professional qualifications reached at a graduate level)

- a subset of the US model that required all students to study specified 'general education' subjects and/or study disciplines from a range of options.

In the end, the Melbourne Model did not conform closely to any of these models. None were exactly right for the University of Melbourne, although they were frequently referred to in the discussions that led to the model that was adopted. The final structure as introduced in 2008 incorporated a number of aspects from all three options. These included:

- six bachelor degrees each of three years duration with the option of studying a fourth year honours program. Each of the six degrees require completion of a 'breadth component', which is generally about 25 per cent of the total degree
- masters or doctoral level professional or specialist programs of two or more years, which are designed to meet accreditation requirements in various disciplines
- research higher degree programs in which students develop advanced research and professional development skills.

Choice and flexibility at the undergraduate level, together with diversity and applicability at the graduate level, are at the heart of the Melbourne Model, which offers considerable advantages for students over the previously existing curriculum structures.

Before the Melbourne Model
In 2006, the year in which the curriculum review occurred, and for around one hundred and fifty years before that, the University of Melbourne offered a curriculum in the traditional mode of the Australian system, which was very much based on the English model. A large number (about one hundred) and a wide range of individual undergraduate degrees were offered, including the Bachelor of Arts and the Bachelor of Science (each providing a

significant range of disciplines from which students could select their preferences), as well as professional degrees in law, medicine, dentistry and engineering, among others. Further study was available through diplomas for graduates who wished to change to a new discipline, postgraduate diplomas and masters degrees for those wishing to enhance the discipline of their undergraduate studies, and masters and doctorates for those interested in pursuing research in their disciplines. Melbourne offered an extensive range of undergraduate combined degrees through which students would frequently study a professional course in conjunction with a more general one (such as Arts/Law or Science/Commerce). These combined courses tended to attract the highest achieving secondary school students with whom they were exceptionally popular. Graduates of these combined degrees were also very attractive to employers.

Given the success of Melbourne's courses and its graduates in gaining employment or going on to further study, the suggestion of a major curriculum change from the traditional to a significantly different model initially beggared belief in the opinion of some, including many of the then students and staff of the University, the parents and teachers of potential students and the employers of graduates. Regardless of whether the University elected the Bologna or the US graduate school model, the proposed curriculum changes would require two or more years of study (and additional costs) beyond a three-year bachelors degree for graduates to achieve qualifications of a professional standard equal to those existing in 2006. In general, the new model required one more year of study than previously. There was great concern that the extended time required to achieve a professional qualification would endanger the University's reputation and result in the loss of high-achieving students to competitor universities.

On the other hand, there was strong support for a new curriculum that was consistent with global movements in higher education and which would better prepare the University's graduates for a changing world. The opportunity to contribute to the design and development of a new curriculum was an attractive challenge to many in the academic community.

Timelines, participation and stakeholders

The University had never before conducted such a wide-ranging review of its curriculum. It would have an impact on all components of the institution's core activity of learning and teaching. It was also expected to be completed in a very short period of time. There was an initial – and short-lived – suggestion that the review, and subsequent development of new courses, could be completed in time for the new model to be introduced early in 2007. By February 2006, a somewhat more realistic, though still very tight, schedule was agreed to, with the 'new generation' undergraduate courses to be introduced under the Melbourne Model in the 2008 academic year. This schedule also took into account the University's obligations to advise prospective students of the requirements for its courses early enough for them to complete any prerequisite subjects in their high school program.

These changes were for the long term: as stated in *Growing Esteem: Strategic Plan 2006*, this was a ten-year project. The introduction of new three-year bachelors degrees in 2008 would be followed by new professional degrees of two or more years. Some of these were available from 2009 while the medical and health based courses began in 2011 and were therefore available for the first graduates of the Melbourne Model degrees as well as graduates of other universities. At the same time, the University needed to meet its obligations to students who had enrolled in 2006 and 2007, or earlier, and allow them to complete their courses in accordance with the conditions given to them when they began.

The Curriculum Commission was established as one of several taskforces when the *Growing Esteem: Strategic Plan 2006* was adopted in February 2006 and was the main body responsible for developing the new undergraduate course structures. The commission, under the chairmanship of then Deputy Vice-Chancellor (Academic) Professor Peter McPhee and with representation from each of the faculties, and from student and other groups, held 25 meetings between February and September 2006. The commission's final report, containing the broad outline of and requirements for the new model of six bachelors degrees and professional as well as research studies at the graduate level, was endorsed by the University's Academic Board and Council in the remaining months of 2006. But this was just the beginning. The detailed work of designing new courses that met the requirements of the Melbourne Model would be undertaken throughout 2007 by six course standing committees, one for each of the six new bachelor's degrees, and by faculty curriculum groups for the new graduate professional degrees. In addition to the academic developments that were integral to the Melbourne Model, there were numerous operational and structural, as well as budgetary, matters that would have to be reviewed. These reviews were undertaken by varied groups made up of representatives of academic units and administrative and professional units who were overseen and directed by 'taskforces' responsible for implementation of the Melbourne Model – especially the Towards the Melbourne Model 2008 (or MM08) Taskforce and its successor, the Melbourne Model Implementation Taskforce (or MMIT) but including many others.

In addition to these committees and groups, a great many individuals participated in the changes and developments, from members of the University Council through to the Vice-Chancellor and others from the University executive group, deans and general managers of faculties, the academic staff members of the course standing committees, professional staff in the numerous administrative units including, eventually, the front-line staff who would be involved in answering questions about the new courses from prospective students, schools and parents. The University also consulted prospective students, their parents and schools, professional and accreditation bodies, alumni, employers of its graduates and relevant government departments. The concerns and views of these people and individuals were all taken into account in developing the new curriculum.[3]

The most intense period of development was in 2006 and 2007. During this time the Curriculum Commission, course standing committees and the MM08 and MMIT with their various subgroups completed their work. Although this story concludes with the introduction of the Melbourne Model early in 2008, the developments continued and are ongoing. Now, however, they are part of the routine fabric of the University's well-developed cycles of planning and review, rather than a significant and unique project of change involving all sectors of the university, which sometimes involved suddenly imposed, urgent and unfamiliar tasks.

The Curriculum Commission and the subsequent committees and groups responsible for putting the Melbourne Model in place encountered a number of difficult moments. Professor McPhee was diligent in keeping the University community informed and involved in the developments, but there was some concern among academic staff that the Melbourne Model would result in the loss of students, damage the University's reputation and take away from its research profile. At times, the debate became heated, if not hostile, and included personal attacks against Professor McPhee. At the same time, some professional accreditation agencies initially opposed the changes – although others were pleased with the proposed initiatives. Some faculties or segments within them argued that the proposed changes were excellent in general but would not be necessary to their own programs, which were already of a high standard.

As well as inspiring opposition of this sort, the workload involved was very heavy for a great number of people and, frequently, many of these had to be involved in each phase of the new developments while continuing the University's normal operations. The frustrations were many – and understandable. The process extracted a considerable personal cost from some participants. But once the University had announced that the new curriculum would be introduced at the beginning of 2008, there was no way the process could be slowed. Even so, there was criticism of the University for the delay in announcing the new courses – even while the number and names of these had yet to be determined.

It is a credit to the large numbers of people involved in the work of the Curriculum Commission and the subsequent implementation groups, especially the course standing committees, that the new courses did have their first intakes in early 2008. It should also be noted that some of those who had been sceptical or hostile during the early developments initiated proposals on alternative approaches for their faculties that resulted in attractive programs consistent with the Melbourne Model.

A story worth telling

The University's website shows little evidence of the hum that existed in 2006 and 2007 over the development, adoption and eventual introduction of the Melbourne Model. The VCE students of those years who were selected to enrol in a Melbourne Model undergraduate degree in 2008 could have completed a bachelor degree in 2010 and may have enrolled in a professional graduate program or in a research degree from 2011. The University has continued on with its normal activities and many staff who began working at the University after 2008 will not be very much aware of the frenzied activity of 2006 and 2007. The University's focus for future directions is currently on its research activities. A discussion paper *Research at Melbourne: Charting the Course to 2025* was released in November 2011 with a strategy to be finalised by August 2012 setting out the objectives and a course of action – which will no doubt follow similar processes to those used for some stages of the Melbourne Model.

But, without doubt, the changes introduced with the Melbourne Model have not only transformed the University's course and curriculum structures but also brought many associated developments: faculty administrative structures, budget policies and processes, graduation ceremonies and committee structures, among other things, have all been affected. A number of initiatives have been introduced, including the establishment of the position and office of the Provost, the development of student learning centres and increased opportunities for students to undertake volunteer work. There are still those who doubt the Melbourne Model was the best way for the University to go. So far, however, measurable outcomes such as numbers of students who have completed their new generation Melbourne Model bachelor degree or numbers and standard of graduates who have proceeded to professional or research graduate programs, are very strong. The University's equity program is greatly enhanced, giving expanded opportunities for students from a more diverse range of economic and cultural backgrounds to be successful in their studies. On the other hand, the median Australian Tertiary Admission Rank (ATAR) in 2011 was 93.10 compared with 94.30 in 2006, in large part because of school leavers who prefer to study clinical and engineering sciences at undergraduate level in other universities.[4] But it is still early days. A more realistic assessment of the success of the Melbourne Model will be possible in another two or three years.

When I started work as the director of the Melbourne Curriculum Project, I reviewed some basic information about change management, the usual steps involved, the expected outcomes, problems to watch out for, and so on.[5] I found several excellent summaries of the outcomes of curriculum reviews undertaken by other universities, especially in the United States. But these summaries and reports were about the policy and pedagogical outcomes; that is, the *content* of the new or revised curriculum. There was scant information on *how* these other institutions had conducted the review, what worked for them and what did not. Given the scale and scope of the changes proposed in the Growing Esteem strategy and the first comprehensive curriculum review in the University's more than 150-year history, it seemed important that there be a record of how the University managed and conducted the changes. Few would argue that some aspects of the review could have been better managed. For example, although communication was extensive and mostly of a high standard, there were still too many existing students and staff who did not feel as though their interests were understood or were being taken into account in the deliberations. In this sense, there may be messages that will help current staff learn from this story about the Melbourne Model and improve review processes used for future activities. Nonetheless, it is important to understand that methods and processes that worked for the University of Melbourne will not necessarily be useful for other institutions. Any change processes and management, and consequent policies, must be attuned to the individual organisation's structure and climate.

Another question, of course, is why should I be the one to tell the story of the Melbourne Model. It's what I asked myself when Professor McPhee invited me to write this book in November 2008. The brief, devised by the Vice-Chancellor, was for 'an objective, informed study of curriculum change at the university, which can be published ... as a record of a significant period in the life of the institution'. I was more than a little surprised – by that time, I was into my retirement and enjoying a more leisurely pace than that experienced in full-time employment. I was also not entirely convinced I was the best person to write the change management story. But there was some logic in my selection as someone who could be relatively objective. All my education had been in the United States; I had worked closely with the Curriculum Commission as director of the Melbourne Curriculum Project; I had considerable knowledge of the University through my various professional appointments; and had not been involved in the implementation of the commission's recommendations. My own role in the Melbourne Model was as something of a 'Jill of all trades' who got things done as needed. My tasks included supporting Professor McPhee in his role as chair of the Curriculum Commission; thinking of issues needing attention or resolution and alerting Professor McPhee and others to these; liaising with faculties, administrative departments and individuals; organising and managing activities relating to the introduction of the model; writing and reviewing discussion, policy and operational papers. I was then closely involved in the processes of developing the model, without having any emotional connection to the elements being transformed. I was deeply familiar with the trajectory of the changes, but also in a position to be objective – which I have aimed to be as much as possible while writing this account. There are some matters on which I have expressed a personal view, but I have included these only after a close review of notes of discussions or consultation with colleagues to ensure the validity of my opinions.

The implementation of the Melbourne Model was multifaceted, with various aspects emerging from developments and discussions at different times and in different ways. In retrospect, one could argue that the implementation was linear, although it did not always seem so at the time. My primary focus here is on the curriculum developments, even though many other organisational matters were in flux at the time. This situation highlights the complexity of the changes, and their interconnections, that were being introduced into the University. My approach may not do justice to the interconnections and relationships between the various groups and the timing of developments, but I hope it does give a sense of the complexity of the changes. As a way of ordering the information, the book has been divided into three parts. The first, Origins, follows the development of the Melbourne Model from the appointment of Glyn Davis as Vice-Chancellor in 2004 to approval of the Growing Esteem strategy in December 2005. Part II, Design, focuses on the work of the Curriculum Commission as it developed the new degrees with the faculties, and explores the commission's impact on various operational matters. Part III, Transition, takes the story through 2007, from the approval of the Curriculum Commission's final report through the launch of the Melbourne Model and the importance of market research to the development of the Melbourne Student Services Model.

The story told here ends with the first student intake into the Melbourne Model degrees in 2008. It has yet to be seen how the changes involved in introducing the model will alter the face of the University, and what their impact at the national and international levels in the longer term might be.[6] The process of fully implementing the Melbourne Model and associated structural changes will take several more years, especially as these have been complicated by the impact on the University of the global financial crisis in the late 2000s and any number of internal and other external factors. For now, I hope this book answers many questions about how academic structures in a large university can be transformed – and about how the Melbourne Model was made.

Part I

Origins 2004–05

1

The Birth of the Melbourne Model

The origins of the Melbourne Model can be found in 2004 when Melbourne University appointed a new vice-chancellor, Professor Glyn Davis. His role in developing a proposal to make significant changes to the course and curriculum structure of the University of Melbourne was crucial. The first part of this book traces how the proposal to review and revise the curriculum grew from a discussion paper – *Growing Esteem: Choices for the University of Melbourne* – released in July 2005 to become an integral and primary part of a new strategic plan. *Growing Esteem: The University of Melbourne Strategic Plan 2006* was published in February 2006 and endorsed by the University Council in March 2006. In less than a year after taking up his post, Professor Davis had proposed a radical change to how courses might be offered at the University of Melbourne and this proposal had been discussed by the University community, fleshed out by working groups and taskforces and endorsed by the University Council. In a move that introduced similarities to higher education structures in the United States and Bologna, the many existing undergraduate degrees would be reduced to six generalist degrees and professional qualifications offered only at graduate level. At the same time, administrative structures and student service provision would be reviewed for improvement.

There had been some discussion during the 1980s and 1990s, and occasionally before, about the university changing its profile to include a higher proportion of postgraduate students, but there had been nothing suggested along the lines of an extensive, University-wide move to a completely different model. But that's what the Growing Esteem papers did, in inspiring what would come to be called the Melbourne Model. What follows is the story of how this model was conceived, designed and put into place.

A new vice-chancellor: 2003

In July 2003 the serving vice-chancellor, Professor Alan Gilbert, tendered his resignation from the University of Melbourne to become Vice-Chancellor of the University of Manchester. His resignation was to take effect from January 2004. On 11 August 2003, the University Council agreed to establish a selection committee for the position of vice-chancellor, with a decision to take place early the following year.[1]

Professor Davis, then vice-chancellor at Griffith University, was interviewed for the position on 16 January 2004. His memories of that interview are less than perfect, but he does recollect arguing in broad terms that the University of Melbourne had an opportunity to offer a distinctive form of education, with a focus on graduate training in professions. He continued:

> This nods toward – but is a long way from – details of what became 'the Melbourne Model'. My aim was simply to signal a view that Melbourne occupied a unique position in Australian higher education, and should use this to break out of the existing institutional mould.[2]

Council adopted the selection committee's recommendation for the appointment of Professor Davis as vice-chancellor on 23 January 2004.[3] Professor Davis remained at Griffith until he took up his appointment at Melbourne in January 2005. Professor Kwong Lee Dow was appointed vice-chancellor for 2004.

The appointment was pivotal. Professor Davis would arrive at the University with clear ideas about what the University community expected of him and a sense of how he would go about helping shape its future. He brought a distinctive, US university, presidential-style approach to developing strategies for the University that contrasted significantly with how such tasks had been undertaken in the past. He engaged consultants from outside the University – and the higher education system – to write about possible future directions for the institution, and chose people to discuss the issues and work with him in developing strategies on the basis of their fresh eyes and approach rather than their deep personal experience of the University. That is not to say he went out on his own. There was wide consultation with the University community during the planning process and the widely publicised opportunity for submissions in response to the discussion paper. The University's structures and well-developed planning and accountability framework provided a range of opportunities for the Vice-Chancellor to feed his ideas into the annual cycle of activities. These included the 2005 February Deans and Heads Conference and the Council Planning Conference, the annual performance reviews of the budget divisions in May 2005, and other components of the University's normal operations and activities at that time.

Getting to know the University of Melbourne: 2004

In May 2004, Vice-Chancellor Elect Professor Davis, after discussion with Professor Lee Dow and Senior Vice-Principal Ian Marshman, commissioned three reviews as a due diligence exercise. These reviews were to provide an independent stocktake of three key activities of the University: administration and finances; teaching and learning; and research and research training. They were conducted independently of each other, by people or agencies outside the University: Phillips KPA for administration and finance; Professor Gregor Ramsey for teaching and learning; and Professor Vicki Sara for research and research training.[4] The reviewers were well known within higher education circles at the time. Professor Sara had recently retired (on 30 June 2004) as CEO of the Australian Research Council (ARC), and had previous experience as Dean of Science at Queensland University of Technology. David Phillips and Peter Wade are experienced directors of Phillips KPA Consultancy, which provides services to the education and training sectors. Dr Ramsey was at that time an independent consultant who had previously held posts with federal and state governments, including as managing director of the NSW TAFE Commission.

The Office of the Senior Vice-Principal managed these reviews. A large volume of background documentation was provided for each by relevant sections of the University, and significant numbers of staff and students were interviewed. The three final reports were presented to the University in October 2004. The 'Report on Due Diligence Reviews' was circulated as background reading for the February 2005 Deans and Heads Conference. The accompanying paper stated, 'the reviewers were to report on the status quo; they were not asked to make recommendations for change or improvements'.[5] Nevertheless, a number of issues were raised that needed attention and or debate and some recommendations were made.

The review of teaching and learning activities was particularly noteworthy for the issues raised rather than conclusions drawn. These included:

> How should the University position itself in relation to the balance between undergraduate and graduate students ... is the aim of the University to become increasingly a research-focused graduate university?

and

> The University has developed a set of 'attributes of the Melbourne Graduate' ... should the first years of undergraduate programs be a common program, which aims to provide a general education developing those graduate attributes?[6]

These questions were particularly pertinent to the University's subsequent decision to undertake an extensive review of its entire curriculum. The report on research and research training activities also raised the question that would become central to that curriculum review: 'What is the University's preferred balance between graduate and undergraduate load?'[7]

February 2005
Deans and Heads Conference

An abbreviated version of the 'Report on Due Diligence Reviews' had been circulated as background reading for the 2005 Deans and Heads Conference, which took place from 7 to 9 February.[8] Since its origins when Professor David Penington was vice-chancellor, the annual February Deans and Heads Conference, originally held in the seaside town of Lorne, has been a popular and important event in the University's strategic planning and accountability program.[9] It provides an opportunity early in the year for the University's academic and professional leaders to come together as colleagues in an informal setting to consider major issues for the University and to share their experiences. The 2005 conference theme was 'Realising the Vision: Positioning Melbourne for a Changing Higher Education Environment'. It was an appropriate event at which to introduce the ideas that would lead to such significant changes at the University.

For Glyn Davis, starting his vice-chancellorship in the first few months of the year had certain advantages. One was that the February conference provided him with an early opportunity to meet and interact with a significant population of the University. The University Council had agreed with Vice-Chancellor Lee Dow's recommendation in 2004 that the University would continue with the 'Melbourne Agenda' (the strategic policy adopted by the University in 1996, during Alan Gilbert's first year as vice-chancellor) as its blueprint for 2005, and an operational plan for the year had been finalised on that basis. The strategic plan and budget for the year had also been determined before the end of the previous year. This allowed Professor Davis to take up his position, accepting operations as they were without any immediate need for major statements about the changes and new directions he may have believed were appropriate.

This does not mean he hadn't been considering the possibilities deeply. Professor Davis recalls that 2004, the interim year during which he was vice-chancellor elect, had 'provided an extensive period for reflection, so I arrived with a reasonably developed set of thoughts about possible future directions'.[10] The reports on the due diligence reviews, mostly favourable to the University's overall operations and key activities, had also provided a great deal of material to consider.

Professor Davis has reported that he 'quietly tested the possible future directions for the University with a range of colleagues' as he sought to understand the University better during the first six months of 2005.[11] The February conference provided him with an excellent opportunity to put some of his ideas to a preliminary test while he mingled with University leaders over the three days, as well as through his formal presentations.

Vice-Chancellor Davis' first presentation to the conference was a comprehensive report on the key findings of the due diligence reviews. His second presentation, 'The Melbourne Agenda: Early Observations', was delivered at the end of the conference. It drew on some of the findings from the due diligence reviews and other observations Professor Davis had made or gleaned from readings and conversations during his brief time in the University. This second presentation represented the new vice-chancellor's own 'stocktake' of the University, encompassing the positive and the not-so-positive aspects, and an outline of what was needed to keep the Melbourne Agenda moving. Professor Davis touched on governance and management, teaching and learning, research and commercialisation, and resources, including people. He also referred to how the Melbourne Agenda had progressed over the past five years, with an argument that the wider context of higher education had changed since 1996 and, therefore, a fresh strategy was needed. He raised two particular questions: 'What is the Melbourne Experience and how does it work?'[12] and 'How does the University define being one of the "finest" universities?' Of the University's student profile, Professor

Davis commented: 'Our student mix across the Uni is uneven. Need the right mix of local and international, postgrad and undergrad, socio-economic.'

The presentation's conclusion listed action to be taken:

> Over the next three months the University community will be invited to reflect on what it means to be 'one of the finest', what we mean by 'the Melbourne Experience' and what our longer-term strategies should be. There will be a discussion paper and consultation meetings, with a report to Council proposing the next iteration of the Melbourne Agenda.[13]

This was a clear indication that the way forward would contain the opportunity for significant change. Professor McPhee recollects the impact of the conference thus:

> The new Vice-Chancellor had both unsettled and challenged us. Any complacency we had that our hard work had us on track to be 'one of the finest universities in the world' was pricked by his courteous but incisive commentary on our shortcomings.[14]

University Council Planning Conference

In 1996, about ten years after the Deans and Heads Conference had become an annual event, the University Council, at the initiative of Vice-Chancellor Gilbert, established its own annual conference planning meetings, usually held around two weeks after the Deans and Heads Conference.[15] Where as the deans and heads discussions range from the strategic level down to grassroots issues, the council's are mostly at the strategic and determining level. Proposals that survive from the Deans and Heads Conference to the Council Conference are likely to carry through into the strategic plan.

In 2005, the University Council Conference took place on 18 and 19 February.[16] The Deans and Heads Conference had been provided with an abbreviated summary of the due diligence review outcomes, while the Council Conference participants received the full, comprehensive reports prepared by the consultants.

A series of presentations on the findings of the reviews were made. The Vice-Chancellor spoke on major issues arising from the reviews; Professor Skene (then president of the Academic Board) on the reactions from the Deans and Heads Conference; the deputy vice-chancellors on research (Deputy Vice-Chancellor (Research) Professor Frank Larkins) and teaching and learning (Deputy Vice-Chancellor (Academic) Professor Peter McPhee); the senior vice-principal Ian Marshman on administration; and the chief financial officer David Percival on finances.

Professor Ramsey's 'Report on Teaching and Learning' included the following pertinent statements in its summary:

> Unimelb is also moving steadily in the direction of increased numbers of graduate courses, the under-graduate program is increasingly cross-faculty in nature...
>
> If Melbourne sees an emphasis on graduate and research programs as its future direction, it could well re-think its undergraduate program in terms of how the general education that provides the foundation for the development of more specific professional skills is organised and delivered. The question ... is when should general education end and when should the focus be specifically on the profession.[17]

Towards the end of the conference, Professor Davis made a presentation on 'The Way Forward' in which he identified nine major actions for attention in 2005. These included questions that had been mooted at the earlier Deans and Heads Conference, such as progressing to the next phase of the Melbourne Agenda (for which there would be a period of consultation with discussion on what it means to be 'one of the finest universities') and how to define and make the 'Melbourne Experience' central to the University's teaching and learning. Action would also be taken in the realms of commercialisation and knowledge transfer, internationalisation, advancement, and public outreach, among others. Again, Professor Davis concluded with a commitment to provide a report to the University Council proposing the next iteration of the Melbourne Agenda.

Maureen O'Keefe, then director of the Vice-Chancellor's Office, prepared a proposal dated 23 February 2005 that set out plans for a consultation process around the Melbourne Agenda, although it is not clear whether this plan was reviewed by any individual or group other than the Vice-Chancellor. The proposal explained that Professor Davis wished to 'test' the Melbourne Agenda, which was then in its sixth year of operation. The vision of the Melbourne Agenda at this time was that the University would be a research-led institution; a learning institution; a liberal institution (where, among other things, academic freedom was protected); an independent institution; an international university and a Melbourne institution. The proposal included that an issues paper be prepared by the end of February, followed by three months of consultations which would cover the level of commitment within the University to this vision and the Melbourne Agenda overall as a strategy; encourage reflection on the Melbourne Agenda; gather information on strengths and weaknesses of the Melbourne Agenda; and identify gaps in the goals and strategies. It was anticipated that a draft strategic plan would be available for consideration by council in July 2005.

This process was followed almost to the letter, although the timetable was out by around three months. The discussion paper was made available in June 2005 when it was distributed to those attending the Planning and Budget Committee Conference, and the consultation period was curtailed slightly for a report to be ready for council in October 2005.

There was a sense of enthusiasm and quiet excitement among participants at the end of this first series of conferences. While there is no doubt that, as Professor McPhee noted, complacency had been shaken, there was also a general view in favour of change and anticipation at the opportunity to contribute to the changes through the consultation process. These opportunities were soon realised, as movements towards change picked up speed.

April 2005
Vice-Chancellor's key performance indicators

At the March 2005 meeting of the University Council, the Chancellor, Mr Ian Renard, had proposed a draft set of key performance indicators (KPIs) for the Vice-Chancellor. The draft indicators were revised in consultation with the Vice-Chancellor and the final KPIs agreed at the April council meeting. The first indicator was agreement on the next phase of the Melbourne Agenda with outcomes of: a) key performance criteria to be adopted by council; b) the alignment of structures with the goals of the University. To achieve these outcomes a discussion paper was to be prepared by April 2005, followed by consultation meetings. It was proposed that council consider the discussion paper by July 2005 after which a stable set of University performance indicators would be specified.[18]

The second KPI was to make the Melbourne Experience central to decision-making within the University and to develop a five-year strategy to ensure that Melbourne was among the best performing Group of 8 (Go8) universities in teaching and student support.[19] This was to be achieved through taking action to:

- establish a Melbourne Experience Taskforce
- investigate closer links between teaching outcomes and budget, staff profile and institutional innovation
- pay attention to University performance in CEQ and PREQ surveys[20]
- work with student and sports organisations on consequences of the implementation of the voluntary student unionism policy.

These KPIs are significant to the development of the new curriculum model in two ways. There is no doubt that the Vice-Chancellor's KPIs were linked to the directions in which he wished to take the University – leading eventually to the Melbourne Model. But it is also important to note that the KPIs were linked closely to the University strategic plan and to the University's accountability obligations at all levels.

Management structures under scrutiny

The Vice-Chancellor's first steps towards change were within the context of management structures. At the April 2005 Planning and Budget Committee meeting, Professor Davis reported that changes had been made to the Senior Executive. A Vice-Chancellor's Advisory Group (VCAG) had been established with a membership of the (then) two deputy vice-chancellors, the president of the Academic Board, the Senior Vice-Principal, and two deans who would also attend Senior Executive meetings.[21] The group was to meet fortnightly and, as the name implies, would advise the Vice-Chancellor.[22]

The 2004 due diligence review of the University administration had implied that membership of the existing Senior Executive was unbalanced. It had around seven vice-principals (professional staff) and four academic staff: the Vice-Chancellor, two deputy vice-chancellors and the president of the Academic Board. It had become reasonably obvious to members of the Senior Executive in early 2005 that the group's composition and operations may not fit with the new Vice-Chancellor's management preferences, although the Vice-Chancellor's concerns were, most likely, more broadly based in management style than the issue of balance.

Professor Davis had already established a 'Matins' group early in 2005, which met for around thirty minutes two or three times each week.[23] Its purpose was to ensure senior managers had an opportunity to discuss the 'hot' issues they were managing and to avoid overlap or lack of knowledge among the group about their work.

After VCAG had been established, the (then) Senior Executive Group, with the addition of two deans, met fortnightly in the alternate weeks from VCAG. There was also a Vice-Chancellor and Deans Group that met fortnightly on the same day, just before the Senior Executive Group. By including two deans as members of VCAG, Professor Davis was perhaps responding to another suggestion from the due diligence review, that effective mechanisms needed to be established to 'ensure cohesion between the senior executive group and the Deans of Faculty and for Deans to contribute effectively in executive decision-making'.[24]

So, what was the significance of the 2005 VCAG, Vice-Chancellor and Deans and Senior Executive groups in the development of the new strategic plan, now more widely known as 'Growing Esteem' and becoming more clearly distinguished from the 'Melbourne Agenda'? It is difficult to fully quantify. Between June and December 2005, the VCAG agendas list items related to Growing Esteem on five occasions, more than occurred for the Senior Executive and the Vice-Chancellor and Deans groups. The record of these meetings consisted of an action sheet, but there were no such sheets for VCAG until the September meeting. Thereafter, they appeared only occasionally. None of the action sheets for the 2005 meetings of VCAG, Vice-Chancellor and Deans Group and the Senior Executive Group includes items related to the Growing Esteem matters that appeared on the agendas. The nature or content of discussions of Growing Esteem issues by any of these three groups at this stage is therefore not available. Over the following two years, however, these groups were among several that had an important role in high-level oversight of the strategy, as is discussed further in Chapter 6. There have since been further changes to the governance and management structures of the University, including those made in 2007 when the position of Provost was established and in mid-2008 when the former Planning and Budget Committee was dissolved in favour of a senior executive 'committee'. Some of these changes are relevant to the development of the Melbourne Model and are discussed in later chapters.

June 2005: Planning and Budget Committee Conference

The University's Planning and Budget Committee was established in 1996, Alan Gilbert's first year as vice-chancellor. The Planning and Budget Committee, with membership from the University's academic and professional senior executives and the deans, was responsible for policy and budget matters that had previously been dealt with separately by two committees of the University Council. In its first year of operation, the Planning and Budget Committee agreed to hold an annual conference that would give preliminary consideration to the budget and operational plan and priorities for the following year, taking into account major internal and external policy issues. This conference provides an opportunity for the University's budget divisions to make proposals for consideration and to discuss, collectively, major projects and matters likely to have an impact on the University budget in the coming year. The conference ends with a formal meeting of the committee, which usually includes approving a draft budget for the next year. The June 2005 Planning and Budget Committee Conference saw significant discussion of Growing Esteem.

The first session of the conference had the theme 'Taking the Melbourne Agenda to the Next Stage'. This session included a draft of the discussion paper 'Growing Esteem: Choices for the University of Melbourne'. The paper had been included in documents distributed to participants just before the conference. Session 5 is listed as dealing with 'Updating the Melbourne Agenda: Confirming the Priorities'; however, there was no paper circulated for this session and no record of any discussion of the topic as part of the conference proceedings.[25]

Session 4 of the conference consisted of small group discussions on the issues and strategies to be proposed to the Academic Board and University Council in relation to taking the Melbourne Agenda to the next stage. Two of the deputy vice-chancellors at that time, Professor McPhee and Professor John McKenzie, were in the same group, with Professor McKenzie as convener. Both, in independent interviews, have referred to discussion within their group of a theoretical scenario involving a graduate school model with consequential effects on undergraduate programs.[26] Professor McPhee also recalls that Professor Ruth Fincher (then Dean of Architecture, Building and Planning) was in the group and had reported on her faculty's discussions about how a graduate school model along the lines of those in US universities would work. Likewise, Professor Michael Crommelin, then Dean of Law, commented on his faculty's recent introduction of the professional graduate-entry Juris Doctor program.

Professor McKenzie recalls that meetings involving the deans held after the conference included further discussion of the graduate school model, with consensus being reached for the University to investigate this option in the context of the Bologna model.[27]

The Vice-Chancellor advised the conference that the final version of the 'Growing Esteem: Choices for the University of Melbourne' paper would be made available to the University community in July, after which there would be a period of consultation and opportunity for submissions to be made up to late August. The Vice-Chancellor also announced this course of action in his regular column in *Uninews*, the University's fortnightly newspaper at that time.[28] As a committee, the Planning and Budget Committee had no further involvement in the discussion and development of the Growing Esteem strategy or the consultation process, but, as will become clear in later chapters, it had a significant role in the implementation phase, especially in relation to the recommendations of the Curriculum Commission.

July 2005: Growing Esteem: Choices

Growing Esteem: Choices for the University of Melbourne: A Discussion Paper that Invites Involvement and Response (hereafter, *Growing Esteem: Choices*) was released to the wider University community in July 2005, having been endorsed by the University Council on 11 July 2005 as the basis for consultation. Professor Davis had prepared the paper with Geoff Sharrock. According to its acknowledgements, it 'benefited from interviews with many senior members of the University, and from comments and contributions from Michael Beaton-Wells, Andrew Norton, Neville Buch, Richard James, David Penington, Maureen O'Keefe and Silvia Dropulich'.[29] Other than Richard James and David Penington, the people named are or were professional staff, mostly within the Office of the Vice-Chancellor. When Professor Davis was asked why these seven were specifically identified, he explained that this was the group who had worked most closely with him and Geoff Sharrock to write the discussion paper. He also indicated that in developing the strategies he thought the University should pursue, he was keen to have advice from people with a 'fresh eye', a preference also apparent in the appointments of relative outsiders Geoff Sharrock and, later, Jane-Frances Kelly.[30]

From February 2005 to February 2006, Geoff Sharrock worked as an adviser in the Office of the Vice-Chancellor with responsibility for writing a discussion paper on the University's options for future directions. Geoff is a graduate of Melbourne University who in 2005 was completing a PhD at RMIT University (he submitted his thesis in August of that year). His main occupation at the time was as a consultant working primarily in the areas of public sector policy, strategy and management development.

Professor Davis did not know Geoff before accepting the vice-chancellorship of the University of Melbourne. In August 2004, Geoff had published a review in *Policy*, the journal of the Centre for Independent Studies, of the Cain and Hewitt book *Off Course* about the University of Melbourne and the establishment of Melbourne University Private during Alan Gilbert's vice-chancellorship.[31] Geoff had received a note from Professor Davis about this article.[32]

After Professor Davis arrived in Melbourne, he asked Geoff to meet him. According to Geoff, it was in this meeting that Professor Davis invited him to write a paper on policy setting in universities – with a focus on Melbourne. Geoff agreed to work on a half-time basis given his other responsibilities. The paper eventually developed into *Growing Esteem: Choices* – a crucial document in arriving at the Melbourne Model, and one that made clear distinctions between the Melbourne Agenda and Growing Esteem.[33]

The discussion paper, its introduction states, 'outlines key challenges and opportunities facing the University, and asks how we might respond. It asks what the University already does well and should keep doing, what needs improvement, what to create and perhaps what to relinquish.' It does so following a structure typical of such documents. A historical perspective, based on the question 'what is a university for?', is followed by an analysis of the changing Australian higher education system. A snapshot of one university is given in the historical section on the defining aim of a university:

> In Paris, the university took an early interest in the professions. Students enrolled for general undergraduate studies in the faculty of philosophy (later to branch into arts and sciences) followed by specialist courses in theology, law or medicine. Graduates would then go out into the world, certified as having the ability and authority (the faculty) to administer to the spiritual, civic and physical needs of the populace.

Around half the paper is devoted to a critique of the Melbourne Agenda as a blueprint for the University. It considers the Melbourne Agenda vision and then each of its five objectives individually. The next section comments on issues seen as missing from the Melbourne Agenda: intellectual leadership; sustainability, including the optimal size and mix of the student body and the best profile of its programs; commercialisation; and organising and managing.

A final section on summary outlook and strategic dilemmas sets out a series of questions, under the subheadings of the five objectives of the Melbourne Agenda, with sustainability and commercialisation added to resources, and the addition of subheadings for intellectual leadership and organising and managing.

The following questions appear under the headings of 'Research Performance' and 'Attracting Scholars':

5. If research contribution is the main basis for the University's international profile, should the University's postgraduate cohort change to include more research students and less coursework students? Overall, what is the optimum profile for the University's academic programs in teaching and research?

6. Are there discipline areas where it makes more sense for all academic staff to combine undergraduate teaching and research roles, and others where it makes more operational sense to separate them? If so, how should this be reflected in program design, and staffing policies?

...

14. Are there too many postgraduate coursework programs, with too few students, occupying too much staff time? If a subject or course is 'non-core' for the discipline, attracting too few students, or available elsewhere in Victoria or online, should it be dropped?[34]

Overall, the paper made it clear that fundamental issues in the University's strategies were being opened for discussion. The strengths of the Melbourne Agenda were recognised, but so too were its weaknesses in the current higher education environment, particularly in terms of curriculum and management structures. The shift in emphasis from the Melbourne Agenda to Growing Esteem was to be far greater than just a change in name.

2

Consultations and Outcomes

Once the *Growing Esteem: Choices* discussion paper had been released, formal consultation with the University community could begin. A dedicated Growing Esteem website, linked to the Vice-Chancellor's website, was set up, through which the paper could be accessed. The existence of the discussion paper, the consultation process and the website were widely publicised through University information channels, including an 'all staff' email from the Vice-Chancellor (who was to use this form of communication frequently throughout the process). Most of the consultation transactions, such as submissions, queries and comments, were made through the website.

July to October 2005
Consultation
Over the period from the release of the discussion paper in June to the publication of the *Report on Growing Esteem Consultation (Broad Summary of the Diverse Perspectives Voiced by Respondents)* (hereafter, *Growing Esteem: Consultation Report*) in October 2005, all members of the community had the opportunity to participate in one or more of the following consultations:

- three public meetings (attended by a total of around seven hundred people)
- five small group briefings
- a 'future scenarios' lunch (12 participants)
- thirteen focus groups (attended by 140: 100 staff, 29 students, 11 residential college heads)
- written responses/submissions (of which there were more than 130, with more than 90 published on the University website with permission from the authors).

In addition to these consultations, the Vice-Chancellor had asked the (then) acting director of the University Planning Office, Michael Beaton-Wells, to prepare a slide pack, all or parts of which were eventually used in various presentations, including one to the Senior Executive Group meeting on 24 July 2005.[1] The slide pack was based on questions raised in the discussion paper. The 11 August 2005 version featured information and data on how to define recognition as 'one of the finest universities in the world', a key question raised in *Growing Esteem: Choices*. The definition was based on comparisons of Melbourne's situation in numbers of students and staff, research outcomes, funding and others, with equivalent traits at some of the top-ranked universities in the world. The pack also included proposals referred to as strategic options, which were covered in the discussion paper. These included options to:

- increase or decrease numbers of students in different fee categories
- reduce total numbers of courses offered and shift to more graduate programs and students
- appoint more staff internationally recognised in their fields to be future leaders and to build teams concentrated in fewer research priorities
- improve teaching and student services, and related actions.

The report on the consultations summarised the views presented in the submissions, quoted from a number of selected submissions and provided a summary of the survey data collected through the focus groups. Written submissions were central to the consultation process and the following section explores the range of responses and people who made them, although these details did not appear in the report. The section also looks in more depth at the Future Scenarios Workshop. This workshop played an important part in shaping the 'Growing Esteem: Strategy' paper, the next development after the consultation report. Both give a good indication of how the University community perceived the suggestion that changes were needed.

Submissions

Change of this scale within a university situation has the potential to affect different participants in many different ways. For students, there are ideological issues of what sort of education will be available to them, as well as practical concerns about the value their education will have on completion and how it might affect future employment options. Academic and professional staff also face the possibility the basis of their employment, and (for academic staff) how and what they teach, could be radically altered by curriculum change and its consequences. Change can cause uncertainty, but it can also offer opportunities, and this became clear in the responses to *Growing Esteem: Choices*. Of the 130 or so written submissions, around 78 (or 60 per cent) were from academic staff responding as individuals or on behalf of their departments. Most of the comments from academics dealt with research issues; in particular, enticements for attracting research scholars and whether or not the University should limit its areas of research. Most respondents who commented on this issue were opposed to any whole-scale restriction of research fields, believing that fields of research likely to be successful (in any sense of the word) cannot be predicted.

Some academics commented in favour of the Bologna or US graduate school models of education but at this stage of the process there was not an overwhelming or apparent stream of support for changing the University's course structure, at least from those who made submissions.[2] There was clear support for a reduction in numbers of students and student to staff ratios. Some academics also favoured reducing the number of individual subjects offered, although others were reluctant to see any dilution of subject diversity.

The leaders of the undergraduate and postgraduate student associations and the Overseas Students Society all made submissions on behalf of their organisations. The undergraduate group expressed the opinion that the University should 'define itself by what it values and not by rankings or numbers'; the postgraduate group felt that if limiting the number of courses resulted in 'better support for those that are offered', the trade-off would be worthwhile; while the Student Representative Council and the Overseas Students Society both submitted the view that campus-based experience and learning should remain central to the education offered by the University and that this should not be undermined by online learning. Otherwise, there were only a handful of submissions made by individual students, alumni (who were not academic or professional staff) and other people. Almost 40 professional staff made submissions as individuals or on behalf of their departments and units. These staff generally conveyed their perceptions of how their departments would be able to contribute to changes to operations that would result if options in the discussion paper were adopted.

A few of the respondents used the opportunity to complain, usually about another department or section of the University that was perceived not to be fulfilling its responsibilities. Many others expressed how much they appreciated the opportunity to make a submission, stating that the approach of involving the community in discussion of the University's future was very welcome and in contrast to their experience in earlier years. Most were also keen that their submission be published on the website. A small number made more than one contact with the section of the Vice-Chancellor's Office responsible for administering the discussion paper and associated activities to particularly advise the Vice-Chancellor they were interested in being involved further.

Future Scenarios Workshop

The Future Scenarios Workshop was held on 24 August 2005 with a select group of participants.[3] It was facilitated by Dr Vin Massaro, who was then a professorial fellow in the University's Centre for the Study of Higher Education (CSHE). The workshop group was provided with four scenarios, three based on rather stringent financial circumstances in the University and the fourth providing a generous income stream. It was thought that this methodology would reliably test whether strategies developed in the first three scenarios would be the same as those developed in a secure financial situation.

The workshop was not required to develop specific strategies or recommendations, but the discussion resulted in a number of suggestions that were taken further. These included the suggestion that the University consider 'reducing the size of the student body strategically to focus on its strengths and change its undergraduate/postgraduate mix'.[4]

A specific response of the workshop about internationalisation suggested that the University should 'become part of the Bologna process through the development of links with European institutions and closer alignment of our program structures'. This suggestion emerged after discussion of particular points in the global competition scenario, including student mobility, mutual recognition of degrees and subjects and increasing presence of US universities in regional markets.

The consultation report

The significance of the undergraduate–postgraduate mix in the University's future plans comes through in section 6.12 (Reviewing) of the *Growing Esteem: Consultation Report* about the balance of undergraduate and postgraduate programs. The opening paragraph states that several submissions 'considered the most radical option floated in the discussion paper, reconfiguring the core curriculum and changing the mix of undergraduate and postgraduate offerings. For some, this made some sense, and was one possible path to rationalisation.'

The extracts selected from the sample submissions to highlight this radical option refer mostly to the US model of an undergraduate generalist degree followed by a professional graduate coursework program. As indicated previously, few of the written submissions made any reference to possible curriculum changes.

Geoff Sharrock, author of the consultation report, states in its conclusions:

While it is clear there are many strengths and much good work to build on, from an institutional perspective, the University currently lacks a coherent strategic direction, and is constrained by internal factors as well as external ones.

At this stage, it appears there is considerable scope for the University to make minor improvements to many aspects of its operations, with tangible benefits for staff, students and the work of the University more generally. But equally clearly, no widely shared, sustainable strategy has yet emerged to make the University 'one of the finest' in the world.[5]

On 10 October 2005, the Vice-Chancellor made a confidential presentation to University Council titled 'The Melbourne Agenda: Next Generation'. It focused on the outcomes of the consultation and covered the general points of the consultation report that was circulated to the University community as a whole. These included that the consultation showed strong support for the aim of being one of the finest universities in the world. Instructions about accessing the consultation report online were provided to the University community through a number of avenues, including a notice in the 14 October 2005 edition of the weekly *StaffNews*.

November 2005
Strategic Directions

The draft (as at 9 November 2005) 'Growing Esteem: Strategic Directions for the University' paper was submitted to University Council at its November meeting as Appendix A to the Vice-Chancellor's report. The council had given strong support to the broad policy directions set out in the paper in its discussions of earlier Growing Esteem documents. This 'Strategic Directions' draft paper, and a presentation made by the Vice-Chancellor, introduced the 'triple helix' metaphor (coined by Geoff Sharrock) to describe the equal, related and intertwined priorities of research, teaching and knowledge transfer. This became a significant aspect of the ultimate Growing Esteem strategy. While the connections between research and teaching had long been recognised, the knowledge transfer aspect had been based on a narrow definition akin to commercialisation, and typically linked with research. The Growing Esteem strategy aimed to have knowledge transfer given a broader definition and to be a third strand of the university's priorities, alongside and equal to research and teaching.[6]

This draft brought together aspects of the original discussion paper, *Growing Esteem: Choices*, on options available to the University and the feedback received from the subsequent consultation process. It concentrated on three core issues, identifying that the University needed to focus the research effort at the University, shift teaching toward a stronger postgraduate profile and define the scope and terms of external engagement. It also indicated that other suggestions made through the consultation process would be included in the final version of the strategic plan, which had yet to be presented to the University community.

The draft introduced a level of substance to the preliminary ideas expressed in the earlier Growing Esteem documents and took into account suggestions and ideas from the consultations. For example, the section of the strategy dealing with learning and teaching referred to the Bologna model, representing the idea of a broad undergraduate degree followed by professional training, in the context of containing the total student population of the University. The Vice-Chancellor's presentation on the strategy highlighted 'internationally transferable qualifications' encompassing one-third of all enrolments at postgraduate level, a graduate school approach, new professional degrees and manageable workloads. There was reference to the changes that would have to be effected by the federal government if the changes proposed by the University were to be successful. These included the government agreeing to move Commonwealth-supported places (CSPs) from undergraduate to graduate level and increasing the FEE-Help cap.[7]

As the following extracts show, a great deal of the draft paper was relevant to the eventual development of the curriculum review and the Curriculum Commission, and gives strong indications of the direction the University had elected to follow. This was based largely on the trends in higher education internationally:

> Higher education is also more clearly a global market. In undergraduate education Australia outperforms most other nations, with overseas students a larger part of its mix. At postgraduate levels, though, in which research prestige looms larger, Australia is behind the United States, part of Europe and emerging university leaders across Asia.
>
> There are international moves to standardize degree structures. The familiar pattern of four-year arts or science degrees followed by graduate school is being echoed by the Bologna Declaration among European nations. The Bologna model, set to become the European standard from 2010, advocates a three-year undergraduate program with advanced courses taught in a two-year masters degree or a three-year doctoral program. If this becomes a global norm but Australia continues to prepare its professionals through undergraduate programs, in the longer term our graduates may no longer be seen as globally competitive.[8]

Within this changing international context, it was important that Australian institutions build on their existing strengths while acting to curb some weaknesses, such as increasing student and course numbers:

> Teaching is the principal means by which the University disseminates knowledge, trains students as scholars and professionals, and prepares the next generation of researchers. Student learning is a crucial strand in the helix, the original and enduring purpose of a university.
>
> Melbourne aspires to offer internationally transferable qualifications to talented students, built on strong

pedagogy and inspired by exceptional scholars. To do this it must first address growth in student numbers and subject options. These were rational responses to a general need for fee revenue and to internal competition for enrolments but with widely recognised negative consequences.

To position for such a future, Melbourne will introduce more graduate programs.

A shift towards greater graduate study poses obvious challenges. In time it should stabilise and even reduce the overall size of the student body.[9]

To become one of the 'world's finest', the University's focus would have to shift. The paper included a section on 'enablers', which set out a number of changes that would be required within the University, and repeated the actions needed on the part of government, if the aims of Growing Esteem were to be successful.

This draft of 'Growing Esteem: Strategic Directions' paper was presented to the November meeting of the Academic Board as an attachment to the Vice-Chancellor's Report. The meeting was attended by 119 board members, more than normal for board meetings.[10] The minutes of the meeting report extensive discussion of the draft strategic directions paper, especially in relation to:

• the 3+2+3 model of teaching and learning
• generalist undergraduate degrees followed by professional graduate programs
• risk assessments having been undertaken on the basis that throughout the 10-year implementation period University income would remain constant while other parameters would improve
• the Deputy Vice-Chancellor (Academic) convening a committee in 2006 that would meet with faculties to determine timelines for any transition to the 3+2+3 model.

The committee mentioned in the final report was eventually named the Curriculum Commission. At the Vice-Chancellor's request, the council appointed Professor McPhee to head up this commission. Professor McPhee was not at the meeting, as he was on long-service leave undertaking research in France at the time. While walking across campus shortly after returning to Melbourne, he was greatly surprised when a colleague called out to him: 'Hello, Commissioner' – and this is how he learned of council's decision. He recalls this as the start of the most significant challenge of his career.

The Vice-Chancellor used an all-staff email on 15 November to report that council had reviewed the 'Growing Esteem: Strategic Directions' paper and would give it further consideration at its December meeting. In the interim, the paper was made available to the University community through the internet. This generated feedback from around 30 people, most of whom were academic staff. The comments were diverse: two expressed concern about what would happen to the honours year; several expressed support for the 3+2 model; some were concerned that there was not a good understanding of the workload implications of the proposed changes, and others commented on research aspects of the draft strategy. One respondent offered, 'Thanks for being a dreamer who dares to dream!'[11]

December 2005: The Growing Esteem strategy is endorsed

A revised draft of the 'Growing Esteem: Strategic Directions' paper was considered at the 12 December 2005 meeting of University Council (as a 'for members only' document). Council adopted the document as the basis for further planning in the University and noted that a strategic plan would be drafted for consideration at the Council Planning Conference to be held in February 2006.

The 12 December 2005 version of 'Growing Esteem: Strategic Directions' was substantially the same as the November version.[12] There was elaboration of some aspects but no change in the substance of the strategies set out in the earlier paper. It is not entirely clear that the decision of council to adopt the Growing Esteem strategy 'as the basis for the University's future planning' was, in fact, endorsing radical change in the curriculum structure such as would be needed to take it towards the Bologna Model. It rather suggests a curriculum review. While the December version of 'Growing Esteem: Strategic Directions' refers to a University taskforce to work with each faculty to plan for the graduate school approach, the council minutes report that the Vice-Chancellor 'advised that as part of the implementation [of the Growing Esteem strategy] beginning in March 2006, there would be a comprehensive and fundamental review of curriculum across the University'. The minutes then refer to a 'University Commission' to be chaired by the Deputy Vice-Chancellor (Academic), which would be 'charged with undertaking the review and reporting to Council in the second half of the year'.[13]

The *Growing Esteem: Strategic Plan 2006,* which was written over a six-week period after council endorsement and published in February 2006, also refers to a curriculum review. But from an early stage it was apparent that the curriculum would not merely be reviewed, it would be redesigned. This was reinforced in the Vice-Chancellor's two 'all-staff' emails of 15 November and 15 December 2005. The first of these described the Growing Esteem proposal that council had considered at its meeting on 14 November, and the second announced that council had 'unanimously endorsed' the Growing Esteem strategy at its meeting on 12 December. Both emails were unequivocal in declaring that the University would be moving to the Bologna Model and offering only a small number of three-year generalist degrees with professional courses at the graduate level.

In discussing with Glyn Davis how the documentation and decision-making appeared to have embraced a curriculum redesign rather than just a review, he suggests that the Curriculum Commission was set up to test the apparent agreement within the University (bar some components of two or three faculties at the outset) for a dramatic change to the course structure and, therefore, the curriculum.[14]

Growing interest in Growing Esteem

It was around this time the term 'Melbourne Model' started to creep into the lexicon. Reference to the proposed curriculum changes under this title had the advantage of showing that it would be distinct from the Bologna or US model of higher education and be developed with specific awareness of the Australian context and the unique position of the University of Melbourne within it. By the time the *Growing Esteem Strategic Plan 2006* draft was circulated for the Deans and Heads Conference (6–8 February 2006), 'Melbourne Model' was being used extensively. Certainly, it was the term most used within the media as interest in what was happening at the University became more widespread.

Awareness of the process and its outcome had been growing outside the University for some time, fueled in part by media reports that could at times be somewhat sensationalist. There had been considerable media interest in the appointment of the new vice-chancellor and speculation on what impact he might have on the University. The Growing Esteem developments were followed in the news media throughout the process from the release of the discussion paper through to the finalisation of the *Growing Esteem: Strategic Plan 2006* and, after that, the work of the Curriculum Commission and subsequent implementation of the Melbourne Model.

As early as 18 July 2005, the *Australian Financial Review* published an article based on the *Growing Esteem: Choices* paper that commented on the growth in numbers of fee-paying students, in part arising from inadequate funding for HECS-based students. There were articles, too, about the discussion paper in the *Australian* and *Campus Review* with the latter reporting that 'controversial proposals could see Melbourne dramatically reshaped with a slashing of its HECS-funded places and a replacing of undergraduates with fee-paying, research-oriented postgraduates'.[15]

The *Growing Esteem: Strategic Directions* paper, released in October 2005, saw another extended round of interest in the proposals continuing into December when the University Council endorsed the proposed strategic directions. The headlines tended towards the dramatic, such as 'Uni wants US-style, full-fee system' and 'Bling it on for degrees of uni cool'.[16] As the *Growing Esteem: Strategic Plan 2006* was released, this interest became more intense, with the words 'Melbourne Model' usually preceded by the descriptors 'contentious' or 'controversial'. At this stage, however, there had been little sign of contention within the process.

January – February 2006
Growing Esteem: Strategic Plan 2006
The Vice-Chancellor employed Jane-Frances Kelly in January 2006 to help write the Growing Esteem strategic plan and assist with setting up its implementation.[17] Between the University Council's endorsement of the Growing Esteem strategy paper in December 2005 and the Deans and Heads Conference in early February 2006, Jane-Frances Kelly and Geoff Sharrock structured and wrote *Growing Esteem: The University of Melbourne Strategic Plan 2006* in consultation with Professor McPhee and others.

As mentioned earlier, a draft of the strategic plan was circulated as a paper for the 2006 Deans and Heads Conference. The plan stated that, by 2015, the Melbourne Model would be in place with two major shifts having occurred: professional programs would be mostly at graduate level and undergraduate programs 'will offer a more coherent general education with fewer courses and subjects, and a range of well-defined pathways into graduate study ... [and will] feature smaller student cohorts'. It anticipated that the student body could grow from the 2005 population of around 42,000 to 50,000 and then, towards 2015, reduce back to about 42,000. The estimate was that 30 to 45 per cent of students would be in professional graduate and research degree programs (about a 20 per cent to 10–15 per cent split).

The well-defined references to the impact the Melbourne Model was expected to have on student numbers had been generated by significant concern in the early years of the twenty-first century – within the University and in higher education institutions more generally – about the rapid growth in student numbers, linked to increases in international students and fee revenue, that had occurred in the 1990s and early 2000s. Although the increase in fee revenue was one of the Melbourne Agenda strategies, it had been expected that other measures would eventually kick in and ease the consequences of ever-increasing student numbers. But, as stated in the *Growing Esteem: Strategic Plan 2006*, it was also expected that the implications of a 3+2+3 model would reach much further than just a reduction in student numbers.

The strategic plan confirmed that a curriculum commission would be established to work with each faculty in planning the transition to new undergraduate and graduate programs under the Melbourne Model, with a report to the Academic Board to be delivered by the end of August 2006. The model was to align with the Bologna Model while taking into account disciplinary differences and Australian professional standards. Some of the anticipated difficulties were referred to, such as convincing prospective students and their parents of the merits of the Melbourne Model, seeking Commonwealth Government support for the professional graduate program approach by allowing the transfer of supported places to graduate level, and supporting staff and managing workloads.

The *Growing Esteem: Strategic Plan 2006* also incorporated operational targets and expected outcomes and dates for completion, which, for a number of years, had been covered in a separate University operational plan. In its appendices, it was explicit in the level of operational detail provided for the three strands of the triple helix. Appendix 1 was the 10-year table of milestones on the path to 2015. Appendix 2 covered the reporting arrangements such as 'the Curriculum Commission will report to the Academic Board through the Planning and Budget Committee', and Appendix 3 set out a table of actions and responsibilities. This latter included several items for the Curriculum Commission in addition to the development of a 10-year plan for the Melbourne Model, including that by the end of 2006 work would have started on a student learning centre in the Engineering precinct, and a Melbourne Experience survey would have been developed and administered to first-year students.[18] Appendix 4 contained the terms of reference for each of the review bodies. While it set the overarching University scene for the three areas of the triple helix, the strategic plan was to be complemented by separate plans for research and research training, learning and teaching and knowledge transfer.

From choices to a plan

In many ways, the leap from the various options put forward in the *Growing Esteem: Choices* paper released in July 2005 to the *Growing Esteem: Strategic Plan 2006* published in February 2006 was huge. In effect, the focus shifted from the fifty-odd questions across activities ranging from research to institutional organisation that were raised in the *Growing Esteem: Consultation Report*, to expectations set out in the terms of reference for each of the taskforces established in the strategic plan (including the Curriculum Commission) that specific design, market and delivery aspects of the strategy would be considered. It is difficult to pinpoint precisely where and when these leaps occurred. As previously indicated, there was no discussion of the *Growing Esteem: Choices* paper or strategy in Planning and Budget Committee meetings. The Academic Board discussed the strategy but was not asked to take a stand or endorse any recommendations. Then, the minutes of the December 2005 University Council meeting referred to the Growing Esteem strategy as the basis of future planning in the University; that is, a strategic plan would be prepared which would incorporate and outline the explicit statements about the 3+2+3 curriculum model, among other things.

Talking to Professor Davis, I commented on how the decision to move to a new course structure and curriculum appeared to evolve without an obvious or defining moment (except, of course, for the December decision of council).[19] Yes, there were the various Growing Esteem documents – the discussion paper, consultation outcomes and strategic directions – and over one hundred submissions in response to the discussion paper. But even after reviewing all the documents and noting comments made about them in the papers of various committees, a question lingered in my mind. How did the University get from the July 2005 *Growing Esteem: Choices* discussion paper, with its suggestion of a curriculum review, to the *Growing Esteem: Strategic Plan 2006* (February 2006) with its proposal to move to generalist undergraduate degrees and graduate schools that would offer professional as well as research degrees? That is, to a proposal for a complete redesign of curriculum structures. And why was there so little debate or dissension arising from these proposals? Was this because there was widespread support for a move to the Bologna or US model of higher education – or was it just a lack of resistance?

Professor Davis responded that he, too, was somewhat taken aback that there were so few apparent objections to such a substantial proposal. It is possible that this was because of a natural or inherent passiveness in academics or, perhaps, their disbelief that such radical change would actually happen. Certainly, the early reaction of some of the professional faculties supports the theory of non-resistance. A senior academic colleague who has worked in several universities offered the explanation that Melbourne has one of the most compliant academic boards he has seen, although it needs to be remembered that the board was not asked to 'vote' on the strategy. Perhaps this was a reflection of the extensive consultation process that had been used.

Whatever the reasons, there is no doubt that the proposals for change had become more ambitious and more far-reaching than originally conceived. The work of the Curriculum Commission, the instrumental body devising the new degree structure, would determine quite how radical this shift would be. The Melbourne Model was now a recognisable entity, with a distinctive name. But what would the model look like?

Part II

Design 2006

3

The Curriculum Commission

The scope of the work undertaken by the Curriculum Commission and the role of its final report in shaping and implementing the Melbourne Model was vast. This part of the book focuses on the commission's work as a major part of the overall story of the Melbourne Model. It looks first at the commission's academic influence – its role in redesigning the University's undergraduate course structure – while taking into account 'operational' issues that required immediate attention with at least an interim, if not longer-term, resolution. To combine an account of the 'academic' and 'operational' planning that occurred would lead to a complicated picture of events and might not accurately reflect the over-riding importance of the commission's academic decisions to the monumental changes the University would adopt. Consequently, in this and the following chapter I describe the core academic work of the commission, with minimal reference to some of the important side issues that were part of its considerations and decision-making, then cover the challenges presented for and by the faculties in Chapter 5. Chapter 6 describes the operational issues associated with the Curriculum Commission and the Melbourne Model, and the varied taskforces and working groups that were established to deal with these.[1] Many of these issues could not be resolved until after the undergraduate course structure had been determined. The comprehensive matters of implementation that began in October 2006 and ran into 2007 and beyond will be detailed in Part III.

According to the Vice-Chancellor, part of the rationale for establishing the Curriculum Commission was to test what the University community response would be to some vital questions around curriculum change. Would there be support for one or two generalist degrees? Would it be possible or feasible for all profes-sional courses to be offered at graduate level? How would serious reservations on the part of some faculties be resolved and, if they could not be, what would the impact be on the overall plan for graduate schools? It was here, as the wider implications for indi-viduals and their departments began to become more apparent, that the first signs of resistance, or dispute, began to emerge.

Aims of the Curriculum Commission

The draft strategic plan referred to a curriculum commission as one of several major review groups that would be established to work through the implementation of the Growing Esteem strategy (the others being the Policy and Advocacy Taskforce, the Know-ledge Transfer and the Research and Research Quality taskforces, the Shared Services Review Implementation Group and the Cross Disciplinary Research Working Group). The final version of *Growing Esteem: Strategic Plan 2006* set out the membership and terms of reference for the commission and the timelines for it to complete the curriculum review. It became the main body for dis-cussing and resolving the questions the plan raised.

The terms of reference for the Curriculum Commission make it clear that it was about redesigning the curriculum and course structure rather than undertaking a curriculum review, although one could argue that this is an issue of semantics.[2] For example, the terms of reference included that the commission would 'rec-ommend a 10-year plan for implementing the Melbourne Model', and 'consider the "design dimensions" including number and type of undergraduate degrees, core knowledge to be covered in each degree, number of core and optional subjects', and so on. Design dimensions also included the aspirational expectation that the Melbourne Model could lead to a stronger student cohort experi-ence, dubbed the Melbourne Experience. According to the out-comes of the student experience surveys, many students (especially those in Arts, Science and, to some extent, Commerce) felt isolated and found it difficult to make friends or feel part of the University community. This experience differed from that of most students in professional courses (Medicine, Dental Science, for example, and even Engineering to some degree). In professional degrees, especially those including laboratory work, significant numbers of students were in the same classes throughout the year or the whole course, giving them opportunities to get to know each other well and socialise together. At this early stage of the Melbourne Model developments, it was thought that there would be smaller classes, leading to students feeling more strongly part of a cohort.

Within only four or so months of the Curriculum Commission beginning its work, the collective University was in motion with multiple spokes of the wheel, making their contribution to the core deliberations and operational matters. The commission, the faculties and academic staff were largely focused on how a new course structure and a new curriculum might best be organised. Others were beginning to consider the multifaceted implications of major course changes and manage questions being raised about the foreshadowed changes. The greatest concerns expressed by the University community at this stage were around what would happen to the fourth-year honours program, whether high achievers would be lost to the University without the lure of the professional undergraduate courses and combined degrees or if students preferred to take their qualification at undergraduate level rather than needing two or more years of a fee-based graduate program, and the potential lowering of the University's reputation as a result. A great deal of thought had to be given to what the consequences of a new course structure might be, and how the new course structure and the component curriculum would be put in place. The challenges ahead were extensive.

Getting started

In December 2005, as director of the Melbourne Curriculum Project, I suggested to Professor McPhee that informal, preliminary meetings with each of the deans would be beneficial. As a result, Professor McPhee, Gioconda Di Lorenzo (project officer in the Office of the Deputy Vice-Chancellor (Academic)) and I formed the Curriculum Commission Coordinating Team. The team visited the deans of all faculties between mid-January and early February 2006, before the commission began its work, to understand how prepared for change each faculty was and what their main issues would be in relation to the proposed curriculum review.

Later, the Curriculum Commission Coordinating Team met weekly to exchange information and, among other things, keep track of progress against the broad objectives for the Curriculum Commission set out in the *Growing Esteem: Strategic Plan 2006* and vet the endless number of reports to various committees that had to be prepared.[3] But the preliminary visits it held at this early stage were extremely valuable in helping set the pace for the Curriculum Commission and ensured the commission had a good idea of faculty concerns from the start. Some segments of the University community were clearly ready to embrace a curriculum redesign, but others, particularly within the faculties that offered professional degrees (such as Engineering and Veterinary Science), had a different attitude. These faculties tended to argue along the lines that while they generally supported curriculum changes for other faculties their own courses should continue with minimal or no change. They felt that their programs were already successful and the proposed curriculum changes would only create problems in their courses' ability to meet accreditation requirements rather than improve them. Further, they believed there was great potential for losing high-achieving students – not only school leavers but also honours and research degree candidates – to competitor universities, and that this would diminish the University's high standing in the community.

There was a wide range of views from the faculties, and the following chapter provides a summary of the main issues that each had to deal with for their courses to conform to the Melbourne Model. Needless to say, the variety of opinions meant Professor McPhee had a challenging task in steering the Curriculum Commission to meet the objectives set out in the strategic plan.

The theme of the 2006 Deans and Heads Conference was 'How to Grow Esteem' – in other words, how would the University implement the three main strands of the Growing Esteem strategy: teaching, research and knowledge transfer? The Curriculum Commission was itself a huge undertaking but there were also critical issues in research, as the federal government at that time proposed to introduce a research assessment exercise (for which the University had already taken important steps in preparation), and the knowledge transfer theme was to prove particularly difficult.[4]

Melbourne Model issues paper

To stimulate discussion of the Melbourne Model and launch the work of the Curriculum Commission, Professor McPhee had prepared an issues paper that was circulated for the Deans and Heads Conference. The paper was to generate thinking about the significant curriculum review, rather than exhaustively cover all issues that might arise. The following summary of the questions raised in the paper provided the basis for a small group discussion session of the conference:

How many undergraduate degrees should the University offer?

What should they be called?

Should all undergraduate degrees have a humanities, a science or some other common component?

How would the University retain its attractiveness to top VCE students?

How could the University improve access by students from a disadvantaged background?

How could the University strengthen its research degrees?

What postgraduate programs should be offered?[5]

These questions not only identified what Professor McPhee considered the central issues the Curriculum Commission would have to resolve, they also formed the framework for its early discussions. The issues paper was another key step in the overall process of curriculum change.

The 2006 University Council Planning Conference was held from 17 to 18 February. As council had already accepted the *Growing Esteem: Strategic Plan 2006* with its triple helix metaphor, including the proposal for a curriculum review under the learning and teaching heading, the conference was strongly focused on research. Nevertheless, the conference papers circulated to participants included the Melbourne Model issues paper previously discussed at the Deans and Heads Conference; Professor McPhee made a presentation on 'The Melbourne Experience' and Professor Skene (then president of the Academic Board) talked about implementing Growing Esteem policies, drawing on discussions from the Deans and Heads Conference.[6] The Vice-Chancellor also gave a report on implementing the Growing Esteem strategy including the tasks to be undertaken by the Curriculum Commission. The scene was now set for the Curriculum Commission to begin its work.

Membership and meeting schedule

The first of the Curriculum Commission's 25 meetings was held on 10 February 2006 and the last on 15 September 2006. Meetings were held on Friday afternoons from 2.00 pm, usually in a boardroom in the Alan Gilbert Building, and normally ran for about two hours.

Membership was set out in the *Growing Esteem: Strategic Plan 2006*. Professor McPhee was the chairman, and the core of the commission was made up of the faculty associate deans (academic) or equivalent, the dean of the School of Graduate Studies, the director of the Centre for the Study of Higher Education, and the presidents of the undergraduate and postgraduate student associations. The chairman of the Academic Programs Committee was a member as the nominee of the president of the Academic Board. The Academic Programs Committee would be integral to the eventual consideration and approval of changes to the curriculum and the introduction of new courses. About midway through the commission's work, the chairman of the Academic Board's Selection Procedures Committee, Associate Professor Barry Hughes, was invited to join the commission to advise on and help with the numerous issues of prerequisites, entry requirements and standards and related matters. A representative of the Melbourne Business School, Associate Professor Jenny George, was also invited to attend meetings of the commission. The Assistant Vice-Chancellor (Teaching and Learning), Associate Professor Susan Elliott, the director of the Melbourne Curriculum Project, Dr Mary Emison, and the Vice-Principal and Academic Registrar, Gillian Luck, were members by virtue of their positions and to facilitate the work of the commission. The commission was fortunate to have Gioconda Di Lorenzo as its secretary. She carried out her responsibilities with good humour and patience and wrote superb records of the Commission's deliberations.[7] In addition to this role (which could be somewhat overwhelming given the almost weekly meetings and the need for papers and minutes to be prepared and distributed to members within exceptionally tight timelines) Gioconda Di Lorenzo also drafted most of the reports from the commission to the various bodies such as Academic Board, the Vice-Chancellor's Advisory Group, Planning and Budget Committee and others.

Almost all members of the commission attended at least 21 of the 25 meetings. One exception was a member of the Vice-Chancellor's Office, who only attended the first seven meetings. Thereafter, a representative of the newly established Growing Esteem Strategy Office (GESO), based within the Vice-Chancellor's Office, attended instead. This representation was to ensure appropriate feedback was provided to the Vice-Chancellor and to help report on the commission's work within the overall communications program developed for the Growing Esteem strategy, for which the GESO was responsible.

The second exception was the nominee of the president of the Academic Board, Professor Jeff Borland, chair of the Academic Programs Committee. Professor Borland attended the first ten meetings of the commission. He did not attend further meetings because of what he perceived to be a conflict of interest. As chair of the Academic Programs Committee, he was expected to take a University-wide perspective on issues associated with the Melbourne Model while, at the same time, he was head of department (Economics) in a faculty that was involved in robust and occasionally heated discussions with Professor McPhee about some aspects of the Melbourne Model – in particular, the proposed breadth component of the new degrees. Professor Borland, and others in the Faculty of Economics and Commerce, argued that the Bachelor of Commerce already met the criteria for the new Melbourne Model degrees, including the breadth component, as students had to select from disciplines ranging from accounting to management. Professor McPhee argued to the contrary. Professor Borland states that he 'found it difficult (impossible)' to represent both the academic programs committee and his faculty simultaneously and, therefore, resigned from the commission.[8]

Although Professor Borland may have felt conflict about his membership of the Curriculum Commission, he was recognised by Professor McPhee and others as an exemplary chair of the Academics Program Committee who maintained a high level of objectivity in dealing with the myriad issues relating to the new-generation course proposals over the late 2006 and 2007 period. His experience is indicative of some of the extreme difficulties that faced commission members who had to deal with both University-wide and faculty-specific concerns.

Modus operandi

The *Growing Esteem: Strategic Plan 2006* stated that the University would move to a common degree structure based

around a few generalist three-year undergraduate degrees leading
to intensive professional or research training at graduate level.
The core of the Melbourne Model would be graduate entry to
professional programs. In retrospect, it is possible to identify four
interlinked strands taken up by the Curriculum Commission to
develop these statements into the Melbourne Model, although this
distinction was not made during its work in 2006. These strands
are dealt with in turn below.

Identifying the components

Deciding how many undergraduate degrees would exist under the
Melbourne Model, and what they would be called, was a vital
part of the commission's deliberations on curriculum reform. The
Melbourne Model issues paper and the Core Principles for
Undergraduate Degrees, which were derived from it, encompassed
the broad or overarching academic issues that would have an
impact on the University as a whole and these documents helped
guide the commission. The commission also dealt with other
academic issues, such as the breadth component and graduate
attributes, resolving the numerous questions and concerns that
were raised and finally reaching consensus on the recommendations that were put forward to the Academic Board in the final
report. Both the *Growing Esteem: Strategic Plan 2006* and the
report of the Curriculum Commission also identified the importance and expectation that the Melbourne Model would involve
stronger and better-defined student cohort experiences within the
'Melbourne Experience'.

Discussing pathways to research degrees

It was understood that the major work of the commission was
to resolve the undergraduate degrees to be offered in 2008 under
the Melbourne Model, but the final report also had to make recommendations on research aspects, including the pathways to
research degrees for graduates of the Melbourne Model courses
and other universities, and consider the characteristics that would
contribute to a distinctive Melbourne PhD experience.

Working with the faculties

It was important for the commission to work with each faculty on the changes it was considering or would be making to its course and curriculum structures to ensure these were in line with the decisions of the commission and the intent of the Growing Esteem strategy. There also were meetings within and between faculties to discuss and resolve the various proposals and issues to reach at least basic agreement on courses to be offered under the Melbourne Model. Chapter 5 gives a brief overview of my perceptions of each faculty's main issues in relation to the work of the commission, but does not give in-depth descriptions and details of the numerous issues on which faculties had to decide.[9]

Managing matters as they arose

A myriad of matters needing attention and decision began to appear by the second or third meeting of the Curriculum Commission and increased over the course of its deliberations. This was partly because the Melbourne Model was to be introduced in 2008 and significant lead times were required to advise prospective students of any foreshadowed changes to course structures and requirements. Some of these issues required interim resolutions; all needed careful review in the context of the Melbourne Model and its longer-term implications.

Professor McPhee and the Curriculum Commission were central to working through these four strands and developing concrete structures for the new courses. Once it had submitted its final report to the Academic Board in September 2006, the commission ceased to exist. By this time, however, both academic and administrative structures had been agreed to or established to take on board the further policy and operational work that would have to occur for the Melbourne Model to be introduced from 2008. The scale and scope of this operational work in the implementation of the Melbourne Model, and the large number of taskforces and working parties it involved, are covered in later chapters.

Structure of meetings and related activities

The commission was responsible for a substantive agenda and many difficult decisions. Because of this, the atmosphere in the meetings was often filled with tension. The interplay between members was almost always collegial but occasionally bordered on becoming fractious. Individual members had to strive to fulfil their obligations as part of a body making decisions with a major impact on the whole University, while also having to manage their deans' expectations that they would 'do the right thing for the faculty'. These obligations were often conflicting, but were successfully managed by commissioners, even though they were extremely tough on some members at a personal level. The two student representatives had a particularly onerous responsibility to their constituents.[10] The student body needed assurance that the courses they would be completing were relevant at the same time as the new courses and curriculum had to be of the same high quality and value. The student representatives' main concern was that their degrees would be seen as inferior to the Melbourne Model degrees or the reverse – that is, Melbourne Model students would end up with degrees of a low standard, or would have to pay exorbitant fees to achieve a professional qualification.

As chair of the commission, Professor McPhee managed, with considerable skill, the difficult task of ensuring that all members had the opportunity to express their views and those of their faculties. At the request of members of the commission I drew up, in consultation with the then and previous chairs of the Academic Programs Committee, a schedule of dates by which critical decisions would have to be made for the commission to have a final report ready for the September meeting of the Academic Board and, in due course, for the Melbourne Model courses to be introduced in 2008. This schedule, which helped Professor McPhee pursue the main agenda, was constantly updated and reinforced. Professor McPhee also kept the commission focused on the main issues by personally drafting and updating the core principles for the new generation undergraduate degrees and writing the commission's report to the Academic Board. He recalls this single authorship as pivotal to avoiding lengthy redrafting by a subcommittee.

There were two predominant sentiments running throughout the meetings of the Curriculum Commission. One was that the University was definitely moving to a new course structure along the lines of the Bologna Model (the issues, then, were how many undergraduate degrees would be on offer, would there be a general education component, and so on) while the other had to do with the timing for these changes. That is, some members thought – and argued – that the commission needed to slow down and take time to have more in-depth discussions about any changes and their ramifications. A third sentiment was reflected in the small number within the community who continued to argue for faculties to have the right to opt out of the changes and continue with their courses as they were.

In parallel with the meetings of the commission, Professor McPhee, sometimes accompanied by Dr Emison and/or Gioconda Di Lorenzo, met with faculty staff to discuss the issues specific to their intended course and curriculum changes. There were also meetings to report on and discuss the work of the Curriculum Commission with other groups at planning days or on other occasions, and information sessions that were open to all members of a faculty or the University community. In time, these parallel activities included many, sometimes very difficult, visits to secondary schools and meetings with principals and schools careers advisers. Following approval of the commission's final report, Professor McPhee made an important visit to Hong Kong, Malaysia and Singapore in November 2006, to explain the Melbourne Model to alumni and prospective international students.[11] Most deans also made visits overseas to meet with prospective international students, their parents and alumni. Given the fees that international students have to pay for their courses, there was real concern – most clearly in Engineering – that requiring another two or more years of study to achieve a professional qualification would destroy

Melbourne's international student market and potentially cause the demise of departments or faculties.

First meetings

The first meetings of the Curriculum Commission set the agenda and the pace for its deliberations over the seven months of its existence. These first few meetings were of vital importance, so a brief description of the matters discussed in each is provided below. After this, the story will turn to an outline of how various key decisions were developed over the course of the commission's meetings.

Meeting 1 (10 February 2006)

The Curriculum Commission hit the ground running. As mentioned earlier, the membership and the terms of reference had been specified in *Growing Esteem: Strategic Plan 2006*; Professor McPhee, Dr Emison and Gioconda Di Lorenzo had had a round of meetings with the deans before the commission meetings began; and Professor McPhee's Melbourne Model issues paper had been discussed at the 2006 Deans and Heads Conference, all before the commission's first meeting.

When the Curriculum Commission did first meet, Professor McPhee spoke about the significant role of members: as representatives of their faculty, for providing the interface between the faculty and the commission and with other faculties, and with obligations to the University as a whole. The commission's terms of reference were considered and several suggestions made for changes. The commission received Professor McPhee's Melbourne Model issues paper, the draft *Growing Esteem: Strategic Plan 2006* and notes on relevant outcomes of discussion at the Deans and Heads Conference.

These outcomes covered various aspects of the new strategy. An important one was to not pursue the strategic plan aim of offering two professional graduate programs by 2007 with the focus instead being on offering quality, generalist undergraduate programs by 2008.[12] Discussion of this issue was around offering six general undergraduate degrees, which might be Arts, Science, Planning/Built Environment, Commerce, Performing/Creative Arts and Biomedical Science. It was noted that general reactions to the proposed Melbourne Model were mixed, with some people expressing support and others showing concerns. There was, for example, considerable support for study abroad, online learning, work experience and knowledge transfer experiences as part of the undergraduate student educational experience and some for a compulsory language requirement or a 'cultural studies' component. At the same time, there was concern that all the programs should be of high quality with a balance between a broad educational experience and adequate professional preparation.

In considering these matters, members of the commission expressed a number of their own issues and concerns, which included:

- the complexities of students taking subjects from other faculties and the meaning of broad, foundation studies
- various issues around the possible requirement for all students to study a language
- whether any subjects should be compulsory
- student workloads, given many students were also in paid employment
- the need for market research
- the need to identify exit points for students in the new curriculum design.

Other documents, including advice on the role of the Policy and Advocacy Taskforce, lists of the single and combined bachelors degrees offered in 2005, and a number of focus questions which faculties were asked to work through to help them consider how they might approach changes as participants in the Melbourne Model were also received by the commission for information.[13] On the basis of this material, Professor McPhee agreed to draft core principles for undergraduate degrees for the second meeting.

Meeting 2 (24 February 2006)
The importance of the Melbourne Model issues paper and the draft core principles that evolved from it (drafted, as requested, by Professor McPhee for this meeting) cannot be overstated. Had he taken the option of allowing fully open discussion in these early meetings of the commission, without having some concrete statements for consideration, it would have taken far longer to home in on the most important elements to be discussed and decided upon within the commission and in the faculties. At the second meeting, the draft core principles were discussed in depth with revisions incorporated and a second draft then prepared for discussion at meeting 3. Other substantive items on the agenda were the final *Growing Esteem: Strategic Plan 2006* and a report by Professor Bebbington (then Assistant Vice-Chancellor, University Relations) on knowledge transfer issues relevant to the commission's work.

Already at this second meeting Professor McPhee stressed how important it was for the University to be able to state as early as possible, for marketing and recruitment purposes, the types of undergraduate degrees it would be offering under the Melbourne Model. Five degree programs across the broad discipline ranges were mooted. Members raised various concerns including reluctance to be too specific about the degrees to be offered until feedback had been received from market research, a definite preference (for some) for only two undergraduate degrees (a Bachelor of Arts and a Bachelor of Science) and a conviction that the University should find a way to continue combined or double degrees, as these tended to attract the highest achieving Victorian Certificate of Education (VCE) students.

A straw vote on the proposal for five undergraduate degrees found most members in favour, although some still preferred the two-degree approach. The Faculty of Medicine, Dentistry and Health Sciences pressed for a biomedical science degree to be added to the five. All faculties supported the 75 points breadth component except Economics and Commerce, which had two particular concerns: that accreditation requirements meant the 75 points breadth requirement would not be possible for Accounting and Actuarial Studies majors and a view that 'a one-size fits all' model for the breadth component would be too restrictive when the scope of the subjects offered within the faculty was taken into account. To meet its goal of introducing students to multiple disciplinary perspectives on major subjects, the commission also agreed to investigate an option for the 75 points breadth component to include a selection of 'core' interdisciplinary University subjects in addition to the faculty-based units.

Meeting 3 (3 March 2006)

By the third meeting of the commission, curiosity among members had increased. A number raised issues – partly in response to the draft core principles but also because faculties were beginning to consider what the Melbourne Model might actually mean for their courses. Of major importance was that administration of the new degrees be simple, while other concerns raised are listed below.

Market research

What was the University doing to find out how the wider community perceived its broad-sweeping curriculum review and what its reactions might be?

Introduction of graduate entry courses

It was understood that the new undergraduate courses would not be introduced until 2008, but would graduate entry programs be offered from 2008 or from 2009?

Breadth subjects

Some thought these should have guidelines that lead to coherence rather than be a random selection of 75 points (or whatever the requirement ended up being).

Fourth-year honours programs

These were critical in some faculties for attracting students from other universities and ensuring that a healthy number of students proceeded to research degrees, but it was not yet clear what would happen to them.

Undergraduate degrees

Would these be faculty based or university wide? What would happen to combined or double degrees and, more importantly, how would the University continue to attract the high-achieving students who generally enrolled in the combined degrees?

Postgraduate coursework enhancement

What did the University propose to offer as the classroom postgraduate coursework experience given the large classes that existed at the time?

School of undergraduate studies

Would there be a 'school of undergraduate studies' for administrative purposes only or consequent to structural changes for the faculties?

At this meeting, the commission also considered responses to the focus questions from the faculties of Law and Medicine, Dentistry and Health Sciences. Law was proposing that, subject to a number of changes, the recently introduced Juris Doctor program would become its professional graduate program. The faculty proposed the revamped program would be three years long, although the possibility of offering it as a two-year or two-and-a-half-year accelerated program was also considered. The government's agreement for Commonwealth-supported places to be transferred from undergraduate to graduate level was critical to the success of the graduate program in Law. It was expected that access to the graduate law program would be more equitable as entrance would not be based solely on performance in the VCE.

The Faculty of Medicine, Dentistry and Health Sciences reported that it was considering a three-year undergraduate program for entry to professional graduate degrees of varying lengths, dependent on the discipline. It anticipated that some discipline studies at undergraduate level would be specified as an entry requirement. The faculty also proposed to offer masters programs in a range of disciplines, which would have pathways to research higher degrees.

Meeting 4 (10 March 2006)

At the fourth meeting, the schedule and critical timelines document referred to previously was refined in consultation with the then and past chairs of the Academic Programs Committee.[14] The schedule had three categories, as listed below.

Undergraduate programs

Decisions required particularly for the general education or breadth component, and about which courses were to be discontinued or continued.

Professional graduate programs

Decisions about which ones would be offered and from what year, what their duration would be and which existing courses would be continued or discontinued.

Related activities

For example, deliberations of the high-level Policy and Advocacy Taskforce, communication strategy for schools, information for VTAC and VICTER guides, market research activities, and so on.

The schedule was updated for later meetings and a companion checklist of matters for decisions normally associated with the development of new courses was also prepared.

Meetings 5, 6 and 7 (17, 24, 31 March 2006)

At the fifth meeting, the updated schedule was presented to the commission for consideration. During discussion of the schedule some commission members expressed concerns about the scope of the market research that was to be conducted and stressed the need to ensure timely advice on the prerequisites required if entry to the new generation degrees was to be introduced in 2008.

The commission considered responses to the focus questions from the remaining faculties in meetings 5 and 6. In response to the submission from the Faculty of Medicine, Dentistry and Health Sciences, the chair suggested that, in addition to the proposed new generation Bachelor of Science, the University would need to offer a separate health or biological sciences degree. This was considered necessary, in part, to ensure that 'bright flight' (the loss of high-achieving VCE students) would be minimal.

In meeting 7, the commission discussed in detail a draft plan for postgraduate coursework and research higher degrees pathways, which had been prepared by Professors Evans and James. The comments of members of the commission were noted and Professor Evans agreed to prepare a revised plan for the next meeting. At meeting 7, the commission also reviewed a schedule of its proposed work activity for the next two months, noting that a communications package on Growing Esteem was being prepared to send to schools and would, doubtless, generate questions from them. It noted that a 'frequently asked questions' website was being developed by Student Access that would also play a role in training faculty staff to manage and track the types of questions being asked.

Role of the Academic Board

While the Curriculum Commission was the main body involved in redesigning the curriculum to create the Melbourne Model, the Academic Board was the main body to consider the recommendations of the Curriculum Commission. The Academic Board is the peak academic decision-making body of the University; it oversees the institution's learning, teaching and research activities.[15] It has around 400 members and in 2006 met monthly from February to December.[16]

The board has a number of committees that report to it on specific academic matters. Committees of the board with particular relevance to the work of the Curriculum Commission included the Academic Programs Committee and the Selection Procedures Committee.[17] These two committees would be especially instrumental in approving the 'new generation' bachelor degrees when developed and their prerequisite and entry standards.

The Teaching and Learning Quality Assurance Committee (TALQAC) would have responsibility for assessing and ensuring the quality of the new degrees after they were introduced.

Over the years, attendance numbers at Academic Board meetings have been a good indication of the importance of various matters to the academic community. Early in my career in the University (in the 1970s), a favourite story about the board was the very large attendance at a meeting sometime in the 1960s when there was to be a vote on 'clinical loadings' for academics with medical qualifications. Reportedly, the council chamber (the venue for board meetings) was overflowing, with members sitting in the aisles, because of the multitude of medically qualified academic members who chose to attend that particular day.

Reports, and eventually recommendations, related to the Growing Esteem issues and discussions, and the work of the Curriculum Commission again inspired significant numbers of board members to attend relevant meetings. Usual attendance figures were in the range of 70 to 80 members. In comparison, the February 2005 meeting, the first attended by Vice-Chancellor Professor Glyn Davis, saw one hundred members present, although there were no particular items on the agenda likely to generate a heated discussion. By chance, the *Age* newspaper had, on the morning of the meeting, run a story on the numbers of domestic fee-paying students enrolled in the University. This resulted in a question being raised in 'question time' (a regular item on the board's agenda during which a member may ask a question about any academic matter of any other member). In response, many members participated in a general discussion of the University's undergraduate enrolment strategies. This issue was one of several discussed in the July *Growing Esteem: Choices* discussion paper, with a focus on the significant increase in international student numbers, which the University had adopted as a revenue-raising exercise from the late 1990s.

Another meeting at which attendance far exceeded the usual numbers took place in November 2005. The attraction at this meeting was the inclusion on the agenda of the draft Growing Esteem strategy paper. As reported previously, the move to the Bologna Model (3+2+3) was a prominent feature of the strategy. One hundred and nineteen board members attended this meeting, which featured a two-hour discussion of the three strands proposed in the Growing Esteem strategy paper. During the discussion, thirty members spoke on the topic.

The first 2006 board meeting, in February, had an attendance of 90 members, although the attraction may have been the two items listed for general discussion – a report on intellectual property statutes and policies and a paper on flexible use of the academic year – rather than the president's debriefing paper on Growing Esteem matters from the Deans and Heads Conference. Nevertheless, it is clear from attendance numbers that board members were particularly interested in developments in the strategy's design, and keen to participate in any discussion about it. As the story works through the deliberations of the Curriculum Commission, I will return to the relevant reports and decisions of the Academic Board when necessary, and indicate attendance numbers.

Within six weeks of starting its meetings, the Curriculum Commission was deeply immersed in the major issues to be considered for its eventual recommendations to the Academic Board: numbers, names and core principles of the undergraduate degrees; requirements for the general education or breadth component; and pathways to research degrees. Operational matters such as market research, advice to schools and prospective students, structures to administer the 'new generation' degrees, and other matters were also on the agenda. The next chapter follows the Curriculum Commission's pathways through making decisions about the major academic matters.

4

Pathways of the Curriculum Commission

The Curriculum Commission was required under its terms of reference to report to the Academic Board in September 2006. This gave it only seven months to complete its work and submit a final report – a very tight schedule, given the tasks involved. The pace and activities of the Curriculum Commission in 2006 cannot be accurately conveyed to those who didn't experience it. There was constant dialogue in committee meetings, one-to-one meetings, telephone discussions and email exchanges, feedback on draft papers covering academic and operational matters, and frequent exchanges between and within faculties as they endeavoured to work through the implications for their students, their courses and their staff.

It was a demanding period, during which these dilemmas took up a great deal of staff time. In addition to the work of the Curriculum Commission and the other Growing Esteem taskforces, the everyday work of the University had to carry on as normal. Many academic and professional staff bore extra work throughout 2006. For a significant number, this continued at an increased level well into 2007 and beyond as the Melbourne Model courses were developed and requirements for the introduction of the new course structure and curriculum were resolved.

There were also moments of relief. The process was given a financial boost when a proposal to establish a 'Growing Esteem Transition Fund' (GETF) was floated at the Planning and Budget Committee Conference in June 2006. The Senior Vice-Principal, Ian Marshman, recalls a discussion in council to the effect that if the University was considering 'a transformational business change, the senior management would need to ensure that all the levers were pointing in the same direction'. He says this got him to thinking about resourcing issues and the need to cover the front-end costs of managing change and the curriculum developments, as well as the costs that faculties would incur over the transition period. The initial proposal that Ian prepared was for a 3:1 matching allocation based on $50 million but later this was increased to $85 million. The funds would be needed to support the faculties in their transition to the Melbourne Model, to fund the extensive marketing that would have to be undertaken to ensure success of the new degrees, and for the introduction of new scholarships.[1] The conference recommended that the Finance Committee seek University Council approval for a fund of $85 million to operate over the period from 2007 to 2012. Council support for using University reserve funds in this way was pivotal to further development of the Melbourne Model. Ian believes the GETF program and its implementation was one of his most creative contributions.[2]

The scope of the Melbourne Model project also provided opportunities for groups outside the taskforces to expand their activities. At Professor McPhee's suggestion, the 2005–06 Academic Women in Leadership Group took on the project of updating and revising the University's graduate attributes, completed in a most successful fashion. Likewise, the 2006 Headstart Group worked to develop a proposal for majors and capstone subjects within the Melbourne Model.[3]

Developing the Melbourne Model

The commission itself focused on the 'design' of the future courses and their academic objectives, leaving some of the non-academic issues for later consideration by other groups. This chapter follows the process by which the academic dimensions of the Melbourne Model were established by the commission, with particular attention to its key decisions. These included the number and names of the 'new generation' undergraduate degrees, the constitution of the breadth component, graduate attributes, majors, knowledge transfer issues and pathways to research degrees.

Specific recommendations in the Curriculum Commission's final report relate to these with the following being most significant (my emphases in italic):

Recommendation 3
That the revised statement of *graduate attributes* be adopted...

...

Recommendation 5
The Curriculum Commission recommends that particular attention be paid to the core characteristics identified for the 'new generation' undergraduate courses, and specifically that the 'new generation' courses:

- are characterised by academic development across the three years;
- focus on first- and final-year cohort experiences;
- *ensure that all students undertake at least one 'major' or equivalent;*
- ensure that multiple postgraduate options are kept open through all three years of the course wherever possible;
- have an exposure to an appropriate research experience;
- *are characterised by a 'knowledge transfer' component, and draw on the advice of an external advisory board;*
- pay explicit attention to e-learning experiences and development; and
- are available as sequential degrees with reciprocal recognition of 100 points of credit.

...

Recommendation 7
That students undertake the minimum of 75 points (or one-quarter of the degree) of *breadth subjects in disciplines which are not available within their core programs.*[4]

In relative terms, most of these requirements were readily accepted after discussion and debate, as they reflect principles that were and are core to the University's teaching and learning. The general education or breadth component, where all degrees would include a compulsory 75 points from another faculty or discipline, proved to be the most contentious requirement, although it was the number of new generation undergraduate degrees, and the names for some of these, that resulted in the most heated debates. As explained later in this chapter, the inclusion of knowledge transfer as a component of the new generation degrees was also problematic.

Broad discipline groups

Determining the number of undergraduate degrees to be offered under the Melbourne Model and what they would be called was the first critical issue for the Curriculum Commission to resolve – and a very difficult one. Professor McPhee's Melbourne Model issues paper referred to perhaps having two undergraduate degrees, a Bachelor of Arts and a Bachelor of Science. Discussion at the Deans and Heads Conference, however, had resulted in the possibility of six 'liberalist' undergraduate degree programs: Arts, Biomedical Science, Commerce, Science, Planning/Built Environment and Performing/Creative Arts. Professor McPhee's discussion paper on the core principles, which drew on the themes developed in the Melbourne Model issues paper, was discussed at the commission's second meeting, held on 24 February 2006. In this discussion there was agreement to the following broad discipline groupings as the basis for the potential development of five degrees:

- humanities/social sciences
- general and biomedical science
- economics and commerce
- technology and the built environment
- visual and performing arts.

Most members of the commission supported the development of five degrees, although a number would have preferred fewer. The Faculty of Medicine, Dentistry and Health Sciences indicated it would prefer a separate biomedical science degree in addition to a general science degree, a recurring theme in the commission's discussions. Whichever of these options prevailed, the number of degrees offered would be markedly fewer than those then available.

In 2006, the University offered more than 40 single bachelor degrees. Many of these were offered in combination with another bachelor degree, bringing the total number of bachelor degrees (excluding honours degrees) with enrolments in 2005 to more than one hundred. The bachelors degree programs were faculty-specific and faculty-administered. In effect, the faculties 'owned' their degrees, and held full responsibility for them. In general terms, the degree names signified the broad discipline area of the faculty, such as Bachelor of Science, Bachelor of Commerce, Bachelor of Agriculture and Bachelor of Education (Primary). Others carried more specific discipline names such as Bachelor of Computer Science and Bachelor of Dental Science.

Many of the highest achieving school leavers who enrolled at the University elected to study a combined degree program – both through interest and to enhance career prospects. Having succeeded in individual subjects from a range of disciplines, students did not always complete the full requirements for the second degree. Single degree students, especially those in Arts and Science, already had the option of taking subjects from other faculties but did not always do so. Students studying undergraduate professional courses were more restricted in their subject choices, in part because of accreditation requirements but sometimes also because of faculty-imposed limitations. According to student feedback surveys, course advice for combined degree students, in particular, was less than optimal; students had to seek course and subject guidance from each of the faculties involved in teaching the disciplines of interest. Consequently, as reported earlier, there was a view within the University community that not only would a new approach lead to Melbourne graduates who were more competitive on the global scene but, also, an added emphasis given to the Melbourne Experience would produce other advantages such as improved services for students. As a former president of the Academic Board, Professor McPhee thought the curriculum changes provided a once-in-a-lifetime opportunity to ensure that all students received consistent advice, support services and academic processes rather than this being dependent on the faculty in which they were enrolled.

The initial intention of the draft *Growing Esteem: Strategic Plan 2006* was for the new undergraduate programs, as well as a small number of professional graduate programs, to be introduced in 2007. This overlooked the extended requirements the University has for notifying prospective students of courses available and their entrance criteria, to say nothing of the significant amount of work that would be required to achieve such a rapid change. Fortunately, some of the pressure on the Curriculum Commission was relieved when it was agreed at the February 2006 Deans and Heads Conference that the generalist undergraduate degrees should be developed in time to be introduced in 2008. The proposal for two professional graduate programs to be introduced in 2007 was put on hold.

By the commission meeting held on 31 March 2006, two changes had been agreed to in the broad discipline groups, now referred to as core fields, for the undergraduate courses. These changes were the inclusion of music with visual and performing arts and the addition of technology with the sciences. The core fields were now:

- the arts, including humanities and the social sciences
- the sciences, including biomedical science and technology
- economics, commerce and business
- the natural and built environment
- music, visual and performing arts.

In discussing faculty responses to the focus questions in the commission's fifth meeting, Professor McPhee proposed there might be a need for the University to offer a separate biomedical or health sciences degree. As already indicated in the previous chapter, this proposal was most likely the result of discussion in the Vice-Chancellor's Advisory Group meeting on 7 March 2006, and a response to continuing concerns about 'bright flight'. Representatives of the faculties of Medicine, Dentistry and Health Sciences and Science indicated they would discuss the issue outside commission meetings.

Around this time, the Vice-Chancellor also suggested the commission might consider an additional degree – a Bachelor of Philosophy, Politics and Economics – modelled on the PPE offered in a number of European and North American institutions. The idea was for an elite degree for high-achieving students interested in progressing to graduate study and careers in financial, public service and business management, among other areas. The faculties that would have provided the degree's core teaching did not support this suggestion, so it did not go ahead.

The commission continued to review and refine the broad discipline groups for the Melbourne Model undergraduate degrees. As well, Professor McPhee provided a report on Curriculum Commission developments to the monthly meetings of the Academic Board. At the March meeting, he told the Academic Board that the commission was working towards developing a broad framework for the undergraduate degrees which would include a general education component. He further reported that the Academic Women in Leadership Group was updating the graduate attributes statement.

April: A four-year degree and Academic Board concerns

In April, at the request of the Vice-Chancellor (and following his email exchange with an academic staff member), the commission considered a proposal for a four-year degree, which could be followed by a two-year professional degree or research studies. Both the Vice-Chancellor and the commission agreed the proposal had merit, but had to concede it was unlikely that the government would provide funding for a broad-scale, four-year degree.

Growing Esteem, including a report from the Curriculum Commission, was listed at the April board meeting as the 'general discussion' item. Professor McPhee reported it was critical for the Curriculum Commission to develop a small number of distinctive, three-year undergraduate degrees that would include a general education component but would also prepare graduates for professional or research postgraduate programs. They also needed to be regarded as strong degrees in themselves. The considerable discussion by Academic Board members (with 92 in attendance), focused on a range of issues. One was the 'risk' of moving medical courses to graduate level and, again, the potential loss of high-achieving school leavers. Melbourne already offered its medical course at school-leaver or graduate-entry levels, while several other Australian universities had moved to graduate-entry only medical courses. Melbourne's sister university, Monash, had a school-leaver entry medical program, and part of the concern about offering only a graduate entry medical degree might have been about the loss of the high-achieving VCE students to the Monash course. Concerns were also expressed about preparations for Open Day – in particular, what advice would be given to prospective students about the potential changes; how the University could ensure that its postgraduate courses would continue to be accessible to graduates from other institutions and the possible disadvantage to individual faculties caused by some of the proposed 'new generation' undergraduate degrees continuing to be faculty-specific while others crossed faculty boundaries.

The Curriculum Commission meeting on 28 April 2006 considered a discussion paper, co-authored by Professor Richard

James and Dr Kerri-Lee Krause from the Centre for the Study of Higher Education, that focused on possibilities and issues associated with the 'general education' component in the Melbourne Model. The paper raised a number of questions for the commission to consider and presented five options for resolving them. The commission discussed this paper at some length and agreed that when minor modifications had been incorporated it should be distributed to faculties for comment back to the commission. After this, the authors would be asked to develop a suggested framework for the general education component in the Melbourne Model. At this meeting, the commission also noted that the Headstart Group would be developing a proposal for 'majors' within the Melbourne Model.

May: Academic Board discusses core principles, numbers and names

The Curriculum Commission meeting on 12 May 2006 considered an updated version of the core principles for undergraduate degrees that the chair proposed to take to the Academic Board meeting on 25 May for comment. Responses from most faculties to the James and Krause paper on the general education component of the Melbourne Model were also listed for discussion. Most faculties now supported the proposed 75 points general education or 'breadth' component, so there was less discussion of this issue, although a few continued to argue for flexibility to include subjects from within the cognate discipline or for a requirement of less than 75 points.

The principles paper included the core fields (unchanged since the end of March) and names for the proposed five bachelors degrees, with some provisos:

The 'new generation' undergraduate courses will be offered from 2008 in five core fields:
1. The arts, including humanities and the social sciences
2. The sciences, including biomedical science and technology

3. Economics, commerce and business
4. The natural and built environment
5. Music, visual and performing arts

Proposed degree nomenclature:
1. Bachelor of Arts*
2. Bachelor of Science**
3. Bachelor of Commerce
4. Bachelor of Natural and Built Environments***
5. Bachelor of Music***[5]

The proposal included the notation 'Some other undergraduate courses will continue to be offered, at least in 2008', as for several courses it was yet to be decided if they would be included in (or transformed for) the Melbourne Model.

For the Curriculum Commission meeting on 19 May 2006, the chair proposed two models for naming the new generation degrees, a generic model and a specific model. The generic model used names such as Bachelor of Arts and Sciences or Bachelor of Arts and Sciences with the core discipline field (for example, music) included in brackets after the degree name. The specific model continued to use the discipline names such as Bachelor of Arts or Bachelor of Commerce, with the Bachelor of Natural and Built Environments having been changed to the Bachelor of Design, Technology and Environments.

The commission agreed that the generic model was a better reflection of the University's intentions in moving to the Melbourne Model but that it was too great a change to sell in the Australian context. The specific names were generally accepted with the exception of the Bachelor of Design, Technology and Environments, which was not supported by the faculties that would be the main contributors to the course. Further discussion was required to resolve the name for this degree to the satisfaction of the participating faculties and the commission.

In the two-week period leading up to the Academic Board meeting on 25 May, there were several meetings and an increase in email exchanges between Professor McPhee and faculty representatives involved in some of the more difficult issues. These included Engineering, Land and Food Resources and Architecture, Building and Planning in relation to the Bachelor of Environments; Engineering about whether it would participate in any of the undergraduate courses of the Melbourne Model for its core disciplines in 2008; and Medicine, Dentistry and Health Sciences and Science over the proposed Bachelor of Biosciences.

The Curriculum Commission report, with the James and Krause discussion paper on the general education component as an attachment, was submitted for consideration at the Academic Board meeting on 25 May 2006. It included the proposed core principles for undergraduate degrees, the five broad core fields (which were unchanged from the commission's mid-May meeting) and these proposed degree names:

- Bachelor of Arts
- Bachelor of Science
- Bachelor of Commerce
- Bachelor of Environment, Design and Technology
- Bachelor of Music

There was also the usual notation, and only minor changes had been made to the conditions associated with the proposed degree names since the previous meeting.

Professor McPhee had identified the following five points to be discussed by the board:

- the number and provisional names of the 'new generation' undergraduate degrees
- the status of these degrees as university programs in the context of Growing Esteem, of particular relevance to multi-faculty programs
- the commission's view that disciplinary breadth was to be achieved by 75 points to be taken outside the core program, respecting both intellectual coherence and student choice

- aligning the degrees with the other strands of the triple helix through distinctive curriculum characteristics
- achieving the requisite balance between disciplinary breadth and academic preparation for postgraduate study.[6]

The president of the Academic Board, Professor Skene, advised members there would be no 'vote' taken on the five items identified for discussion. With more than one hundred members in attendance at this meeting, the board had a lively and wide-ranging discussion of the Curriculum Commission report, particularly on the proposed breadth component, equity and access issues and the importance of student advice to the success of the Melbourne Model. The topic was one that aroused deep emotional feeling around specific points and, while always civilised, featured some passionate arguments. One of the most frequent pleas at board meetings during this period was for more time to consider and debate the proposals. But, of course, this was just not possible given the tight timeframes to which the University was working.

At its meeting on the following day (26 May 2006), the Curriculum Commission heard a report on the board's discussion of the core principles and proposed degree names. The commission noted that names for the human biosciences degree, if the course was approved, and the natural and built environment program would have to be resolved soon and certainly by the time documents were printed for distribution on Open Day in August 2006.

June: Names for five – or six – new generation degrees
At the Curriculum Committee meeting on 2 June 2006, Professor McPhee, as chair, stated that he wished to have resolved for report to the Academic Board meeting scheduled for 22 June the proposed names for all new generation undergraduate degrees and confirmation the faculties of Science and Medicine, Dentistry and Health Sciences had agreed there should be an undergraduate biosciences degree. The chair also reported that the Faculty of Engineering had agreed that its core discipline streams would most

likely be offered through the Bachelor of Science, and that the name of the degree for the core field of 'natural and built environment' would be Bachelor of Environment(s), subject to the approval of the Faculty of Architecture, Building and Planning. Members noted that students would have the option of studying biosciences through the Bachelor of Science as well as through the Bachelor of Bioscience degree.

By the next meeting (held on 9 June 2006), the proposed names of the six 'new generation' degrees that had been endorsed by the commission had been refined to:

- Bachelor of Arts
- Bachelor of Science
- Bachelor of Bioscience
- Bachelor of Commerce
- Bachelor of Environments *or* Bachelor of Environments and Design
- Bachelor of Music

Debate over the name for the Bachelor of Environments or Bachelor of Environments and Design continued. Professor McPhee had encouraged the commission to be consistent in naming the degrees and supported Bachelor of Environments as a single word that would encapsulate its scope.

The Curriculum Commission noted that over the previous week several media reports had indicated the federal Minister for Education had given in-principle approval to the University's proposal to transfer some of its undergraduate Commonwealth-supported places to the postgraduate level. Nevertheless, the University had not yet received written confirmation of this approval.

At this 9 June meeting, the commission heard a presentation on the graduate attributes project from the Academic Women in Leadership Group and discussed a proposed list of attributes under five categories. A number of suggestions were made and the commission noted that the Academic Women in Leadership Group would present their report to Professor McPhee before the end of June and eventually to the Vice-Chancellor. A comprehensive report that included the proposed attributes would be brought to the commission for consideration in August.

As in May, the June meeting of the Academic Board, with just under one hundred members in attendance, saw another lively and wide-ranging discussion of the proposed names for the new generation undergraduate degrees. Before the report from the Curriculum Commission was discussed, the Dean of Engineering, Professor Jannie van Deventer, read a statement advising that his faculty had 'concluded that it was in the best interest of engineering education at the University of Melbourne to offer a redesigned four-year Bachelor of Engineering program', and would delay a move to the Melbourne Model until such time as the faculty had been able to work through what it perceived to be serious financial and marketing issues. He went on to say that the faculty did look forward to moving to the Melbourne Model in due course. Nevertheless, the faculty had agreed that the discipline of geomatics would be offered through the new Bachelor of Environments. Much of the board discussion of the commission's recommendation for nomenclature of the new generation undergraduate degrees was focused on the pros and cons associated with the University offering both a Bachelor of Science and a Bachelor of Bioscience. The discussion, which became quite heated, included comments on what some members considered were pragmatic reasons for offering the two degrees: that it would satisfy a perceived community expectation for the University to have a biosciences course, and would continue to attract high-achieving school leavers. A vote on the motion resulted in the names proposed for the six new generation degrees being endorsed by a substantial majority.

The proposal to include a bioscience as well as a science degree in the Melbourne Model was complex and related to student numbers and academic issues. That is, there were concerns that a bioscience degree would detract students from the core physical and mathematical science disciplines in favour of preclinical biological sciences taught by the Faculty of Medicine, Dentistry and Health Sciences. Alternatively, some in the Faculty of Medicine, Dentistry and Health Sciences were concerned that only subjects taught by the faculty could adequately prepare students for a medical degree. As indicated, these concerns appeared early in the deliberations of the Curriculum Commission and, although some would argue that a single science degree might have been a more satisfactory outcome, the two faculties worked collaboratively in reaching agreement on discipline options available in the two degrees.

July: Challenge to Academic Board June meeting minutes

The intensity of the Academic Board's discussion of the proposal for both a science and a bioscience degree to be included in the new generation suite of courses was reflected in the July meeting when a member questioned the accuracy of the minute (number 14.2) of the June meeting that referred to the discussion. The statement in question was: 'The Board then voted, by a substantial majority, to approve the names of new generation undergraduate degrees to be introduced under the Melbourne Model'.

The outcome of this query was reported in the minutes of the 27 July meeting:

> The minutes of meeting 5.06 held on 22 June 2006 were confirmed without amendment although several members commented that to describe the vote in favour of the names of the new generation degrees (minute 14.2) as being carried 'by a substantial majority' was an overstatement given the closeness of the vote. The President noted that it is not Board practice to record voting numbers in the minutes where voting is done by a show of hands but the vote was roughly 2:1 in favour.[7]

But this was not the end of the challenge. In the August board meeting, the president, Professor Loane Skene, reported that several members had made representations to her following the July meeting, again with concerns about the words 'by a substantial majority' used in minute 14.2 of the June meeting. On the basis of these concerns, the president suggested it would be desirable for the minutes to be amended with minute 8.3 of the August meeting to read:

> The Board resolved that the words 'by a substantial majority' be deleted from the penultimate paragraph of minute 14.2 of the minutes of meeting 5.06 of the Academic Board held on 22 June 2006 and that the following sentence be added to the paragraph: 'A majority of those members who voted were in favour of the motion'.[8]

July: Visitors from Harvard and the University of Queensland

Early in 2006, Professor McPhee had invited Professor James Wilkinson, Director of the Derek Bok Center for Teaching and Learning at Harvard University, to visit Melbourne in relation to the curriculum review. Harvard was undergoing its own curriculum review, which had begun in 2002 but had not been resolved by early 2006. Lunch for the Curriculum Commission with Professor Wilkinson was a pleasant occasion for reflection on progress, as was an earlier dinner at which commission members were encouraged to enjoy a social occasion without reference to their challenges. In addition, Associate Professor Fred D'Agostino, Director of Studies in the Faculty of Arts and Director of the Contemporary Studies Program at the University of Queensland, who was working on a project relevant to the curriculum review at that time, was also invited to visit.

Professor Wilkinson visited during the week of 10 to 14 July. During this time he gave the Menzies Oration and participated in several activities related to the work of the Curriculum

Commission. He attended the meeting of the commission on 14 July 2006 and shared his knowledge and experiences at Harvard on a range of issues relevant to the commission's deliberations. His comments on issues surrounding the breadth component of the model were of particular interest. He emphasised the need for expert and accurate course advice as integral to students getting maximum benefit from the breadth component.

Associate Professor D'Agostino attended the Curriculum Commission meeting of 21 July 2006. He spoke about his project for conveners of majors and sequences of study, emphasising that universities should aim to develop general principles for how majors programs might be 'fit for purpose', which could then be adapted for individual disciplines, and also to introduce students to core knowledge and disciplinary culture as early as possible in their courses. This clarity in majors would be important for the new generation degrees under the Melbourne Model.

July: New generation course descriptions and entry requirements

Discussion about the breadth component continued, especially at the faculty level, with the Curriculum Commission noting at its meeting on 7 July 2006 that it would be important to distinguish the 75 points breadth component from 'majors'. The commission agreed to clarify this point for the next iteration of the core principles.

Also at this meeting, the commission reviewed a draft outline of the content proposed for Open Day product sheets on each of the new generation undergraduate degrees. These descriptions had to include prerequisite requirements for each of the degrees and comments on pathways to further study or employment when the degrees had been completed. The Student Entry Pathways Subcommittee was in the process of considering the prerequisite requirements. No changes to the prerequisites for the existing courses were expected for the new generation degrees in Arts, Commerce and Music, but prerequisites had yet to be determined for the new Bachelor of Environments and those for the Science and Bioscience degrees had not been finalised.

Preparing these new generation course descriptions was an important step in shaping future developments. The long lead times for informing students about course prerequisites and other requirements for individual courses places considerable constraints on the timing of any changes an institution may wish to make. As a participant in the Victorian Tertiary Education Commission (VTAC) process for the selection of students into tertiary courses, the University has to satisfy a number of criteria and requirements in relation to both content and timing. Already, the University was in the situation of wishing to introduce new undergraduate courses in 2008 when the prerequisites for 2008 course admissions had been finalised and communicated to students in 2005.

The next phase of discussions over the draft descriptions of the six new generation courses took place at the July Academic Board meeting. While individual faculties had strong views about the wording of the descriptions, the board discussion was focused on the proposed entrance requirements for the new Bachelor of Environments, the Bachelor of Science and the Bachelor of Bioscience. The prerequisite requirements for the Bachelor of Environments were straightforward, with the participating faculties reaching agreement that there would be 'assumed knowledge' of mathematics for some majors offered in this degree instead of a rigid mathematics prerequisite.

The more difficult decision came with the variation in prerequisites proposed for the Bachelor of Science and the Bachelor of Bioscience. There was difference not only in the subject requirements but also in the standard of achievement expected. For example, all applicants for admission to the University must satisfy an English language requirement, this being VCE English for Victorian school leavers. The proposal for five of the new generation courses was to continue with an achievement standard of 25 in English, while 35 was proposed for the Bioscience degree, not only for English but also for the other prerequisite subjects (Chemistry and one of Mathematical Methods, Specialist Maths or Physics). VCE Biology was included as one of the optional prerequisites for the Science degree while it was excluded from the prerequisites for Bioscience.

Discussion in the board meeting pointed out the proposed variations in prerequisite requirements seemed at odds with the message of coherence inherent in the Melbourne Model. Some members thought the proposed prerequisites for the Bioscience degree gave an impression that it would be a 'pre-med' course and not one of the Melbourne Model new generation degrees. Others argued that prerequisites needed to be more open to achieve equity in admissions, suggesting that common prerequisites across the six degrees would be preferable to the maze of subject requirements for selection into the existing undergraduate degrees.

The discussion concluded with the adoption of this motion:

> That the Board approves entry criteria for the six new generation degrees for 2008 ... subject to the revision of the Science prerequisites as outlined above and that further discussions on the Bioscience prerequisites take place between SEPSC and relevant Deans with a view to the introduction of VCE Biology as a prerequisite and changing prerequisite scores from 35 to 25, with the Academic Board President approving any such changes on behalf of the Board. The Board notes that all prerequisites will require the approval of VTAC and will also need to be reviewed towards the end of 2006 in developing entrance requirements for 2009.[9]

As in the June meeting, at which it was decided the Melbourne Model would comprise six new generation degrees, the July meeting had a healthy attendance of just over 90 members and, because of the importance of the discussion on the course descriptions and prerequisites, ran almost an hour more than its standard limit of two hours. A fundamental issue had been resolved. The simplicity of prerequisites would be an important step in enabling the University to meet its target of broadening access to university entry.

August: The breadth component

With content of the written material about the Melbourne Model for use on Open Day resolved, in early August the Curriculum Commission returned to finalising the policy for the breadth component. To aid this process, Professor James prepared a draft framework to guide faculties on how to develop breadth subjects and sequences for the new generation degrees. The draft included a statement that explained the rationale for breadth subjects to students, identified learning objectives for the subjects, and demonstrated how the breadth component might contribute to the new curriculum in its interdisciplinary content and learning objectives and the teaching methods to be used.

At this 4 August meeting, the commission also considered a discussion paper on the status of languages in the new curriculum, prepared by a Faculty of Arts subcommittee on languages. In the earliest stages of the commission's deliberations the prospect had been raised that all students might be required to study a language as part of their degree course in the Melbourne Model. This latest paper focused on languages as an option for the breadth component of the new generation degrees. After debating the proposal, the commission agreed that a sequence of 75 points of language studies would satisfy the breadth component if the focus was on cross-cultural knowledge as much as on language acquisition.

At its meeting on 11 August 2006 the Curriculum Commission discussed a first draft of its report to the Academic Board which named the new generation degrees to be offered in 2008 as:

- Bachelor of Arts
- Bachelor of Bioscience
- Bachelor of Commerce

- Bachelor of Environments
- Bachelor of Music* (*Name of degree to be reviewed when courses at the VCA move to the Melbourne Model)
- Bachelor of Science.

The commission had extensive discussion at this meeting on the proposed requirements for the breadth component. A member suggested that the final report would need to emphasise both the depth and the breadth in the new generation degrees. Others suggested that trying to achieve depth as well as breadth was an oxymoron. The term 'deep generalist degree' was proposed as the preferred description for the new generation degrees – as opposed to 'liberal education' or 'generalist', which implied that the new degrees would not prepare employable graduates. Fortunately, the contradictory term did not survive long enough to be included in the Melbourne Model definitions in Appendix 12 of the Curriculum Commission's final report.

The next major discussions of the draft occurred at a mid-year Deans and Heads Conference on 23 August 2006 (held explicitly to discuss developments in the Melbourne Model including the commission's draft report) and at the Curriculum Commission meeting on 25 August. The Deans and Heads Conference was generally favourable towards the draft report and participants were especially interested in the proposed Board of Undergraduate Studies (BUGS), which will be discussed in a later chapter.

The commission took feedback from the Deans and Heads Conference into account and resolved the outstanding issues within the breadth component, which included establishing the core principles defining breadth; deciding that, in a small number of cases, there would have to be an exception to the disciplines from which the breadth subjects were selected; and that students should be able to select from a range of custom-designed 'University' breadth subjects, which would be interdisciplinary and available to all undergraduate students.

August: Knowledge transfer

As indicated previously, the new generation degrees in the Melbourne Model were to include a knowledge transfer component. The complexity of this third strand of the 2006 Growing Esteem strategy's 'triple helix' has continued to the present time.

The Curriculum Commission grappled with the issue in its deliberations. At the same time, the Knowledge Transfer Taskforce was working to resolve the issues of defining knowledge transfer and other matters parallel with the Curriculum Commission and the other Growing Esteem taskforces. The commission heard presentations and discussed various written materials on knowledge transfer developments at several meetings. Professor Bebbington met with the commission in February 2006 and provided a definition and then, at the next meeting, several examples of knowledge transfer were made available. These included work experience placements and internships in professional settings; tutoring and practice teaching assignments in schools; applied research projects examining an external problem or testing a solution in the field. There was further discussion at meetings in May and in July. At the meeting on 28 July 2006 Professor Pattison, who was also a member of the Knowledge Transfer Taskforce, commented on a paper from the taskforce. The paper articulated the ways knowledge transfer was already embedded in the University's teaching and learning activities. Some members of the commission argued that the examples given were just part of the normal day-to-day teaching and learning program and it seemed inappropriate to refer to these as knowledge transfer activities.

The commission further considered the knowledge transfer issue when discussing its final report. It concluded it would not be possible to mandate knowledge transfer activities for the new generation degrees for practical and equity reasons. For example, it would be neither appropriate nor equitable to insist that all undergraduate students should have a study abroad or other overseas experience during their degree at Melbourne. Likewise, not all courses would provide work experience. Nevertheless, the soon-to-be established course standing committees would be expected to take knowledge transfer activities into account when designing specific Melbourne Model courses.

Professor Pattison revised the Knowledge Transfer Taskforce paper in light of the commission's discussion. The paper appeared in the final report of the commission as Appendix 6, 'Knowledge Transfer and the Curriculum: A Discussion Paper'.

Pathways to research higher degrees in the Melbourne Model

Much of the commission's focus was on discussing and resolving vital aspects of the new generation undergraduate degrees, but it also participated in considering issues around higher degrees. The importance of the University's research training activities and performance was included in the Curriculum Commission's terms of reference for the design dimensions with two items listed for consideration: explicit pathways for research higher degree programs and mechanisms for transition between research and 'professional' pathways, and exceptions to the typical 3+2+3 structure for bachelors/masters/doctorate in the Melbourne Model (for example, honours years).

The *Growing Esteem: Strategic Plan 2006* included establishing a research taskforce to consider the broader implications of research and 'make recommendations to improve the quality and impact of University research and research training by the end of September 2006'.[10]

As a member of the Curriculum Commission, Professor Barbara Evans, then Dean of the School of Graduate Studies, in cooperation with the Research Higher Degrees Committee and the Associate Deans (Research Training), took the lead in considering these items and eventually bringing proposals to the Curriculum Commission. The first discussion of the pathways issue in the commission (at the 3 March 2006 meeting) was based on annotations to the Melbourne Model core principles paper to highlight or add in matters specific to research higher degrees. One point related to the suggestion that, taking into account research higher degrees, it would be preferable to think of the Melbourne Model in terms of eight years of study – that is, 4+4 – as opposed to the 3+2+3 model. Members had ongoing concerns that constant reference to the proposed undergraduate degrees as 'generalist' could be misleading and that it would be preferable to use alternative terminology that emphasised the academic quality of the proposed programs. General opinion was that the pathway should be flexible and provide adequate academic preparation, regardless of whether it would lead to a professional program or to a research degree. These suggestions were incorporated into later iterations of the core principles paper.

Over the next several weeks, Professor Evans continued to consult members of the academic community; in particular, the Associate Deans, the Research and Research Training Committee and the Research Higher Degrees Committee. These consultations helped shape the various versions of the research pathways papers.

By the end of March, Professor Evans and Professor James had prepared a discussion paper, 'Research Higher Degree Pathways within the Melbourne Model', which emphasised the importance of ensuring a flexible undergraduate curricula to accommodate students whether they elected to follow a research path or a professional one. The paper also stressed that the pathways should continue to cater for students from other universities who wished to pursue research degrees at Melbourne, or Melbourne graduates who might pursue further study at another Australian or overseas university.

Consistent with the brief to develop recommendations to improve the quality of the University's research training, the paper suggested that the Melbourne Model provided an opportunity for developing a 'distinctive Melbourne PhD', which might include high-level 'coursework' and that would fit into an eight-year program. This would be the 4+4 model with the undergraduate fourth year as honours followed by a four-year combined masters and PhD. For this option to be successful the University would have to persuade the Commonwealth Government to increase research scholarship funding from three and a half years to four years to cover the additional six months of candidature. Several faculties supported the two-year masters, which they considered would offer a stronger preparation for the PhD.

After further consultation with deans and associate deans, the Research Higher Degrees Committee Working Group prepared a revised paper, 'Growing Esteem, the Melbourne Model and Research Higher Degrees'. This paper, which was reviewed by the Curriculum Commission in late May, continued with the earlier themes of flexibility and an honours year under the umbrella of a 4+4 model for research higher degrees. The paper elaborated on the proposed optional advanced studies program for PhD students, which would comprise 50 points or the equivalent of one semester of full-time study. The commission discussed the paper in detail and some members expressed support for the advanced studies program as a feasible way for the University to do something truly distinctive. Some faculties also expressed strong support for continuing the honours year.

The next iteration was a research higher degrees pathways key issues paper in which the following three items of concern were identified: that the new generation degrees may leave students insufficiently prepared in discipline areas to undertake honours or postgraduate programs; that students taking new generation undergraduate degrees and then proceeding to professional graduate programs may be discouraged from pursuing research higher degrees because of the increased costs and time involved; and that an advanced studies program would lengthen the PhD and compromise the University's capacity to improve PhD completion rates. The paper suggested several solutions to these problems but the commission, when it discussed the paper, did not agree on any of them.

A later iteration of the higher degrees pathways paper (discussed by the commission in its meeting on 18 August 2006) had two components: 'Principal pathways into research higher degrees in the Melbourne Model' and 'Providing a distinctive Melbourne PhD Experience'. The paper proposed the alternative paths of an honours year or two-year masters to research higher degrees. The distinctive Melbourne PhD would be based on all PhD students being strongly encouraged and funded to have an international experience during their candidature, and to complete a Melbourne Advanced Studies Program, although neither of these would be a compulsory requirement.

While some members supported the honours year as a pathway to research higher degrees, the commission agreed that departments and faculties would be best placed to determine the most appropriate pathway for their students. The commission supported flexible pathways and agreed that within the breadth component of the new generation degrees, there could be a generic 'research orientation stream' of 25 or 37.5 points made available to all undergraduate students.

The papers outlining these options were discussed at the Academic Board meeting on 24 August 2006. Before this meeting, discussions of the Melbourne Model and the Curriculum Commission deliberations at the board had been concerned with the undergraduate courses, although there were also questions about the future of the honours year. The discussion was wide-ranging and included questions or comments on honours as a pathway to research degrees or as an endpoint; the necessity to provide bridging programs for students who lacked research experience in their professional graduate course but who wished to progress to a research degree; concern about which committee would have final say on honours year requirements and structure; support for the advanced studies program but a preference for it not to be referred to as a certificate; and ensuring the pathways were flexible enough to cater for students from varying backgrounds and qualifications.

The papers were revised again, taking into account feedback from the board discussion and the August Deans and Heads Conference. Following further discussion in the commission

meeting held on 1 September 2006, revisions of the two papers
were included in the commission's final report with a brief description and seven recommendations, four related to research pathways and three to a distinctive Melbourne PhD experience.

September 2006: The final report

At its twenty-third meeting, on 1 September 2006, the Curriculum
Commission heard a presentation by the Headstart Group, which
had been considering whether majors and capstone subjects
should be a part of the new generation degrees and, if so, how a
major should be constituted. The commission supported the recommendations in the report that related to the principle of depth
(majors) in the new generation degrees, but acknowledged that
capstone subjects might not be relevant to all disciplines. The
commission also discussed an updated draft of its final report, and
clarified particular aspects relating to the breadth component and
various references in the report about implementing the Melbourne
Model. In its meeting on 8 September 2006, the commission discussed the next iteration of its final report and determined that,
while its view was that a 'major' should be a requirement for each
of the undergraduate degrees, it did not wish to define tight
requirements for them.

The preceding paragraphs show how the intensity of the work
undertaken by the Curriculum Commission continued through to
its final few meetings. Even in the last two meetings, held on 8 and
15 September, further key academic issues were considered. These
were the proposal from Professor Ian Anderson and Professor
Marcia Langton for a vision statement for Indigenous studies
under the Melbourne Model, and a revised version of the report on
English language requirements for the new generation degrees, presented by Professor Pattison.

The commission supported the recommendations in both
these reports. It noted, in regard to Indigenous studies, that a
sequence of subjects from existing, revised or new developments could form a breadth component in the new generation
degrees, and that the English language proposals would be most

appropriately considered further by the proposed Board of Undergraduate Studies. Commission members continued to have concerns about the breadth component of the degrees, which is reflected in attempts to refine the description of this aspect of the Melbourne Model in the commission's final report.

The final meeting of the Curriculum Commission was held on 15 September 2006. Following it, members attended a party in the Gatekeeper's Cottage (the location at that time of the Office of the Provost) for an informal celebration of the final draft of the report to the Academic Board. The occasion was distinguished by the great sense of relief felt by all members after seven incredibly intense months spent discussing and developing the Melbourne Model. It was also an occasion for good humour, and some unforgettable *bon mots* made by commission members during meetings were recalled. My favourites included the preferred titles for Arts degrees – the Bachelor of Lifestyle, the Master of Lifestyle and the Degree of Doctor of Lifestyle, but the comments 'Isn't there just one environment?' (in response to the proposed name of Bachelor of Environments) and 'Our "major" streams are so broad that we need the 75 points for some depth' and the question 'What is a deep generalist?' also resonated strongly.

All involved knew that implementing the Melbourne Model would be a huge task for the University, but the collegiality and compromise that had been shown in reaching agreement on the final report were more than just significant. It showed that members of the University community could work together through conflict to produce a basis for major change.

Academic Board adopts the Curriculum Commission's final report

The Planning and Budget Committee reviewed the Curriculum Commission's draft report at its meeting on 13 September 2006, and agreed to recommend its adoption to the Academic Board.

The Academic Board considered the commission's final report, *The Melbourne Model: Report of the Curriculum Commission*, on 21 September 2006. Just under one hundred members and about twelve observers, including members of the Curriculum Commission who were not members of the Academic Board, attended this meeting. Professor McPhee introduced the report with a brief summary of its development and the detailed work of the previous seven months. He thanked members of the commission and others who had facilitated its work. In conclusion, Professor McPhee highlighted the central recommendations and then moved that the report and its recommendations be adopted.

A diverse range of matters was discussed, from the absence in the report of any specific recommendations for reviews of new courses after two or three years of operation, to the uncertainty of government approval for Commonwealth-supported places to be transferred from undergraduate to postgraduate courses. There was no strong focus on any of the academic recommendations made in the report. This is perhaps not surprising, given several major decisions had already been endorsed by the board, including the number and names of the Melbourne Model undergraduate degrees, the requirement for the breadth component and course prerequisites. This is a reflection on the collegial and consultative process usually followed by the University in developing and finalising major decisions. It is a good practice of leadership to ensure that by the time a final decision is to be made there are no surprises in the recommendations!

Nevertheless, the Academic Board's adoption of the report was one of the most significant milestones in the history of curriculum developments in the University of Melbourne. The board's minutes record that when the outcome of the vote was known:

> the Vice-Chancellor then thanked the members of the Curriculum Commission and the PBC Working Group for their dedication and hard work and the Board for its strong endorsement of the two reports. He noted that the process had been accomplished in a relatively short period of time and under the University's usual

governance procedures. He paid particular tribute to the leadership of the Deputy Vice-Chancellor (Academic), a view strongly supported by the Board which acknowledged his work through a spontaneous and sustained round of applause.[11]

The Curriculum Commission's final report and the Planning and Budget Committee report of the Implementing the Melbourne Model Working Group were approved by the University Council on 9 October 2006. These approvals formalised the introduction of the Melbourne Model from 2008 – and opened the gate to the long and difficult path of implementation.

5

The Faculties

We have seen how the Curriculum Commission worked with the faculties to resolve important questions about the design of the new courses. This chapter delves more deeply into the specific concerns of the individual faculties, all of which were coming to the idea of the Melbourne Model from a slightly different position in existing course structures, plans for the future and financial situation. As indicated earlier, before the Melbourne Model faculties considered they 'owned' the degrees that they managed (for example, the Faculty of Engineering was fully responsible for all the various Bachelor of Engineering degrees, Economics and Commerce likewise 'owned' the Bachelor of Commerce, Science owned the Bachelor of Science and so on). Although the degrees were actually University degrees – in that they were approved by University Council and awarded by the University, not by a faculty – this sense of ownership and responsibility was central to faculty responses to the introduction of the Melbourne Model.

The *Growing Esteem: Strategic Plan 2006* stated that the Curriculum Commission, through its chair, would work with each of the faculties in the redesign of its courses to determine how they would fit in with the Melbourne Model over time. Given the diversity among the faculties in the disciplines they cover and the complexity of the structures in place in 2005 and 2006, it is not surprising that, in the early meetings of Professor McPhee and Dr Emison, the initial reactions of deans and faculty general managers to the proposed curriculum review varied dramatically. Nevertheless, it was equally striking that most were in favour of moving to the graduate school or Bologna model while only a small number had serious reservations. These initial positions were clarified and challenged as the Curriculum Commission defined what the courses and course structures would be for the University as a whole. As with any large-scale institutional reform, the general support for the objectives of the Melbourne Model became more muted, or evaporated altogether, once individuals and faculties realised how the changes would affect their long-established curricula and academic practices of which they were proud.

Early discussion

Early discussions of the Growing Esteem strategy and the Bologna Model–style curriculum that it proposed suggested a broad education in the arts and sciences. Many concluded the ultimate degrees would be a Bachelor of Arts and a Bachelor of Science, as tends to be the pattern in many US universities. This would have been an extraordinary outcome for an institution with strong professional faculties who had control of their degrees and the content of these for 'their' students. To some extent, it was a significant achievement that the recommendation in the commission's final report was for only six new generation undergraduate degrees. Much of the early discussion with individual faculties focused on what undergraduate degrees would be offered under the rubric of the Melbourne Model and with which of these degrees the faculties would have an involvement. It was a moment of revelation when one startled dean stated: 'But there are twelve faculties and only six undergraduate degrees proposed!'[1]

As the deliberations of the Curriculum Commission progressed, Professor McPhee continued to meet faculty groups to discuss developments and options as well as concerns. Most of these meetings were congenial, as all parties had genuine interest in exploring the possibilities of such major change in the University's course and curriculum structures. But some of the meetings were rather intimidating – if not decidedly hostile. The executive of the Faculty of Medicine, Dentistry and Health Sciences, for example, can be confronting to those who are not familiar with the overall size and structure of the faculty itself. It is very large. Professor McPhee, Dr Emison and Gioconda Di Lorenzo met the executive in mid-May 2006. Behaviour was cordial, but there was an atmosphere of tension and resistance throughout the meeting. This was where several of the 25 or so present first made it clear that, if there was to be any change to their course structure and curriculum, there was a strong preference for a 'human biosciences' undergraduate degree, especially among the clinical departments. Arguments to support this included a perceived need to maintain a teaching and research nexus lest there be a loss of students proceeding to research degrees, and a desire to let students who 'know' they wish to pursue a career in medicine enrol in human biology as an undergraduate. As reported in the previous chapter, the faculty was forceful in arguing the case for the biomedicine degree – and they were ultimately successful.

The Faculty of Engineering also had serious reservations about the Melbourne Model, which were made particularly clear in a meeting held in mid-April 2006 with the Curriculum Commission and staff in the Department of Electrical and Electronic Engineering. At that time, the faculty's and department's preference, if there was to be any curriculum change at all, was for an undergraduate degree in which students would undertake a common first year and then proceed to their preferred branch of engineering studies (not unlike the situation that had prevailed in earlier years) or a 3+2 structure that would result in a separate Bachelor of Applied Science and a Master of Engineering. In his presentation to the meeting, the head of the department, Professor Iven Mareels, made a number of points to back the department's opposition to the Melbourne Model. These included the importance of engineering in today's society, which was not in dispute; reference to new engineering courses at Harvard and MIT as models that could be followed; and the Bologna Model treatment of engineering as an 'entry' discipline.

The faculty had very valid concerns, especially when it came to the possible impact of the Melbourne Model on international student intakes and the income these provided. They also faced issues of accreditation, loss of high achievers and a diminished population from which to draw students into research degrees. The faculty found it hard to understand why there would continue to be a Bachelor of Commerce while the Engineering degree would have to be taken at graduate level. The discussion became heated to the point that some staff implied Professor McPhee was personally responsible for creating the situation in which they found themselves.

Faculty issues

Issues that emerged in the discussions that appeared to be of concern to most, if not all, faculties included:

- the need for market research to show whether the new undergraduate and professional graduate school model would be attractive to prospective students and their parents (for undergraduates)
- whether the new structures would enable the University to maintain and strengthen its position with research higher degrees
- the need to ensure the new courses would satisfy accreditation requirements of the professional bodies
- who would 'own' the new generation undergraduate degrees and who would have responsibility for their administration
- access to and equity in the professional graduate programs and whether Commonwealth-supported places would be available for students in these courses
- opportunities under the Melbourne Model for interdisciplinary teaching and research collaboration.

What follows is my interpretation of the issues and ideas posed by the faculties. The faculties themselves may have quite a different account of the issues. Certainly, there are political nuances in some of the discussions related and, although I have not explained all these in full, it is impossible to write such a story without touching on several.

Law

To an extent, the Faculty of Law led the rest of the University in moving towards a graduate model. As long ago as the late 1960s and early 1970s, the University had considered a proposal for adopting the American graduate school model for its law course. Of course, to accept such a proposal at that time would have been an extremely radical move and it did not occur. However, the idea continued to lurk in the background, and was reinforced by the faculty's close links with law schools in Canadian and US universities.

A first step in the eventual transition of Law to a professional graduate qualification came in May 2000 with introduction of the Juris Doctor, a small-intake, fee-based graduate entry course that had already been introduced at some other Australian universities. In line with the University's requirements, the subjects in this course had to be taken at the graduate level, as opposed to undergraduate subjects offered as part of a graduate entry program. While the name of the course is consistent with nomenclature in the northern hemisphere, it is technically a masters-level course and had been approved as such by the then Commonwealth Department of Education Science and Training (DEST) when it was introduced.

A second factor that influenced the readiness of Law to move its prime course to graduate level came about during the international review of the Faculty of Law in 2005, where the Vice-Chancellor had raised the question of how the faculty would react to the option of moving to a graduate school model with the chair of the review panel, Professor McPhee. This was well in advance of the Growing Esteem discussion paper and the University's decision to adopt a version of the Bologna Model. Initially, there was reluctance among the review panel to such a move but a recommendation in the review's final report included that this option be pursued over the following few months.

The Melbourne Model proposals, then, were neither alien nor unwelcome to the direction the Faculty of Law was heading under the leadership of its dean, Michael Crommelin. The undergraduate Bachelor of Laws degree had been the University's most successful course in attracting high-achieving students, most of whom studied combined courses (Law combined with Arts, Science, Commerce or another degree). The decision to move to a graduate school model was seen by the faculty as one way to improve equity opportunities; that is, students who wished to apply to study Law would no longer have to rely solely on the results achieved in their VCE as school leavers.

The initial Juris Doctor was a successful course that was readily modified to become the principal professional graduate qualification in Law under the Melbourne Model, but there were still two main issues of concern. First, there was the uncertainty about whether the federal government would agree to transfer Commonwealth-supported places from undergraduate to graduate courses and, second, the question of whether the University, to maintain its attraction for high-achieving students, should introduce a guaranteed entry scheme for school leavers interested in proceeding to a Law qualification. It was unrealistic to expect the graduate program to be competitive if the Juris Doctor was available only on a fees basis. This hurdle, which was one of the issues pursued by the Policy and Advocacy Taskforce, was overcome with the government's verbal agreement for the University to transfer some of its Commonwealth-supported places from undergraduate to graduate programs, although a formal letter specifying the individual graduate courses that had been approved for Commonwealth-supported places was not received until December 2007.[2] Law again showed leadership in accepting 50 per cent as the minimum number of Commonwealth-supported places it would have in the Juris Doctor. This provided a strong marketing opportunity for the University to use for the new generation degrees.

Accreditation of the Juris Doctor was another issue that had to be resolved. There was also concern there might be a professional backlash against discontinuation of the Bachelor of Laws. However, these matters were carefully managed through communication between the faculty and the profession, with open support for the move from some in the profession. Certainly, there was no blatant public opposition to the University's proposed changes to the law course level and structure. This successful transition from a professional undergraduate to a professional graduate program of one of the University's highest profile courses was significant in setting the tone for other courses.

Architecture, Building and Planning

Like Law, Architecture, Building and Planning, which already had a two-tier structure for some of its courses, had been exploring the possibility of a change in course model. For around a year, the faculty had been discussing options that included moving to a graduate school–type program with a semi-generalist undergraduate course that focused on 'design'. By February 2006, the faculty had already mapped out a 'foundation' first year, in what could be developed as a Bachelor of Design that would feed into various discipline streams in the later years. There was some concern that discipline-based professional masters courses (architecture, construction management and so on) of only two years might not be enough on top of a wholly generalist undergraduate program or for accreditation purposes, while students were likely to consider a three-year professional masters too long after a three-year undergraduate degree. There were also concerns that students coming from other courses or institutions might need to take 'catch-up' subjects, which would lengthen the total program – as would the faculty's preference to continue with a one-year 'practical' work experience, although the professional requirement was for only 26 weeks.

The picture was complicated further as support grew for the Curriculum Commission's proposal that a single degree cover the natural and built environment. Such a degree would mean the faculty jointly developing a course involving at least four other faculties given the location (which was based on the budgeting faculty for a department or school) of the relevant departments or disciplines. These faculties included Arts (Geography), Science (most disciplines), Land and Food Resources and Engineering (Chemical, Civil and Environmental, and Geomatics). Issues particular to the Faculty of Land and Food Resources and to the Faculty of Engineering, which will be dealt with later in this chapter, further added to the difficulty of leadership, cooperation and decision-making for the group designated to develop an undergraduate course.

Professor Ruth Fincher, then Dean of Architecture, Building and Planning, chaired the early multi-faculty groups formed to develop the new generation undergraduate course. She, along with other leaders in the faculty, played a crucial role in balancing the constraints of accreditation within a 3+2 structure with their genuine commitment to a multi-faculty, collaborative degree with multiple graduate pathways. Gaining international acceptance for the March 2008 intake would be a challenging demand for her successor.

Arts

The Arts degree was already considered somewhat generalist in nature, with so many of its students in combined degree programs, and the requirement for a major area of study was not strictly enforced. The faculty was open to its students taking a quarter of the points for the degree from other faculties and thought a requirement for all students to study a language would be desirable. Initially, academic staff in the languages were resistant to such a proposal, concerned they would become language instructors rather than teachers of culture and society as well as language. As it has turned out, large numbers of students have opted to study languages and there has been no need to make a language compulsory. Students have also been able to take a language as a concurrent diploma.[3]

A major concern for Arts was how to achieve enough depth in a new generation degree to ensure students had sufficient grounding for the fourth-year honours course at Melbourne or at other universities. In reverse, the faculty wished to ensure that graduates from other universities would continue to be eligible for honours and research programs at Melbourne. The faculty felt it was desirable that all students undertake some studies in humanities and wanted to avoid a situation where most students aimed for a professional graduate program and did not proceed to honours or other research study in the humanities. The future of the 'honours year' was a frequent question.

Long before the change to the Melbourne Model had been proposed, the Faculty of Arts had been facing the dual issues of large numbers of subjects and looming financial problems arising from a variety of unrelated circumstances, including the decrease in numbers of fee-paying international study abroad and full-course students. These issues continued during the Melbourne Model development process. The faculty had indicated early in discussions that it wished to reduce its large number of first year subjects. With the introduction of the new generation Bachelor of Arts, several subjects were revamped, with the content combined (including Professor McPhee's own longstanding subjects on the American and French revolutions), and a number of new interdisciplinary foundation subjects were developed. The faculty used the Curriculum Commission to reinforce plans for greater coherence in its courses, including obligatory majors with capstone subjects and a clear progression across three levels of study. Regardless of these complications, it was important that the new generation Bachelor of Arts attract large numbers of applicants.

The faculty indicated that it would convert its only professionally accredited course, the Bachelor of Social Work, to a two-year professional masters degree. Discussions about the timing of the conversion and related issues resulted in the eventual transfer of the Department of Social Work from the Faculty of Arts to the Faculty of Medicine, Dentistry and Health Sciences (in the School of Nursing and Social Work) for budgeting purposes. The Bachelor of Social Work had its last intake in 2009 while the new professional graduate program, the Master of Social Work, had its first intake in 2010. The Bachelor of Arts (Media and Communications) had its last first-year intake in 2010 and from that same year became available as a major or minor discipline within the new generation Bachelor of Arts.

Economics and Commerce

Before the end of November 2005, Professor Maggie Abernethy, the Dean of the Faculty of Economics and Commerce, had indicated to the Vice-Chancellor that the faculty would have difficulty with the breadth component of the Melbourne Model proposals because of the extensive accreditation requirements for the accounting qualification. The faculty was concerned that students should continue to be able to satisfy requirements for this accreditation without further study; in this context, a requirement for one-quarter of the degree to come from subjects outside the faculty was seen as problematic. On the other hand, the dean reported that the Master of Applied Commerce already met the requirement of a professional graduate course, accepting students with any undergraduate degree, and could be adjusted to better suit the Melbourne Model. The faculty also wished to retain an honours year to ensure a flow of students to postgraduate and research programs.

Throughout the deliberations of the Curriculum Commission, the faculty did not change its stance about the breadth component and accreditation requirements, and in fact extended it to Actuarial Studies as well as Accounting. The faculty's preference for a breadth component was 37.5 points with some students being permitted to extend this up to 50 points. A primary argument made by the faculty was that 'breadth' could be covered adequately from within its range of disciplines (Accounting through to Marketing and Management). Others within the University did not agree. Eventually, following some heated discussions, the faculty agreed to endorse the 75 points breadth requirement. The compromise agreed with the faculty was that students pursuing accreditation in Actuarial Studies be exempted from the breadth requirement. Instead, they are required to take 75 points from outside the core program, including several specified subjects, in order to satisfy accreditation requirements. In addition, students pursuing accreditation in Accounting, while required to satisfy the 75 points breadth component, have to include three specified law subjects in their selection.

Music[4]

In 2005, the University Council had approved full integration of the Victorian College of the Arts (VCA) with the University, to take effect from the beginning of 2007. Consequently, the VCA and the Faculty of Music were attempting to work through the issues of integration as well as the curriculum review throughout 2006, although the VCA had been granted an extension of five years – until 2012 – before it had to participate in the Melbourne Model. This meant it did not have to develop new courses for introduction in 2008.

On the other hand, the Acting Dean of the Faculty of Music, Cathy Falk, made a strong case to the Curriculum Commission to proceed with developing a new generation three-year Bachelor of Music. The faculty also took the lead in designing new breadth subjects specifically to cater for or attract students from other degrees. The faculty stressed how important it was for the University to continue its highly successful music therapy program either as a continuing bachelor degree or as a new professional masters course, with the latter option eventually being adopted.

The Faculty of the VCA and Music was established in April 2009 and saw the creation of a single School of Music. In 2012, the new faculty continues to offer the new generation Bachelor of Music for students who wish to specialise in performance, composition, musicology or ethnomusicology, and the Bachelor of Fine Arts (Contemporary Music) for students wishing to focus on commercially driven cross-art modes of composition.

Medicine, Dentistry and Health Sciences

The Faculty of Medicine, Dentistry and Health Sciences faced a plethora of issues related to the Melbourne Model, ranging from how the government would react if there was a one- or two-year transition period during which the University had no intake into its medical course, through a resoundingly negative reaction from the Australian Dental Association to dentistry becoming a graduate program, to undue concerns about 'bright flight' from the medical course. While Physiotherapy and Nursing were keen to move to graduate programs, Psychology, a discipline offered primarily through the Bachelor of Arts and Bachelor of Science courses, was beset with serious concerns about which of the proposed Melbourne Model courses would be appropriate for prospective psychologists, and what length the Melbourne Model courses would need to be to meet professional qualification requirements. The faculty also had to consider the financial implications of years in which there would be no intake of students – in order to resolve workload issues, as well as to maintain expected numbers of graduates in the various disciplines during the transition period. The threat of 'fallow years' because of constraints on clinical placement numbers was critical. In addition, each of the faculty's major discipline areas presented their own specific challenges.

Nursing

Compared to several other universities, Melbourne was a latecomer in offering courses in nursing when it started at the postgraduate level in 1996. It was only in 2002 that an undergraduate Bachelor of Nursing was introduced at the Shepparton campus with the course becoming available at Parkville in the mid-2000s. With increasing numbers of university-level nursing courses across the country, demand for the undergraduate course was not strong and the quality of intakes was of some concern. Steps had been taken even before the work of the Curriculum Commission to revamp the nursing program in line with the University's expertise. Consequently, the three-year bachelor degree had its last intake in 2006 and in the accelerated two-year program in 2007. From 2008, the nursing programs, including a range of studies in specialist areas, were available to new students only at the graduate level.

Physiotherapy

The University first offered an undergraduate physiotherapy course in 1991. It was a popular course but the quality of the intakes varied as external factors, including the introduction of similar courses in other universities, created fluctuations in demand. Consequently, the introduction of the Melbourne Model and the opportunity to move to a graduate program was seen as timely. The School of Physiotherapy was keen to introduce a graduate program from 2008 but financial and other complexities resulted in further undergraduate intakes in 2008 and 2009, with the graduate Doctor of Physiotherapy introduced from 2011.

Dentistry

Before the end of March 2006, the Australian Dental Association Victorian branch (ADAV) had publicly declared its opposition to the University's proposal to move professional courses to graduate level. The association claimed that dentistry was already taught at a very high level and it would be far too expensive to offer as a graduate course. Dental Health Services Victoria (DHSV), the body responsible for providing clinical places for dental students, was also opposed to any move to graduate programs. The DHSV was most concerned about the Bachelor of Oral Health, a three-year undergraduate course introduced from 2005 (when it replaced a two-year diploma course that had been available for several years) to train dental hygienists and therapists. It was agreed that this course was not appropriate for graduate level and the University continues to offer it as an undergraduate course with no indication that it will be discontinued in the foreseeable future. Eventually, discussions with the ADAV were settled when the faculty and the University agreed that the Bachelor of Dental Science would have its last new student intake in 2009 with a new graduate Doctor of Dental Surgery to be introduced from 2011.

Medicine

From 2000, the undergraduate medical course had been available to school leavers or as a graduate entry course. Several other universities had already introduced the option of graduate entry to the medical course. Consequently, the pattern was for some universities to have only school leaver intakes, while others had changed to graduate entry only and some retained both, as was the case at Melbourne. The numbers of domestic students enrolled in the Bachelor of Medicine, Bachelor of Surgery (MBBS) course were determined by the Commonwealth Department of Human Services and Ageing to ensure that there would be adequate places for the clinical training years, among other reasons.

In early December 2005, the Medicine, Dentistry and Health Sciences Education Unit had prepared a briefing paper in response to Growing Esteem called 'A New Direction for Health Sciences Education', to inform the faculty's discussion of the Melbourne Model proposals. The main emphasis of the paper was for the faculty to develop and offer a three-year Human Biological Sciences undergraduate degree. Admission requirements for this new degree would be based on school leaver performance and the highest achieving applicants would be assured places in the professional graduate programs in the various disciplines within the faculty, subject to achieving results at a satisfactory level as specified by the faculty. The principal argument for the degree was based on maintaining the faculty's capacity to attract the highest achieving school leavers for the medical course. This approach varied from that of the Faculty of Law, which saw that offering professional graduate programs could perhaps enhance equity options for students. In later comments, the Faculty of Medicine, Dentistry and Health Sciences recognised that access might be more equitable under the Melbourne Model because of the graduate entry option for professional courses. Other points made in the paper indicated the faculty's overall perspective. These included that combined degrees would not continue; the degree would not be a return to the first three years of the 'old' medical course; and the undergraduate degree would not reproduce the current Biomedical Sciences degree.[5]

Discussions held early in 2006 and during the first several meetings of the Curriculum Commission appeared to favour the

Bachelor of Science as the principal science-based undergraduate course that would feed into professional graduate programs in science, medical and health sciences and related disciplines. However, early in March the Vice-Chancellor's Advisory Group had agreed that a model should be developed showing what a separate biomedical science degree would look like.[6] There is no recorded explanation for this decision, although it probably arose from concerns about 'bright flight' among other issues.

The December 2005 proposal was for a human biological course made up of subjects taught by departments in the Faculty of Medicine, Dentistry and Health Sciences. However, following discussion with other faculties and in meetings of the Curriculum Commission, both the name and the content of the course evolved to fit better with the core principles of the Melbourne Model. A critical meeting to resolve the concerns of the two key faculties, Science and Medicine, Dentistry and Health Sciences, took place in January 2007, during which the two deans, Professor Angus and Professor Rathjen, agreed that the new generation Bachelor of Science and Bachelor of Bioscience would be marketed as 'Sciences at Melbourne' and would operate as joint pathways into the health and other professions. The Faculty of Medicine, Dentistry and Health Sciences also agreed to adopt the professional graduate school pattern of the Melbourne Model, which Professor McPhee recalls as one of the breakthrough moments in the Melbourne Model story. The name finally agreed for this sixth new generation undergraduate course was Bachelor of Biomedicine, in part to distinguish the course from the Bachelor of Science. The content includes basic subjects in Chemistry, Physics and Mathematics or Mathematics and Engineering Design dependent on the particular stream students wish to follow. The same or equivalent curriculum may be taken through the Bachelor of Science.

The MBBS course had its last school leaver intake in 2008 and its last graduate entry intake in 2009. The faculty introduced its new four-year Doctor of Medicine course in 2011.

Psychology

There were some early concerns about how psychology would be positioned as a discipline area within the Melbourne Model scheme. The course standing committees resolved these with recommendations endorsed by the faculties and the Academic Programs Committee in 2007. University management did discuss whether the School of Behavioural Sciences, which includes Psychology, was best located, from a budget and administrative position, in the Faculty of Medicine, Dentistry and Health Sciences or elsewhere. The predecessor Department of Psychology was located in the Faculty of Arts for budget purposes, although there were discussions from time to time that it might have been better placed within the Faculty of Science. Under the Melbourne Model, a major in Psychology may be completed through a Bachelor of Arts or a Bachelor of Science, and substantial studies in the discipline may be undertaken to satisfy the breadth component of the Bachelor of Commerce. Issues of accreditation and major requirements for Psychology are discussed in a later chapter.

Veterinary Science

In 2005, the Faculty of Veterinary Science had only recently gained accreditation from the American Veterinary Society for its undergraduate Bachelor of Veterinary Science course. Most students accepted into the Bachelor of Veterinary Science were admitted once they had completed a year in the Bachelor of Science (or equivalent studies) with only a small number accepted directly as school leavers. The professional qualification in the United States is a graduate program. Moving to a graduate school model would be consistent with the North American model, but there was concern within the faculty that the reaction from the profession and prospective students would be negative, because of the higher cost and greater time required to achieve the qualification. Consequently, the main argument for retaining the Bachelor of Veterinary Science, at least in the short term, was to allow time for market research. In the interim, various options were mooted such as a 3+3 if the undergraduate program was a 'vet stream' offered through a generalist science degree or, alternatively, a four-year graduate program. The appointment of Professor Ken Hinchcliff, an alumnus with extensive experience in the United States, as the new dean of the faculty was a central factor in resolving the issue. It was agreed that intakes into the Bachelor of Veterinary Science would be retained up to and including 2010 with a new professional graduate program, the Doctor of Veterinary Medicine, to be introduced from 2011. The undergraduate pathway into the Doctor of Veterinary Medicine would be the new generation Bachelor of Science or equivalent.

Land and Food Resources

This was another faculty with a range of difficult issues to resolve in addition to the curriculum review. A combination of factors, including the amalgamation of the Victorian College of Agriculture and Horticulture with the faculty, a decline in student demand for the higher education courses (not unique to Australia), and three major restructures and several changes in the deanship over a ten-year period had left the faculty in an unstable position. In 2005, the faculty had been running a budget deficit for many years. With the declining student enrolments, the University could no longer maintain the several campuses teaching technical and further education (TAFE) courses. This was not the University's first attempt to rationalise the number of campuses and courses in the Faculty of Land and Food Resources. On previous attempts, community and political pressures, among other things, had dominated and only minimal changes had taken place rather than the drastic steps that may have resulted in earlier resolution of some of the financial issues. Nevertheless, there had been various organisational restructuring and curriculum changes in attempts to improve the situation.

The late, highly respected Professor Bob Richardson, dean from 2000, had retired at the end of 2004. Professor Frank Larkins was acting dean in 2005, concurrent with his position as Deputy Vice-Chancellor (Research). Another acting dean, Professor Ron Slocombe from Veterinary Science, was appointed for 2006 while the University continued its search for a new dean. Professor Rick Roush was appointed dean from 2007.

All these continuing pressures brought a high degree of uncertainty to the faculty, but there was considerable enthusiasm as well as concern at the prospect of the Melbourne Model. Government and community emphasis on issues of the global environment was thought to bode well for the development of high-standard coursework masters programs and undergraduate breadth subjects. As well, with the faculty's long-standing record of success in research, the shift to specialist graduate programs appeared to be a logical step. As for Law, however, the success of the graduate school approach would hinge, in part, on the government's approval for the University to offer Commonwealth-supported places to postgraduate students.

The situation was far from simple. The faculty still had problems with the courses taught at the Dookie campus near Shepparton and at the Burnley campus. What would be the fate of these campuses if the Bachelor of Agriculture (Dookie) and the Bachelor of Horticulture (Burnley) were replaced by broader undergraduate degrees? The prospects for graduate entry courses in agriculture, horticulture and forestry were strong, but the long-standing problems of low student demand and lack of financial security were ever present in the discussions.

Also, other faculties (Architecture, Building and Planning, Science, Engineering) had leading roles in the development of the new generation Bachelor of Science and Bachelor of Environment. The Faculty of Land and Food Resources did not believe it was in a strong position compared to these larger and more stable faculties, although the acting dean and the faculty representative on the Curriculum Commission put forward a strong case for the faculty's participation in the Melbourne Model.

The faculty agreed in time for the Curriculum Commission's final report that the Bachelor of Agriculture would be revamped, with part of the course to be offered at Dookie, and the Associate Degree in Horticulture would continue to be taught at Burnley. Other disciplines, such as agricultural science and food science, were developed as majors within the new generation Bachelor of Science and landscape management within the new generation Bachelor of Environment.

Science

The Faculty of Science viewed the Melbourne Model as providing opportunities and challenges and, while there was support for a reduction in the number of undergraduate programs offered, there was a preference that the 'honours' year be retained in some form to ensure a flow of students into research programs. The faculty was also interested in the future of niche degrees such as Biomedical Science and Information Systems and how the many students who completed combined degrees would be catered for under the Melbourne Model.

Various options were considered for the Bachelor of Optometry under the Melbourne Model. There was some concern that moving to a graduate 3+4 program would discourage prospective students, although the faculty had introduced a five-year undergraduate program for optometry in 2001. There was also concern that students who had completed a first degree at another institution would not have taken the requisite subjects – which would require a level of creativity in designing the prerequisite subjects for admission to a Doctor of Optometry. The Bachelor of Optometry had its last school leaver intake in 2009 and the four-year professional Doctor of Optometry was introduced in 2011.

The faculty had significant interactions about course developments with the faculties of Engineering, Land and Food Resources, Medicine Dentistry and Health Sciences and, eventually, Veterinary Science to ensure that the new generation Bachelor of Science would provide pathways for students interested in progressing to postgraduate study in these professions. While none of the interactions were straightforward, perhaps the most complex one was with the Faculty of Medicine, Dentistry and Health Sciences. A number of preclinical departments in Medicine, Dentistry and Health Sciences had taught into the Bachelor of Science for many years and were accustomed to attracting significant numbers of Science graduates into their honours and research higher degree programs. With the close liaison, which had been tested from time to time over the years, there was an expectation among some academics in both faculties that the new generation Bachelor of Science would be the logical track for students interested in pursuing a career in medicine and health sciences disciplines. However, as reported elsewhere, there was also considerable concern within Medicine, Dentistry and Health Sciences that the loss of the high-achieving school leaver population would be damaging to the faculty and to the University in the longer term. Medicine, Dentistry and Health Sciences was also of the view that a graduate entry medical course required a level of previous studies in human biology that would be best taught by its departments.

Fortunately, as with most of the difficult issues that were discussed in development of the Melbourne Model, these matters were resolved to ensure the best outcome for students through discussion and compromise by all parties. As mentioned earlier, the new generation Bachelor of Biomedicine offers a number of major options that involve teaching by various departments in the faculties of Engineering and Science as well as Medicine, Dentistry and Health Sciences.

The Faculty of Science was instrumental in resolving an interim arrangement for the Faculty of Engineering's participation in the Melbourne Model when it agreed, in late August 2007, to be party to developing a three-year Bachelor of Science and a two-year Master of Engineering, with Engineering to also continue offering a four-year Bachelor of Engineering, at least in the short term. The Bachelor of Science, while satisfying the conditions for a new generation undergraduate degree, would include sufficient engineering content to allow the subsequent Master of Engineering to be completed in two years. Final agreement to this proposal was reached in September 2007.

Before the Melbourne Model, Science tended to have a
narrow perspective on masters programs, thinking they were for
those who did not meet the standards for the PhD. However, with
the introduction of the Melbourne Model, Science and Engineering
worked together to develop a successful suite of two-year inter-
locking professional masters programs for career scientists.

Education

The situation for Education was particularly interesting. It had
offered 'graduate' and 'graduate entry' programs before the 1989
merger of the Melbourne College of Advanced Education with the
University. The University had also offered the Bachelor of Science
(Education) as a four-year bachelors degree in conjunction with
the Secondary Teachers College for a number of years. The faculty's predominant course had been the Graduate Diploma in
Education, which satisfied the requirements for an initial teacher
qualification and was popular with graduates, particularly those
with degrees in Arts and Science. Early Childhood and Primary
Education degrees had variable popularity according to market
demand. The University had introduced the two-year, graduate
entry Bachelor of Teaching in an effort to improve teacher training
but the degree was not competitive with the one-year Diploma of
Education. Also, the Bachelor of Teaching was at a disadvantage
compared with courses at other universities because state governments had not endorsed it as the preferred teacher training
qualification. Student numbers remained low and many converted
to the Diploma of Education after one year of study.

The Dean of Education, Professor Field Rickards, remained
concerned that prospective students would not support the graduate school model unless Commonwealth-supported places were
available. Areas needing particular attention included teacher
registration requirements and early learning or early childhood
qualifications. Notwithstanding these issues, it was logical for the
faculty to become a graduate school with the two major bachelor
programs, Primary and Early Childhood, to be phased out after
the last intakes in 2008 and a new suite of graduate programs to

be developed and introduced. The concern about the costs to the faculty of offering a 'practitioners' or clinical model of teacher education was alleviated by an allocation of $7.96 million by the federal Department of Education, Employment and Workplace Relations through the Diversity and Structural Adjustment Fund to establish and teach the Master of Teaching over the period of 2009 to 2011, and the Education Investment Funding to build teaching spaces for graduate students.

Engineering

In 2006, the Engineering Faculty comprised six departments, each with either its own major stream in the Bachelor of Engineering or a specialist degree like the Bachelor of Computer Science or Bachelor of Geomatic Engineering. The faculty had large numbers of international students who provided considerable income as well as a high proportion of domestic students who studied combined degrees. These factors, along with the four-year undergraduate degree being the norm for engineering accreditation in the United States and the United Kingdom, made the Melbourne Model look decidedly unattractive to many within the faculty and there was a general reluctance to move towards it. There was a strong view within the faculty that a 3+2 model for achieving engineering accreditation would be unpopular with students, and their parents, from both a time and a cost perspective.

An external review of the faculty in January 2006, commissioned by the Vice-Chancellor, added another level of complexity. Recommendations from the review related to teaching and learning emphasised the faculty needed to review its curriculum in the context of participating in the Melbourne Model and also offer an engineering course that would be challenging and interesting to students. There was a small contingent within the faculty who believed it would be valuable for the faculty to consider the curriculum changes as recommended in the review outcomes, because the faculty's track record with student feedback on quality of teaching was not good.

As mentioned earlier in this chapter, the commission's discussions with the Faculty of Engineering were not easy. Professor

McPhee had more email exchanges about the curriculum review and the Melbourne Model with Engineering staff, and more meetings to discuss Melbourne Model options for the faculty to consider, than with any other faculty. The faculty was divided throughout most of 2006 on the direction it would take, although, as reported in the section on the Faculty of Science, an interim resolution resulting in the 3+2 Bachelor of Science + Master of Engineering was agreed on just in time for Academic Board approval of the Curriculum Commission's report in September 2006. Under this arrangement, there would be continuing intakes into the then Bachelor of Engineering degree up to and including first semester 2010. A range of engineering disciplines may be studied in four of the new generation bachelor degrees and, if followed by a two-year Master of Engineering, engineering accreditation requirements will have been satisfied.

Victorian College of the Arts

The integration of the VCA with the University, which took effect from the beginning of 2007, has already been mentioned. One aspect of the agreement for the integration was that the VCA would have a five-year guarantee preserving its status quo; that is, the VCA would have until 2012 before it would have to introduce courses in line with the Melbourne Model.

The college had much work to do in 2006 to meet the requirements for the integration but it was also an active participant on the Curriculum Commission. Early in the deliberations of the commission, there was some support in the VCA for the graduate school model for several of its courses, particularly those with a number of students who had already completed prior studies or were older than the school leavers who made up most new students in many other undergraduate courses at the University. However, the college gave little active consideration to the 3+2 model, although it would have provided students with more study options, and students in other degrees could have enrolled in VCA subjects for their breadth component. The college was also not enthusiastic about the suggestion that any graduate school in the performing and creative arts would be based at the Parkville campus.

The college and the subsequent Faculty of the VCA and Music, which was established in April 2009, experienced a considerable period of turmoil involving a range of issues, including whether or not to participate in the Melbourne Model. A decision had been made at the 2007 Planning and Budget Committee Conference for a review of the Faculty of Music in order to resolve further problems associated with the integration with the VCA. The recommendations of this review were endorsed by the University Council but implementation was difficult because of a range of other issues, not least of which was the continuing problem of funding for the VCA and a student and staff backlash against any participation in the Melbourne Model. The University then commissioned Dr Switkowski, a former Telstra CEO who was at that time chair of Opera Australia, to lead a review of the newly established Faculty of the VCA and Music.

The report of this review was completed in May 2010 and the recommendations endorsed by University Council in July. The recommendations included a proposal for the Faculty of the VCA and Music to continue as a single faculty with two distinct components: the VCA and the Melbourne Conservatorium of Music. Each component would have its own director who would report to the Dean of the Faculty of the VCA and Music. The major recommendation for the curriculum was that introduction of the Melbourne Model for the visual and performing arts disciplines based at the Southbank campus be suspended until a new process had considered the faculty's courses and teaching practices – with the report due by 31 December 2010. A considerable boost to the future of the VCA was welcomed in August 2010 when the state government agreed to provide $6 million per annum for four years and the Commonwealth government agreed to top up the Commonwealth Grants Scheme funding by $5.1 million per annum. Professor Barry Conyngham's appointment as the new dean was announced in December 2010.

School of Graduate Studies

The School of Graduate Studies is considered equivalent to a faculty for the purposes of some aspects of the management of the PhD degree, but its contributions to the work of the Curriculum Commission covered a much broader range of honours and postgraduate studies options, as described in the previous chapter. In 2007, the school was renamed the School of Graduate Research and, with the introduction in 2010 of a new student system, some aspects of management of PhD candidature were devolved to the faculties and graduate schools. The School of Graduate Research continues to oversee admissions and the examination of theses, and to provide enrichment activities and support for the University's research students.

As this chapter has shown, the introduction of the Melbourne Model presented difficult situations for most faculties to work through, but the nature of these situations varied considerably. Law was in a category of its own and quite comfortable about the change, and Commerce, Medicine Dentistry and Health Sciences, Science and Arts to some extent maintained their position through the names of the new generation bachelor degrees. But issues around balancing the requirements for breadth subjects with professional accreditation requirements was a major problem for some faculties and the small number of degrees to be offered left several feeling disempowered. The Curriculum Commission's work with the faculties involved negotiating very sensitive issues around faculty-specific concerns and ambitions and the aims of the University and its new strategic plan as a whole. To do so was essential to developing new academic structures, at the core of the success of the new model. Although the process was at times fraught, the Curriculum Commission achieved this aim with some skill. As it did so, however, it produced or revealed many further issues on the operational side that needed to be considered and resolved. The next chapter explores these in more detail.

6

The Curriculum Commission and Operational Matters

The proposed radical reconfiguration of academic structures that had been endorsed by the University Council was unique in the history of Australian universities. The stakes would have been very high for any university, but they were particularly so for one of Melbourne's standing. So were the demands, for the Curriculum Commission was operating within a competitive tertiary environment with considerable constraints of timing, all the more sensitive because of a sceptical, and sometimes negative, local media. The design of the courses was a vital part of creating and selling the new model – and of clarifying what the new model actually was – and we have seen how the Curriculum Commission worked with the faculties to arrive at the final list of six undergraduate degrees. But there were a multitude of operational matters related to or generated by the work of the Curriculum Commission that required consideration in parallel with the deliberations over curriculum structure. Decisions regarding many of these were made by a series of taskforces and working groups established for the purpose, some of which replaced, subsumed or superseded others during the planning period. In most instances, Professor McPhee, as chair of the Curriculum Commission, and I, as director of the Melbourne Curriculum Project, were involved in some capacity.

In addition to the numerous operational matters that required attention, planning for *how* implementation would proceed, once the Academic Board and University Council had approved the recommendations, was on the agenda as early as March 2006. Although most members of the commission and others in the University community may have thought the curriculum review was progressing far too quickly, it would be fair to say that trying to stay ahead of the various 'operational' matters needing attention was equally difficult.

Looking back now at the events that took place in 2006, and at the various groups that were involved, the climate seems one of chaos, with many decisions made on an *ad hoc* basis. But it needs to be remembered that at this stage it was not absolutely certain the Melbourne Model proposal would be endorsed by the Academic Board or, if endorsed, what it would look like. Because of this, deans and others in the academic community were reluctant to agree to firm structures to deal with the myriad issues any earlier. Issues were considered as they arose, by the people involved in developing the Melbourne Model and by others who were expert in the area in question, as necessary. As a result, a number of the task forces and working groups were set up on the run, as it became apparent they were needed, which caused some tension. The middle months of 2006 were particularly charged. As the school communities realised what was being proposed for 2008, and as faculties absorbed what the changes would mean for each of them, so the intensity of questioning increased. The easy way out would have been to delay the changes to 2009 or 2010, but this would have exacerbated feelings of confusion and resistance to change. Professor McPhee recalls several decisive discussions with the Vice-Chancellor, who supported his view that the risks were far higher if the University leadership was seen to be hesitating or equivocating.

Checklists and critical timelines

In December 2005, shortly after learning I would become director of the Melbourne Curriculum Project from January 2006, I drew up a list of all the broad headings that might be affected by new courses and curricula – which included everything from course entry requirements and standards to student progression rates and the impact on faculty trust fund prizes and awards. A number of items on the list, such as discipline majors and whether the Melbourne Model should include an option for sequential degrees, were intertwined with core discussions on academic content of the

Curriculum Commission. The list eventually formed the basis of a checklist developed for members of the commission and others involved in establishing the Melbourne Model. The checklist also formed a companion to the schedule that members of the commission had requested; it let them know the timelines by which relevant decisions and actions would have to be taken for new courses to be introduced in 2008. Further, modified versions of the checklist provided a starting point for discussion in later groups responsible for putting the Melbourne Model into place, and for documents prepared to help work through steps in the implementation phase.

The schedule was updated on a regular basis and made available to the commission at subsequent meetings. It initially had three components: undergraduate programs, professional graduate programs and related activities. The latter took into account the deliberations of the Policy and Advocacy Taskforce, VTAC deadlines, and issues that were to be considered by Academic Board and other committees. By mid-May 2006, a list of key matters to be resolved in the Melbourne Model had been drawn up, with meeting dates scheduled for the various committees that would have to be consulted in the approval process.

Professor McPhee was steering the Curriculum Commission through an ordered and methodical process, at least for the academic aspects of the review. Taking the same controlled approach to the operational aspects was more difficult. There was a wide range of operational issues that needed attention and a large number of enthusiastic professional staff who were keen to be involved and to act on possible changes in which they would be involved. In particular, if substantial changes were to be implemented in 2008, prospective students, their parents and other stakeholders needed to know what these changes and the requirements for the new courses would be some time in advance. It was important to maintain a balance between preserving the status quo if the proposed changes were not approved, and preparing for a very different environment if they were.

Within the Curriculum Commission and the wider University community, there continued to be considerable concern about the lack of market research into the views of stakeholders on such a dramatic shift. This situation became somewhat frenzied, fuelled by the University's very public profile. As shown earlier, significant media interest began with the new vice-chancellor's arrival in 2005 and continued with the subsequent public release of Professor Davis' strategic review discussion paper and the *Growing Esteem: Strategic Plan 2006*. Melbourne University is one of the country's most prestigious and successful universities, and there is always interest in its leaders and directions. It is not possible to keep major activities under wraps for more than short periods, especially when the outcomes will have a major impact on the entire institution and all its stakeholders. In the case of the Melbourne Model, the University would definitely benefit if it could conduct market research before media versions of events became widespread. Even more importantly, there was a need for market research feedback that endorsed the University's approach to a new curriculum and ensured that high-achieving students (and their parents and schools) would continue to preference Melbourne as their 'university of choice'. While there was a gut feeling that this would be the case, the more concrete reassurance that could be provided through collected data was needed. Market research, then, became a priority among the operational matters, as did communication – what, when and how stakeholders would be told about the moves being mooted. These were two of the key issues, which also included negotiations with the federal government and determining detailed management structures for the new undergraduate degrees.

Main issues

The checklist and timeline, then, helped clarify the main operational issues during the time of the Curriculum Commission. These can be categorised into the following four topics, some of which continued to be major themes in the implementation phase.

Communication with stakeholders
Deciding how and what information should the University provide to its staff and students and the wider community, especially prospective students, their parents and the schools.

Market research
Establishing how the wider community would react to the proposed curriculum changes.

Negotiation with the federal government
The Policy and Advocacy Taskforce coordinated government negotiations regarding the University's student profile and its request to shift funds from undergraduate to postgraduate places.

Responsibility for the new generation undergraduate degrees
Determining who would be responsible for developing and implementing these degrees, and for their management and governance, and the timelines for these activities.

The complexity of these issues and the interactions between the significant numbers of individuals and organisational units involved cannot be overstated. Gaining federal government agreement to Melbourne's proposal was essential for the success of the Melbourne Model and would also affect communications with stakeholders. Likewise, if market research showed serious and extensive reservations about the curriculum changes, these would also have an impact on the University's communications with its stakeholders, and would have to be taken into account before any final decisions could be made on the proposed changes. The interconnectedness of the four issues was a recurrent theme of the Curriculum Commission's deliberations and continued throughout the implementation phase. In the rest of this chapter I look at the groups that handled each issue and at how they went about it.

Communications

The first 'Melbourne Model Taskforce' (active March 2006)
As mentioned earlier, the University's professional staff members were overwhelmingly enthusiastic about being involved in and making a contribution to the work of the Curriculum Commission. There were no guidelines or precedents to follow for such a major change exercise, with such a significant University-wide impact. Consequently, at times it became difficult for the commission to deal with staff keen for the specific information that would allow them to get on with their work, stay ahead of the demands and ensure that decisions were made and deadlines met – the specific information just wasn't available.

An example of this came up around the middle of February 2006 when the (then) director of Student Access, Carmel Murphy, contacted the Senior Vice-Principal, Ian Marshman, about the end-of-May deadline for updating information included in *VICTER 2009*.[1] This is an important document outlining requirements for tertiary courses, aimed primarily at Year 10 students planning their subjects for university entrance two years hence – another indication of the long lead times involved. After emails between Carmel, the Senior Vice-Principal, Professor McPhee and others, this led to the first Melbourne Model Taskforce being established, with membership of Admissions Office and faculty staff, to ensure we would all be giving prospective local and international students and other stakeholders the same information about the Melbourne Model.[2] This was also driven, in part, by an (optimistic) expectation held by some players that University Council would decide on the Melbourne Model degree programs at its meeting scheduled for 6 March 2006.[3] At about this same time, the Growing Esteem Strategy Office (GESO) was being established within the Vice-Chancellor's Office; its main responsibilities were internal and external communications related to the *Growing Esteem: Strategic Plan 2006,* including the Melbourne Model.

Recruitment and admissions staff liaised with Jane-Frances Kelly in the Vice-Chancellor's Office, who was establishing the

GESO, about the work to be undertaken by the Melbourne Model Taskforce. There was a further link between the (then) Vice-Principal (International Development), Bruce Bayley, and the taskforce about the need for market research, and the importance of feedback from the University's stakeholders – both locally and internationally. Bruce had also had discussions with a senior member of Trinity, one of the university's residential colleges, who had expressed concerns about how the Melbourne Model would affect the VCE-level international students taught by the college. The Trinity program was – and is – a prime feeder of international students into Melbourne's undergraduate programs.

The Melbourne Model Taskforce was short lived, with four meetings in March 2006. Minutes of the second meeting of the taskforce (held on 8 March 2006), stated that the taskforce had been formed as a result of a request by Ian Marshman for Student Access, in conjunction with faculties, and its purpose was to develop 'first level identification of stakeholders affected by the Melbourne Model; identification of public commitments made and deadlines to be met affected by the Melbourne Model'. The minutes continued: 'The Vice-Chancellor's Office is responsible for the development and running of the University's communication strategy. The Taskforce's role is to provide information to the Vice-Chancellor's Office to inform the strategy.'[4]

Most of the taskforce's efforts over its short lifetime went into drafting and refining various documents, including a stakeholders list that indicated the type of information that needed to be provided and when, who should be responsible for providing it, and the draft of a letter that would be from the Vice-Chancellor to stakeholders (particularly school principals). By the group's final meeting, Jane-Frances Kelly had drafted the objectives and a schedule for the Growing Esteem communications strategy. A further meeting of the taskforce had been scheduled for 12 April but this was cancelled. The group was no longer necessary, as it was superseded by the GESO and its activities, and, eventually, by the establishment of the Market Research Steering Committee and the New Generation Course Approvals Working Group.

Growing Esteem Strategy Office (active April 2006 to November 2007)

The Growing Esteem Strategy Office (GESO) was established in April 2006 in response to a suggestion made by Jane-Frances Kelly to the Vice-Chancellor. Her rationale for the office was that it 'was clear that Growing Esteem was going to be a major change management challenge, requiring coordination and communication from the centre of the university'.[5] Originally, it was thought the office would be needed for around six months, but the scale of the Growing Esteem strategy, and the potential changes caused by the introduction of the Melbourne Model, resulted in the office continuing to exist until the end of November 2007. From this time, some of the GESO responsibilities were transferred to the newly established Office of the Provost and others to the newly established Vice-Chancellor's Strategy Unit.

The role of the GESO was refined over time, but is well summarised by the paragraph that appeared on the Growing Esteem website and in *Growing Esteem Implementation Update 19*:

> GESO is based in the Office of the Vice-Chancellor. Its role is to coordinate the implementation process, manage the *Growing Esteem* communication strategy and to provide support to taskforces, committees, departments and faculties in the implementation of the *Growing Esteem* strategy.[6]

Membership of the GESO consisted of professional staff from several central and faculty departments who were seconded for short-term appointments in the office, and Dr Pat McLean, who was appointed as manager of the office for the duration of its existence. Dr McLean, a member of the senior professional staff in the student services area, was recommended for the role by the Senior Vice-Principal following a request for nominees from the Vice-Chancellor.

The learning curve for GESO staff was steep. Time was needed to become familiar with the range of work being undertaken by the various taskforces; at the same time, they established the Growing Esteem website, implemented the communications strategy and managed its other activities. The GESO was not established until after the Growing Esteem taskforces – the Curriculum Commission, the Policy and Advocacy Taskforce, the Research Taskforce and the Knowledge Transfer Taskforce – had started their work, and the executive officers (or equivalents) of these taskforces were somewhat hesitant about the early approach of the GESO staff to provide support for them. The executive officers had been appointed before GESO was established, so there was an element of confusion about respective roles. In hindsight, this may have been alleviated if the executive officers had been considered members of the GESO and more directly included in its activities, at least in the early stages. Over time, roles were clarified, although executive officers remained concerned that they were not included in some crucial discussions, and that feedback from senior management through GESO was sometimes inadequate. The pace of activity and the lack of clearly defined roles played a part in this, and also contributed to the several revisions of the GESO's responsibilities.

In any case, the overarching role of GESO was to develop and manage the Growing Esteem communications strategy, and perhaps the title 'Communications Coordination Office' would have better reflected the unit's purpose. Over the course of its existence, the GESO also coordinated or had a role in a number of other activities which included those listed below.

Developing and maintaining the Growing Esteem website
The Growing Esteem website was linked to the University's homepage and included information such as the strategic plan, implementation updates, frequently asked questions, audio files of the Growing Esteem forums and ways of commenting on aspects of the Growing Esteem strategy. Over time, there were links to other critical sites such as Future Students and a restricted access link for staff, which provided more detailed information than was available to the general community. The website was generally

considered to be of a high quality and of benefit to the community for communicating information about how the *Growing Esteem: Strategic Plan 2006* was being implemented throughout the critical years of 2006 and 2007.

Developing and implementing the communications strategy for Growing Esteem

This strategy covered both internal and external audiences and encompassed a number of flow-on activities. These included working with staff in other departments of the University to develop the main messages and materials for use in publications; preparing briefing notes and PowerPoint presentations for the Vice-Chancellor and other senior University officers to use both within the University and to external groups (particularly schools); developing and maintaining a schedule of presentations on the *Growing Esteem: Strategic Plan 2006* to be made by the Vice-Chancellor and other senior officers to various groups within the University or to external groups.

Coordinating and preparing reports (Growing Esteem updates)

Reports on activities of the Growing Esteem taskforces were prepared for the University Council, Academic Board and Planning and Budget Committee, as well as for the Growing Esteem website. In 2006, each of the taskforces was required to complete a biweekly report according to a set template from which GESO then compiled the comprehensive reports for the committees and the website. In early 2007, the reporting was changed to a monthly basis with relevant people providing information to GESO.

Coordinating and organising events

Events included the Vice-Chancellor's lunchtime forums; breakfast and dinner sessions with school principals, industry leaders and others; visits to schools, and the launch of the Melbourne Model. The Recruitment and Admissions Office provided advice to the GESO and was actively involved in arranging and carrying out visits to schools and events for the principals and careers advisers.

Planning and preparing information for open days in 2006 and 2007
Melbourne Model information packs were prepared in conjunction
with other departments to ensure that complex questions about the
new generation degrees could be answered with confidence.

Liaison with taskforce executive officers
The GESO manager, together with other GESO staff, had fortnightly meetings with the executive officers of the taskforces from
April to the end of September 2006. Thereafter, the GESO link
with the taskforces or bodies that evolved from them was through
its representation on committees such as the Markets Working
Group and the administration and support it provided for these
groups.

In operational terms, a GESO member represented the Vice-
Chancellor's Office at meetings of the various taskforces and their
successor bodies to provide feedback to the Vice-Chancellor –
consistent with the initial purpose of GESO to ensure the Vice-
Chancellor's Office had a central role in the Growing Esteem
activities and developments. Some of this role was also undertaken through the various management committees and groups,
such as VCAG, Matins and so on. In effect, the GESO was another
path of management through the Vice-Chancellor's Office. The
GESO manager, together with the director of the Vice-Chancellor's
Office, met weekly with the Vice-Chancellor to provide an implementation update on Growing Esteem. Topics discussed at these
meetings ranged from relevant forthcoming events to development
and outcomes of the staff pulse survey to staff concerns about
workloads arising from the Growing Esteem strategy. As well, the
manager attended weekly 'communications' meetings.[7]

Communications strategy
To help establish the GESO and kick-start the communications
activities, Jane-Frances Kelly had prepared a draft communications strategy plan of the following four items by 24 March 2006.

Implementation updates

Growing Esteem would be a standing agenda item for meetings of VCAG, Planning and Budget Committee, Academic Board and University Council. In addition, fortnightly updates would be prepared for the Growing Esteem website to cater for internal and external audiences, for meetings of deans and heads and the vice-principals and faculty general managers.

Core materials

These were aimed at stakeholders on the basis that other communications would be consistent with them. The materials were to increase understanding of the Growing Esteem strategy, explain why the proposed curriculum change was necessary, demonstrate the connection between decisions and the external environment, and provide the community with the opportunity to comment. The media used for communicating these core materials were wide-ranging and included the Growing Esteem website, *UniNews*, *Staff News*, 'all staff' and 'all student' emails and forums, implementation updates, the *Growing Esteem: Strategic Plan 2006*, electronic downloadable presentations, Vice-Chancellor's breakfasts with heads of colleges, industry leaders and research institutes, and a glossy Growing Esteem brochure sent to various groups with a letter from the Vice-Chancellor.

Specific materials

This referred to additional communication required for specific internal and external stakeholder groups, including coordinating responses to media coverage of the Melbourne Model. The most sensitive and complex groups to be addressed about the Growing Esteem initiatives were the schools community – principals, careers advisers, and prospective students and their parents. The University wished to be as open and informative as possible but there were risks in providing details at too early a stage. Providing information before certain decisions had been made by the Curriculum Commission and the Academic Board could force the

University into decisions by default, or risk losing the faith of the schools' communities if information proposing a particular course of action was released, but then withdrawn. The advice provided by the Recruitment and Admissions Office was critical to the University's relations with the schools community.

Timelines
The dates for the rollout of key events over the coming weeks and months.

The sensitivity of these matters was highlighted in an information session for school careers advisers conducted by the University in May 2006. At that stage, neither the numbers nor names of the new generation undergraduate degrees had been determined, although the core discipline fields were named. The advisers were quite hostile in their questions and comments. The uncertainty of the Melbourne Model at that time was undermining the significant role careers advisers had in providing advice to students about the requirements for, and their chances of getting in to, particular courses. The situation was complicated when the Vice-Chancellor began his presentation with a few slides on universities' reduced funding, with some of the advisers interpreting the University's rationale for the course changes as being purely financial. A fair amount of 'patching up relations' with the careers advisers was needed after this session. A presentation to school principals in July 2006, after the Academic Board had agreed to the names for the six new generation undergraduate degrees, excluded the slides on funding.

Another aspect of the communications strategy involved establishing a Growing Esteem Query InBox. This electronic facility replaced a Curriculum Commission email hotline, arranged by the director of the Melbourne Curriculum Project in mid-February 2006 to cater for queries and comments from both the internal and external community. The Query InBox could be used for making queries or comments to the University about any aspect of the Growing Esteem strategy. The GESO received the queries and forwarded them on most frequently to the executive officer of the relevant Growing Esteem taskforce for response or advice. As director of the Curriculum Project, I received a fair number of these queries, mostly from prospective students but also from University staff and alumni. The GESO manager has advised that more than 600 enquiries were received through the Query InBox, and almost all had to do with the Melbourne Model.[8]

Market research
Market Research Steering Committee (May to September 2006) and Growing Esteem Markets Working Group (May 2006 to June 2007)
The Curriculum Commission minutes for the meeting on 17 March 2006 noted that a 'Market Research Standing Committee' would meet in the week of 20 March. However, it was not until early April, after the newly appointed Vice-Principal (Marketing and Communications), Pat Freeland-Small, had taken up his position, that a briefing document was drafted to invite tenders for a market research project into the changes proposed under the Melbourne Model. The document was prepared with input from Professor McPhee, the Vice-Principal (International Development), Bruce Bayley, and myself as director of the Melbourne Curriculum Project. The briefing paper was considered at a Matins meeting on 6 April 2006 and forwarded to the Planning and Budget Committee to be considered at its meeting on 12 April.[9] The Planning and Budget Committee agreed to the proposal and endorsed an allocation of $500,000 from the 2006 Teaching and Learning Fund as funding towards a market research program.[10]

Beaton Consulting were the successful bidders, with a proposal presented to a senior management group on 5 May 2006. The Melbourne Model Market Research Steering Committee, which was managed through the Office of the Vice-Principal (Marketing and Communications), met on 15 May to consider the proposed research by Beaton Consulting on 'Market Testing of the Melbourne Model'.[11] The meeting also identified key documents for the consultants to review and people to be interviewed and/or surveyed.

The Growing Esteem Markets Working Group was established in parallel with the Market Research Steering Committee and had its first meeting in late May 2006 (see Appendix 4a for membership of both the working group and the steering committee). This working group was managed through the GESO, as its brief would be part of the communications strategy. While the Markets Steering Committee was focused on market research and testing to gauge reactions to the Melbourne Model, the Markets Working Group had a wide brief with a strong focus on the 'how and when' of the University's marketing activity. Its principal term of reference was: 'The working group will ensure the University manages its student and other markets to maintain and improve its position in them in implementing Growing Esteem.'

In line with this brief, the working group used updates on the market research, its close links with the GESO, and other sources to guide the content and timing of its communications. Most of its discussions were related to matters such as:

- the overall communication strategy taking into account outcomes from the market research as appropriate
- content and timing of communications with the schools; for example, information sessions for Year 10 students, the Vice-Chancellor's letters to principals, feedback from school careers advisers, Vice-Chancellor's dinners with the principals
- internal communication for staff and for enrolled students
- international markets
- preparations and communications for Open Day
- content and production of a video on the Melbourne Model
- interaction with and release of information to the media.

The Growing Esteem Markets Working Group met approximately fortnightly and more frequently in the two months before Open

Day, which was scheduled for 20 August 2006. After Open Day, the meetings were roughly monthly to the end of 2006.

The Market Research Steering Committee had another four or five meetings after May, the last being in early August. These meetings generally discussed market research, identified appropriate groups and individuals to be surveyed and interviewed, and heard reports on outcomes of the research and testing that had been completed. Beaton Consulting representatives reported on outcomes of the market research at Curriculum Commission meetings on four occasions. Some of the issues highlighted from the first report included the perceived need for more information to be provided to both the internal and external community. This was not possible as critical matters were still under discussion and few major decisions had yet been made.

A second report on market research outcomes was provided in early August and the third report was delivered to a meeting in late August. These provided detailed outcomes from focus group interviews for individual faculties, local and overseas alumni, international agents, employer groups and careers advisers. The final presentation by Beaton Consulting to the Curriculum Commission, on 15 September 2006, indicated that the main features of the Melbourne Model would be exceptionally challenging to implement, but that in general there was broad support across the community for the University's approach, and enthusiasm for the knowledge transfer component, especially volunteering. Professor McPhee remembers that one of the senior consultants put it this way: 'We think this is a remarkably difficult and ambitious challenge; we also think you should go for it.'[12]

Beaton also presented outcomes of the market research to the Planning and Budget Committee Conference in June and to the Planning and Budget Committee and the VCAG in mid-September. A final report on the market research was presented to University Council in October, as part of the package of reports related to the Melbourne Model; that is, alongside the Curriculum Commission and the Planning and Budget Committee Implementation Working

Group reports. The Senior Vice-Principal agreed to bring a communications plan for the Melbourne Model to the next meeting of council in light of the market research outcomes.

Government liaison
Policy and Advocacy Taskforce (March 2006 to February 2007)
The Policy and Advocacy Taskforce, with a membership of senior-level staff (see Appendix 4a for details) was established to liaise with high-level government officials and discuss policies relevant to the success of the Melbourne Model. The taskforce's terms of reference stated its role was to 'develop policy options to ensure affordability and the widest possible access and support for talented students, regardless of their background or circumstances'. These included:

- the transfer of some Commonwealth-supported places (CSP) from undergraduate to graduate programs
- increasing the amount students can borrow through FEE-HELP to match tuition costs for full-fee places at both undergraduate and graduate level
- extending youth allowances and Austudy entitlements to graduate study
- removing the cap on Higher Education Contribution Scheme (HECS) contributions for CSPs
- reallocating undergraduate CSPs identified as surplus by the University to other Victorian institutions to ensure the pool of government subsidised places did not diminish
- providing University financial support for students for expenses other than tuition
- extending the Access Melbourne program to graduate study
- seeking greater philanthropic support to finance scholarships
- developing mechanisms to encourage wider accessibility for merit-based selection into undergraduate and postgraduate programs.

The taskforce met on six occasions between March 2006 and February 2007, during which it considered each of the items listed above. As well as identifying approaches it might take to lobby federal and state government ministers on these matters, the group was involved in other discussions and activities within the University on fundraising and in considering options to increase the numbers of students assisted by the Access Melbourne program.

From around May 2006, following a meeting of University representatives with the then Minister for Education, Science and Training (DEST), Julie Bishop, there were indications that the Australian Government supported the University's intention to move to the Melbourne Model and backed the most critical issue of giving approval for the University to transfer Commonwealth-supported places from undergraduate to graduate students. However, there was no firm statement from the Department of Education, Science and Training showing support for the University's request until March 2007.[13] In December 2007, the University finally received a letter from DEST advising it had approved the University's request for the allocation of Commonwealth-supported places to specific professional masters programs.

The new generation degrees
New Generation Course Approvals Working Group (June to December 2006)

This group was established to manage some of the issues origi-nally intended for the first Melbourne Model Taskforce, and to work through the timelines for approval of the new generation degree programs, especially in the lead up to the 2006 Open Day. Its membership is given in Appendix 4a. Most of the critical dates and issues to be resolved were included in the checklist and schedule that had been prepared for the Curriculum Commission and both these documents were available to the working group. The first of the working group's five meetings was held in June 2006 and the last in December 2006. Its discussions focused on these matters:

- timelines for approval of the new generation courses and revisions to the 'Blue Book', which would be necessary for the new generation undergraduate courses[14]
- resolving prerequisite requirements for the six new generation undergraduate degrees for the 2008 intake of students, although most of these matters had already been dealt with by the chair of the Curriculum Commission in consultation with the chair of the Academic Board's Selection Procedures Committee, and with the relevant faculty staff
- identifying, with the faculties, which of the (then) existing undergraduate courses would have a mid-year intake in 2007. This information was necessary for advising prospective students and to be available on Open Day
- establishing a separate Academic Board Postgraduate Coursework Programs Committee to replace a sub-committee of the Academic Programs Committee with the same name
- ensuring legislation and academic policy amendments would be considered by the appropriate bodies
- discussing developments related to establishing the Board of Undergraduate Studies (BUGS) and the course standing committees (CSCs), the groups that would eventually assume responsibility for some of the issues that the New Generation Course Approvals Working Group had attempted to identify and resolve.

The New Generation Course Approvals Working Group appears in various diagrams prepared by the Boston Consulting Group in relation to its Melbourne Model implementation critical path plan, but it had no meetings in 2007, as its responsibilities had by then been subsumed by the interim Board of Undergraduate Studies (iBUGS) and the CSCs.

Planning and Budget Committee Implementing the Melbourne Model Working Group (July to September 2006)
At its 2006 conference, the Planning and Budget Committee agreed to establish an Implementing the Melbourne Model Working Group

(see Appendix 4a for membership details), which was to provide a preliminary report in August and a final report in September, at the same time the Curriculum Commission would submit its final report. This agreement came about in response to two papers: one written by Richard James in consultation with others that proposed establishing a College of Undergraduate Studies, similar to those that exist in a number of universities in the United States, to focus on the 'Melbourne Experience'; and a second one written by the Senior Vice-Principal and others that put forward three models for delivering the Melbourne Model, including a 'college' option. The aim of having a 'University body' responsible for overall management of courses and students was to ensure that all undergraduate students would have a classroom and campus experience of equivalent quality; in other words, a 'whole of University' approach to student services regardless of the course studied.[15]

The working group's purpose, as stated in its draft terms of reference, was: 'To consider issues around the new generation degrees and make recommendations on the best way of delivering and managing these programs in the future which meets the needs of students and optimises their Melbourne Experience under the Melbourne Model.' The group met on six occasions between 12 July 2006 and the end of August 2006. It was instrumental in shaping the subsequent deliberations on the academic and administrative structures required to implement the recommendations of the Curriculum Commission. The scope of the working group's eventual recommendations was to be in two parts: the academic management of the new generation undergraduate degrees to encompass development, management, monitoring, resourcing and continuous improvement of the degrees, and the administrative arrangements that would best support the delivery framework for the Melbourne Model. Because of its significance, the nature and course of its discussions over its short existence from July to delivery of the final report in September 2006 are described in detail below.

First meeting (12 July 2006)

The background documents available for the working group's first meeting were *Growing Esteem: Strategic Plan 2006*, 'Implementing the Melbourne Model' (a discussion paper from the 2006 Planning and Budget Committee Conference) and 'Core Principles for Undergraduate Courses' (a Curriculum Commission draft paper that had been presented to the Academic Board on 25 May 2006). These would already have been quite familiar to the working group's members, as they were all deans and professional staff who had been involved in developing the papers.

In addition, the agenda included a draft paper outlining principles to guide the implementation of new generation courses in the Melbourne Model. The working group's discussion of these draft principles drew out a number of issues, some of them recurring themes as the new generation courses developed and the Melbourne Model was implemented. These included:

- whether subjects 'belonged' to departments or faculties when considered in the context of interfaculty and interdisciplinary teaching
- arrangements for managing the courses that were to be 'taught out' while the new generation courses were being developed and offered
- that standardised policies and course rules would be critical for the University to provide excellent coordination of the University degrees and to ensure that students received consistent and accurate advice
- the need for a University training program to prepare future course advisers for their roles under the Melbourne Model
- that course advice be degree-based and mindful of graduate pathways, rather than faculty-based
- implementation of the Melbourne Model as an opportunity for the University's course administration to become 'student-centred' rather than continue as 'provider-centred' as it had been for quite some time.

Second meeting (20 July 2006)

At its second meeting, the working group reviewed its revised terms of reference and membership (to now include the president of the Academic Board), a revised set of guiding principles, following discussion of the previous draft at the first meeting, and three items listed under the broad heading of 'Melbourne Model Management and Delivery Framework'. These were draft terms of reference for a Board of Undergraduate Studies (BUGS) and course committees; a discussion paper on a proposed structure for a University of Melbourne Undergraduate College and the 'Outline of Delivery Model and Implications for the Management of New Generation Courses and Students'.

The delivery model outline provided a framework for possible governance and management arrangements of the new generation degrees, and presented tables with a description, questions, risks and issues for each feature or perspective. The features and perspectives included matters such as a board of undergraduate studies, course committees, academic structures, and so on.

Third meeting (31 July 2006)

For this meeting, held less than three weeks after the first one, a draft proposal for implementation of the Melbourne Model had been prepared for consideration by Planning and Budget Committee. It set out draft terms of reference for the proposed Board of Undergraduate Studies and the course committees, and proposals for further working groups to consider implementation matters in greater detail. There were also sections on the importance of and possible models for providing course advice, course management and ensuring a high quality 'Melbourne Experience' under the Melbourne Model. The course management component recommended that a dean or director of Undergraduate Studies be appointed who, together with directors of each course and year level, would coordinate the overall framework proposed for the Board of Undergraduate Studies.

The Planning and Budget Committee discussed the draft interim report of the working group at a meeting on 9 August. The

Dean of Economics and Commerce, Professor Abernethy, was concerned that the proposed Board of Undergraduate Studies would duplicate and remove authorities and duties from faculties and the Academic Board. She was supported by several other deans in these arguments, some of whom raised other issues as well. Although Professor McPhee assured members that the Academic Board and its committees would continue to have an important role in course approvals and quality assurance, he advised that the working group would issue a revised document that incorporated the feedback from the Planning and Budget Committee.

Fourth meeting (11 August 2006)
The working group considered a revised draft of its report that took into account the discussion at the Planning and Budget Committee. The working group agreed to amend the terms of reference for the Board of Undergraduate Studies in line with suggestions made by the Dean of Economics and Commerce.

Fifth and sixth meetings (17 and 29 August 2006)
The working group considered more revisions to the draft report, including further discussion of the 'planning principles'. The principles as they appeared in the working group's final report were:

(i) The Melbourne Model is student centred; the first priority in implementing the Model will be to ensure that the present and anticipated future educational and administrative needs of undergraduate and postgraduate students are met and services are delivered in a manner that best meets those needs.

(ii) Teaching informed by research, and student exposure to a research experience, is a critical part of a student's educational experience.

(iii) The formation, development, monitoring and continuous improvement of the discipline content of the new generation courses will be the province of academic staff from the relevant disciplines and delivered within a cohesive curriculum.

(iv) The University will plan for a delivery framework of the Melbourne Model which is optimal in approximately 2015, and will develop transition arrangements which minimises disruption to the University in the interim period and which take account of the internal and external environment.

(v) Decisions about the best framework for delivering the academic and administrative support aspects of the Melbourne Model will be based on the need to optimise the quality of the future programs and their modes of delivery and will not be determined by current organisational and budget arrangements; existing academic and administrative support arrangements will be reviewed and, if and as necessary, modified as part of a systematic transition plan involving all interested parties.[16]

A statement that had appeared in the original draft of the principles, but which did not survive to the final draft because of its contentious implication, was: 'The new generation undergraduate degrees are courses of the University.'[17] The working group's final report to the Planning and Budget Committee did include a qualifying statement in the section on the planning principles, which included the sentence:

Some consequences of the Melbourne Model and these principles for the new-generation undergraduate degrees, which are built on more inter-faculty contributions than in the past, are that a University-wide framework for managing the courses which allows the faculties to act in concert is required, with faculties continuing to have a fundamental role in contributing to the design, development and teaching of these degrees.[18]

The group also worked to realise the vision of student administration, advice and support services that would be more efficient and consistent across all faculties and courses. A paper prepared by the Vice-Principal and Academic Registrar on 'Course-Based Student Service Centres' at the request of the working group was also discussed. This focused on resources to support the chairs of the BUGS and the CSCs, and draft criteria for postgraduate courses. In the interval between meetings 5 and 6 of the working group, the mid-year Deans and Heads Conference had been held and its feedback on a draft interim report was also taken into account when the final report was prepared.

The Planning and Budget Committee supported nine of the ten recommendations included in the working group's final report at its meeting on 13 September 2006 and agreed to forward the report to the Academic Board for its meeting on 21 September, and then on to University Council. The one recommendation that was not supported had to do with postgraduate courses, on the basis that the working group had not had enough time to give full consideration to this matter. The University Council approved the final report on 9 October 2006 and its main recommendations are listed, and their ramifications explored, in Part III of this book.

Shared services review

At the annual Planning and Budget Committee conference in June 2005, the committee approved a proposal for a review of service areas to ensure they supported the University's core activities effectively. The University administration had proposed that fundamental 'whole of University' evaluations should be held of major administrative programs to find out if the current administrative structures across the centres, faculties and departments were cost-effective. There was a strong focus on information technology in shared services and facilities, which resulted in the Planning and Budget Committee agreeing to provide significant funding for transition to an improved business model. Four other program reviews were proposed for the finance, marketing and development, academic services and international administrative areas. The reviews were conducted in the second half of 2005 and the Planning and Budget Committee accepted recommendations from the four panels of review in December 2005. The final report on the review of the international area was postponed to April 2006. The agreed recommendations were to be implemented in 2006.

The Shared Services Review Implementation Group was one outcome of these recommendations. It was established as one of the six taskforces described in *Growing Esteem: Strategic Plan 2006* to support the development and implementation of the Growing Esteem initiatives. The role of the shared services program was to 'oversee the development and implementation of a "whole of university" approach to administration, which ensures alignment between administrative capacities and Growing Esteem priorities'.[19] The implementation group held the first of eleven meetings in 2006 in March, and a further three meetings between March and June 2007.

The early meetings in 2006 focused on reports from reference groups that were working through the recommendations approved in December 2006. The notes for the Shared Services Review Implementation Group meetings refer to a hiatus for the academic services review given the work of the Curriculum Commission and uncertainty about the final outcome of the major curriculum changes. There was also an indication that the administration should see the curriculum changes as a 'once in a lifetime opportunity' for the University, in providing services, to change from a provider-centred approach to a student-centred one.

The Shared Services Taskforce report to the July 2006 VCAG retreat noted that an important issue for the Shared Services Review Implementation Group was the framework for delivering the Melbourne Model. It also indicated that when the framework was clarified, the administrative support mechanisms to ensure students received high-quality student-centred management and support could be planned and implemented during 2007. By the time the implementation group met in late August 2006, the members would have had an opportunity to review the draft reports of the Curriculum Commission and the PBC Implementing the Melbourne Model Working Group. With this information, the implementation group was to prepare a report to the Planning and Budget Committee 'outlining priorities, scope and mechanisms for reviewing academic administration to support the Melbourne Model'.[20] The report was also to indicate that the University needed to conduct an activity-based costing for its administrative activities. In light of the involvement of consultants from Boston Consulting, the report to PBC was held over, initially due to absences of key staff and also because further thought was to be given to methods of collecting cost data.[21]

At the Shared Services Review Implementation Group October meeting, Ian Marshman reported on a meeting held with senior officers of the Boston Consulting Group (hereafter, Boston), on 10 October 2006, to discuss the scope of work necessary to put the Melbourne Model in place and options for Boston involvement. Boston had already undertaken several weeks of background work on how the proposed model might be implemented so it would be in a position to finalise a critical path proposal for the University as soon as possible after the Curriculum Commission's final report had been approved. This was essential given that the timelines for developing and introducing the new generation Melbourne Model courses would be less than eighteen months from this time and introduction of the courses in March 2008. Boston's role will be discussed in more detail in Part III.

With the work that had been completed by some of the Shared Services Review groups and the sweeping changes that the University was embarking upon with the Melbourne Model, including new structures, the work of the Shared Services Review Implementation Group was much diminished in 2007. There were three meetings between March and December. A meeting scheduled for June was cancelled and the final meeting was held in December 2007.

Existing groups

As well as the groups set up to handle specific aspects of designing and implementing the Melbourne Model as they arose, a number of existing bodies were also involved in crucial aspects of the project.

Vice-Chancellor's Advisory Group (VCAG) (May 2005 to May 2008)

The origin of VCAG, as an initiative of Vice-Chancellor Davis in 2005, and its role in that year were reported in Chapter 1. By early 2006, VCAG membership had been expanded to include the Assistant and Pro-Vice Chancellors. In 2006, VCAG met more or less weekly during term time and monthly to fortnightly at other times of the year. In 2007, meetings were weekly for most of the year. The usual agenda for VCAG meetings in 2006 was:

- Action sheet from previous meeting
- Vice-Chancellor's items
- Advisory Group items
- For noting (this item included a brief report on government and political issues prepared by the Vice-Chancellor's Policy and Government Relations Adviser, and dates of leave/absence of senior officers from the University).

Although there was an agenda and action sheet as well as supporting documents for some of the items listed, there were no minutes taken of the meetings. Consequently, there is no public record of any discussion of Growing Esteem items, even though, according to the Growing Esteem communications strategy, these were to be included on the agenda as a standing item. As there were few matters related to Growing Esteem listed in the action sheet, my assumption is that the 'communication' involved oral reports of progress and discussion of issues that needed attention. Professor McPhee states that VCAG was one of the forums, like Matins, where he was able to sound out senior colleagues informally on the contentious issues he was confronting. In this sense, VCAG had a significant role, throughout its existence but especially in 2006 and 2007, as the body with an overarching role in discussing strategic issues and their resolutions.

There were two matters that may have been discussed at some length (or at least were considered to merit further attention), as they were included on the action sheets for relevant meetings. The first of these was the entry for an early March meeting of VCAG, on investigating the possibility of having a separate biomedical science degree as one of the new generation degrees cluster.[22] A proposal for such a degree was considered at the VCAG meeting on 13 June 2006, which was less than two weeks before the Academic Board endorsed Bioscience as the sixth of the proposed new generation degrees. The second matter encompassed a number of individual items on the October and November agendas related to the Melbourne Model after the Curriculum Commission report had been endorsed by the Academic Board. For one of the August 2006 meetings, an item appears on the action sheet titled 'coordination of major change in the University' with a comment that there would be a presentation to the Vice-Chancellor and Deans' Group, but there is no record of what this contained.

In addition to regular meetings, there were three VCAG 'retreat' meetings in 2006: one in each of April, July and October. Each of these ran for four to five hours during which a number of significant matters were discussed in detail, with a strong focus on the full range of Growing Esteem activities. For the Growing Esteem taskforces, the documentation and discussion included a progress report against the objectives for each of the groups, identification of specific issues under consideration at the time, and a discussion of forthcoming issues and how they would be managed. The executive officers of the taskforces were invited to attend these meetings. The retreats provided an opportunity to take stock of the state of play of each component of the Growing Esteem strategy, and to plan for the next stages of development.

At the April retreat, the Senior Vice-Principal presented a paper on 'Administrative Reform and Shared Service', the first outline of plans to 'achieve administrative reform and improvements to support and enable the University's new Strategic Plan, Growing Esteem'. The paper built on achievements from a 2005 program of shared services reviews and outcomes but indicated that, with the developing curriculum reforms, there would be further opportunities for business improvements in administrative services and systems. It set out the mission and objectives for the University administration and strategies for achieving those objectives. The paper stated that the Shared Services Review Implementation Group would oversee the strategies, but also recommended that a professional project manager be appointed to the GESO to support achieving the vision of Growing Esteem.[23] Perhaps even more significantly, the paper reported that the University had made an application for $1.8 million in funding under the federal government's Workplace Productivity Program (WPP) to support the proposed program of academic administration reform and planning tools, and to appoint consultants to work with the University. This funding is discussed further in Appendix 5.

VCAG 2007
The VCAG 2007 meetings operated with a somewhat changed agenda from that followed in 2006:
• Action sheet from previous meeting
• Vice-Chancellor's urgent issues
• Strategic issues
• Items needing resolution

- Briefings (these included the government and political issues and leave/absences from the 'for noting' items on 2006 agendas).

There were few items included under the 'Vice-Chancellor's urgent issues' heading during the year. Only a small number of items were listed under 'items needing resolution', of which five directly related to the Melbourne Model although other relevant items may have been discussed as 'strategic issues'. The five that did make it to the agenda were funding for the University's extensive 'Dreamlarge' advertising campaign for the Melbourne Model, nomenclature of graduate schools, orientation for new undergraduates in 2008, and the naming and branding of the student centres. On the other hand, a considerable number of items related to the Melbourne Model were listed under 'strategic issues', including marketing the Melbourne Model, the Melbourne Student Services Model (which will be described further in Chapter 9), Open Day arrangements, revised university structures consequent to the adoption and introduction of the Melbourne Model and several others.

There were two VCAG retreats in 2007, one in May and a second in July. In addition to reviewing progress against the 2007 University Plan, the May retreat had two major items to consider: the strategic implications of the Commonwealth budget and academic structures. The latter item involved a lengthy process of investigation and review (discussed in Chapter 8) that led to the position of Deputy Vice-Chancellor (Academic) being converted to that of Provost, and to a revised structure for managing the Melbourne Model. The main item considered at the July retreat was 'whole-of-University' marketing, a discussion in which a number of professional staff from the marketing and recruitment departments had been invited to participate.

Vice-Chancellor and Deans
The Vice-Chancellor's Consultative Committee had been initiated by Professor David Penington during his tenure as vice-chancellor.

The group met monthly and, as a result of Professor Davis' initiative, from May 2005 the first half-hour was a deans' closed session, with the Vice-Chancellor and the Senior Vice-Principal then joining the deans for an hour. The Vice-Principal and Head of Administration, Liz Bare, also attended the meetings from November 2006 (when the Head of Administration position was created).

Matters related to the Melbourne Model under the standing agenda heading 'Vice-Chancellor's items' included Growing Esteem; Growing Esteem and change management; Open Day feedback; access to funding under the Growing Esteem Transition Fund; 2008 entry scores, and Melbourne Model implementation arrangements. Under the standing agenda heading 'Deans' items' for the meeting on 21 July 2006 was a general discussion of the Melbourne Model, including Open Day arrangements.

Only two items directly related to the Melbourne Model – Melbourne Model launch details and the Melbourne Model Student Services Model Project – were listed on the agenda for Vice-Chancellor and Deans' meetings in 2007. The last meeting of this group appears to have occurred in November 2007 as the December 2007 and the March and April 2008 meetings were cancelled. In May 2008, a new management structure was adopted with the establishment of a Senior Executive Committee that replaced the Planning and Budget Committee, the VCAG and the Vice-Chancellor and Deans' Group.

The work conducted by the various taskforces during 2006 and 2007 had sorted out a great many issues. The course design was now clear and endorsed, market research had been undertaken that showed the changes were viable (though difficult) and information about the changes and what they would mean had been communicated to various stakeholders. As far as possible, potential future students, their parents and schools knew what the new degree structure would involve. The task for the University now was to ensure the new generation degrees, and the appropriate student services, were ready in time for the first students to enrol in 2008. The year 2007 was all about implementing the model. This year of remarkably rapid, and at times frenzied, transition is explored in Part III of this book.

Part III

Transition 2007

7

Launching the Melbourne Model

On 17 April 2007, the Melbourne Model was officially launched. A month earlier, on 22 March, a meeting of the Academic Board (with around a hundred members in attendance) had approved the objectives and core programs for the six new generation undergraduate degrees, on the recommendation of its Undergraduate Programs Committee. In his report, Professor Davis emphasised the historic role of the meeting in approving the courses – just over a year since the Curriculum Commission had held its first meeting. The Vice-Chancellor also reported that he had finally received advice from DEST that it had approved the transfer of undergraduate Commonwealth-supported places to postgraduate places. And the Senior Vice-Principal reported on the University's enhanced scholarships program, which comprised three elements: recognition of merit; support of access and equity; and minimisation of 'bright flight'.[1] These three things went a long way to ensure that the Melbourne Model could be successfully implemented – and appropriately launched. But the vote to approve the six degrees had not been unanimous. The student representatives on the Academic Board raised questions in this meeting about why Gender Studies would be available only as a minor in the new Bachelor of Arts instead of a full-fledged major.[2] The three student representatives subsequently voted against the motion to approve the six degrees – the only members of the Academic Board to do so.

Launch day
The launch of the Melbourne Model gave the University the opportunity to showcase the new generation degrees and aspects of its broader agenda to the community, to respond to specific

questions about the structure of the degrees and confidently outline the rationale behind them. It was a day of formal speeches and ceremony, with many associated activities planned for the weeks to follow. The target audience was wide: federal and state government politicians and officials through school principals, prospective students and their parents to current staff and students of the University. The aim was to ensure that all segments of the community were provided with necessary information about the Melbourne Model in preparation for Open Day in August and the VTAC end-of-September closing date for prospective students to apply for admission to the new generation degrees in 2008.

Launch day began its invitation-only formal morning program in the David Penington Building with speeches by Chancellor Ian Renard and Vice-Chancellor Professor Davis. The Vice-Chancellor outlined the thinking behind the Melbourne Model curriculum and the benefits, as well as the magnitude, of the changes involved. He also introduced the new student scholarships, particularly the Kwong Lee Dow Young Scholars Program.[3] The Vice-Chancellor reported that the Melbourne Access program would be extended to the new graduate programs so that at least 20 per cent of places in each of the Melbourne Model undergraduate and professional graduate degrees would be reserved for students who had suffered prior educational disadvantage as a result of their social or economic circumstances. Ms Sana Nakata, a student at the time, spoke about her vision of the benefits of the Melbourne Model. She defined the advantages of a generalist education before specialisation, claiming that 'most of us arrive at university feeling very much like travellers in a strange country', that 'Tertiary education is the opportunity to engage more critically with what we know' and:

> Before it sends us out into the world as lawyers and other professionals, it demands first that we know ourselves. And from there we might choose to add lawyer, doctor, or architect to the list.

It is this rich and valuable education that the Melbourne Model offers its students.[4]

After these formal morning activities, deans met with their staff to express appreciation for the tremendous team effort that had gone into the achievements leading up to and including the launch. The deans then introduced a video of the morning's launch activities, after which staff were invited to a celebratory barbecue, put on at three locations: University Square, the Concrete Lawn and the South Lawn.

The occasion was also used to introduce the Dreamlarge advertising campaign, which evoked varied reactions. Melbourne University had not previously used television media and cinemas for marketing, although several other universities had been doing so for some time. Further, the Dreamlarge indirect approach for publicising the University's programs was against the expectations of many. The Dreamlarge campaign aimed to present education not just as a means to an end but as an opportunity to think through who we are and what we value, and the role we want to play in the creation and transmission of knowledge.[5] Some staff, students and members of the general community considered it outrageous that so much was to be spent on advertising, while others thought it was a highly innovative campaign that provided a good reflection of the bold approach the University was taking with its new curriculum.[6]

The launch-day activities were to culminate with a grand dinner at University House.[7] Members of the internal and external community and, in particular, school principals had been invited. The event was thrown into disarray when about 50 students picketed and demonstrated outside University House in protest about a range of issues, of which the proposed closure of the Department of Creative Arts and prospective course changes at the VCA were prominent.[8] The decision to terminate the Bachelor of Creative Arts course in question had been taken long before the Melbourne Model, but had become a focus of discontent. Lauren Hutchison, the Melbourne University student union arts officer, was later quoted as saying, 'So many third-year subjects are being cut in creative arts that it is impossible for many students to finish their course.'[9] Because of the protest, around one hundred of the invited guests were unable to enter University House for the dinner. It was disappointing for many involved in planning the launch that this protest was reported more widely in the media than the otherwise successful day's main proceedings.

The University took various measures to make sure those who had missed the dinner had an opportunity, in the days just after the launch, to attend other functions and to receive information outlining the Melbourne Model. Around the same time, Professor McPhee convened a general meeting of students to address issues that concerned them. This meeting was disrupted by the same groups who had protested at the launch dinner. These incidents served to highlight a shortcoming in the Melbourne Model implementation, particularly from the perspective of some students who believed issues central to teaching out the existing courses had been poorly handled. Such had been the attention devoted to the design and implementation of the new generation courses that the interests of some students enrolled in degrees that would be discontinued had not been met. Recommendation 2 in the Curriculum Commission final report had emphasised just this priority, and the recommendation was well understood, but there were so many other pressing issues and such limited time that this key aspect had been somewhat neglected. One move to deal with the problem was the appointment of Liz Sonenberg to oversee 'teaching out' issues on behalf of the Melbourne Model Implementation Taskforce, which is discussed further in Chapter 9. The launch demonstrated the strength of the model and the clarity of the vision behind it – and showed up some weaknesses in implementation that would need to be remedied.

Lead up to the launch

In the six months between the September 2006 approval of the Curriculum Commission's final report and April 2007 there had been considerable work, by both existing and newly created bodies, to ensure that implementation of the Melbourne Model had progressed enough for the launch to take place. But there was a great deal more to be done to prepare for the first intake of new generation degree students in 2008. Once the Curriculum Commission's final report had been endorsed by the Academic Board and the University Council in September 2006, the ground had shifted significantly. Whereas 2006 had been a time of ambitious and bold discussion and design, now attention had to turn to the detailed, exacting work of implementation. Time was of the essence. There was less than a year available for the new generation degrees to be developed and approved if accurate details were to be available for the prospective 2008 intake of students. Twelve formerly undergraduate degrees with professional accreditation were shifting to graduate entry in 2008; they, with other new graduate programs planned for 2011, also had to be redesigned.

Preparation for the launch, overseen by the MM08 Taskforce (described in the next chapter) with the involvement of other groups such as the VCAG, was just one focus. The Growing Esteem Markets Working Group, discussed in Chapter 6, continued its work in the first half of 2007, with two priorities being the Dreamlarge advertising campaign and preparing for the Melbourne Model launch.[10] Preparations included a marketing plan and strategy, not only for the launch but also for all of 2007, and communication with schools and the wider community about the Melbourne Model. Marketing the Bachelor of Environments and the Bachelor of Science, both of which would involve teaching from three or more faculties, continued to be of particular concern. To prepare for the launch, academic programs managers were provided with training and key staff were given lists of 'frequently asked questions and answers'. Another priority was Open Day in August 2007 – an important deadline for which it was essential accurate course and promotional material be available.

Putting the academic elements of the Melbourne Model in place was made more complex by the University's commitment that the model would improve overall student experience, partly through student learning centres or hubs. These complications were dealt with by a number of new groups and guidelines, as well as some that already existed. This final part of the book discusses the activities of these various groups, new and old, and their roles in the transition to the Melbourne Model. The focus in the rest of this chapter is on the continued finetuning of the academic framework for the new generation degrees (largely through the interim Board of Undergraduate Studies and the course standing committees) and the University's management structures, in the months between September 2006 and June 2007. The following chapters look at the further work undertaken during this period and beyond to implement the Melbourne Model and to ensure that the changes involved were managed efficiently and well from all angles. In particular, this includes an outline of related changes to University administration and organisational structures, and the development of the new generation 'Melbourne Experience' – soon to be an integral part of the Melbourne Student Services Model. Through these events we follow the story through the year of transition, from the end of 2006 to the first intake of students in February 2008.

Academic framework

The recommendations (Appendix 6a) in the final report of the Curriculum Commission set out the academic framework for the new generation degrees that would form the basis of the Melbourne Model. The recommendations from the report of the PBC Implementing the Melbourne Model Working Group provided a framework for what had to be achieved for these degrees to be operational and the key structures needed to carry out the tasks.

The central recommendations of the working group appear below.

Recommendation 1
That a University-wide framework is required for planning, designing, implementing and managing the

new generation undergraduate degrees and that this should be achieved through the establishment of:

(i) Course Standing Committees for each new generation undergraduate degree with responsibility for designing and developing the courses, with membership and terms of reference as described in Appendix 2.

(ii) A Board of Undergraduate Studies (BUGS), which is the primary mechanism for the faculties to act in concert to ensure the recommendations from the course Standing Committees adhere to the new generation degree core principles and University policies, and makes recommendations on the courses to the Academic Board via its subcommittees (terms of reference described in Appendix 3).

...

Recommendation 6
That all course advisers for new generation undergraduate degree students undergo a University training program to ensure that student-centred and high quality, expert course advice across all degrees is available to students.

...

Recommendation 8
That faculties are strongly encouraged to develop and refine proposals for Graduate Schools which are responsive to cross disciplinary programs, financial sustainability, postgraduate student experience, and market expectations, and that these matters are canvassed in faculty business plans so that the Planning and Budget Committee can consider the appropriate

framework for Graduate Schools in the second quarter of 2007 after the first round of faculty planning.

Recommendation 9
That the new generation courses will operate under a common set of rules and policies which will be applied consistently across the University.[11]

Re-reading these recommendations more than five years after they were written, what stands out is the simplicity of the structure proposed for the core tasks to be completed before the new generation degrees would be ready for their first intakes. Also, two of the recommendations especially highlight the significant changes being wrought by the Melbourne Model on functions of the University quite apart from the curriculum structure: that all student course advisers would have to undergo a training program, and that 'the new generation courses will operate under a common set of rules and policies which will be applied consistently across the University'. A universal standard was something that had not previously existed in student service provision, and although this aspect of the Melbourne Model sometimes seemed secondary, it was and remains a highly significant part of it.

Throughout the Curriculum Commission discussions, frequent reference had been made to the need for students to receive course advice of the highest quality and depth. It was considered essential that students receive sound advice from which to make the best choices for their studies if the Melbourne Model was to be successful. Student surveys on the quality of teaching and student services, introduced by the University in the late 1990s, had regularly shown significant levels of dissatisfaction with the variable policies maintained, and advice given, between faculties. The quality of course advice provided by administrative staff and the quality of some student services frequently rated low, raising concerns that these units were underperforming. Combined degree students who frequently had to seek course advice from two or more faculties were particularly dissatisfied. Consequently, with six 'University' degrees, common rules and policies would be essential to avoid the local variations in services and practices that had occurred previously. This was a rare opportunity to make improvements with student satisfaction in mind.

What is *not* reflected in the PBC working group recommendations is the complexity of the tasks that had to be completed and how the introduction of the Melbourne Model would change the face of the University over the longer term. The University's operations in 2007, in its early efforts to implement the Melbourne Model, and since, have left virtually no stone unturned. Everything was up for review, from the core elements of change associated with the Melbourne Model new generation degrees that are the theme of this story, to the way the University interacted with its students, to organisational structures and practices for the longer term. As will become clearer, these operations heralded a series of consequences that, when combined with other internal and external developments, were far more substantial – and created far more upheaval – in changing the face of the University than had been imagined or anticipated.

One of the consequences, already touched on briefly, was the establishment of the Board of Undergraduate Studies and the course standing committees. The proposed structure of both BUGS and the CSCs was contentious from the start. The debate intensified when the 'college of undergraduate studies' discussion paper, written in March and April 2006, was considered at the Planning and Budget Committee Conference, leading to the creation of the PBC Implementing the Melbourne Model Working Group, and continued into 2007. The 'college' model – whereby the academics who taught into the undergraduate degrees, the administrative students services staff and others would form the college responsible for the new degrees and related academic services, with a budget to go with it – presented a new and radically different structure. Faculties saw it as a potential threat to their independence, with some arguing that such a structure was not necessary and, further, would undermine the authority not only of the faculties but also of the committees of the Academic Board. A number of academic staff held strong views that their faculty undergraduate committees or equivalent groups were more than adequate for developing the curricula for the new generation degrees. Other faculties – especially those who were unlikely to have 'management ownership' of one of the new degrees – were less confident. Professor McPhee had urged academic staff to focus on the quality of the degrees, not on funding issues, but he had frequent meetings during 2007 with faculty staff who were convinced they were being 'locked out' of course design discussions with consequent concerns about student numbers and funding. A particular question for Professor McPhee was whether the proposed BUGS would be able to stop the 'student numbers wars' of the past.

The Academic Board was also concerned it might be left without a key role in considering and approving the new generation and other degrees. These concerns continued to be raised in the deliberations of the BUGS and various other groups. It was clear that the course standing committees would be responsible for developing the curriculum for the new generation degrees, but there was less certainty about who would ensure that a common set of rules and policies was developed for the six Melbourne Model new generation degrees and, eventually, for degrees at the graduate level.

The Board of Undergraduate Studies

Professor McPhee, as Deputy Vice-Chancellor (Academic), convened the first meeting of the interim BUGS on 29 September 2006, just over a week after the Academic Board endorsed the final report of the Curriculum Commission. It was designated as an 'interim' body for the simple reason that the tight timeframes for development and approval of the new generation degrees meant the board had to begin its work before the University was able to ensure BUGS and the standing committees were legally constituted. This interim arrangement was endorsed by the University Council in October 2006, after iBUGS, as it was called from then on, had held its first meeting. As it turned out, BUGS never existed in other than an interim form.

At this time, the iBUGS had a potential membership of 22, including eleven deans and six chairs of the standing committees but excluding the provision for two co-optees. Eleven members attended the first meeting, including the nominees of six deans (no dean attended in their own right). Technically, the six chairs of the standing committees had not yet been appointed and, consequently, could not have attended this first iBUGS meeting. Meetings of the standing committees followed in October and November and thereafter.

Professor McPhee discussed the iBUGS terms of reference at this meeting, taking care to elaborate on the relationship of iBUGS with the Academic Board – a major point of concern to the deans. In particular, he explained that iBUGS would 'oversee a range of policy matters, including the design, development and delivery of the "new generation" degrees'. He went on to say that the role of iBUGS should not be confused with that of the Academic Board:

> The iBUGS will make recommendations to the Academic Board, with advice from course standing committees, on matters affecting undergraduate study in the University including academic and administrative arrangements and strategic considerations.[12]

Professor McPhee sought to reassure those present that the board would have a continuing role in course approvals and quality assurance. The iBUGS terms of reference also stated that its reporting relationships were to the Planning and Budget Committee on financial matters and to the Academic Board, through board committees, on academic matters including quality of education. It was, therefore, answerable to these two bodies.

In further discussion of the terms of reference, it was noted that iBUGS would recommend the development of policies in particular areas but would not be responsible for drafting these policies. The iBUGS also considered what its role would be – and whether it would have one – in developing the graduate schools and advising the Academic Board on matters of policy that would affect undergraduate programs outside the Melbourne Model. It was agreed at this meeting that the iBUGS work plan over the next four to five months would focus on pathways for students returning to study or those from other institutions, possibilities for majors of common size and structure, concurrent diplomas, University 'breadth' subjects and other related issues.

The iBUGS noted that a new Melbourne Model Implementation Taskforce (known as MM08 and not to be confused with the original taskforce) had been established and that the Boston Consulting Group would provide advice on implementation structures. These groups were both central in this stage of the implementation process, and will be discussed further in the next chapter.

The second iBUGS meeting, held in early November 2006, had an improved attendance with a total of 22 members present, the maximum possible excluding co-optees. Attending were seven deans, including two who were also chairs of standing committees, nominees of four other deans and the remaining four chairs of standing committees and some from other categories of membership. Professor McPhee, as chair, explained that iBUGS would have a role in the divisional business planning that was underway within the University. This would be true especially for the distribution of the then-existing student course load into the new generation degrees, and in providing advice on student support offered by central units. The iBUGS received and discussed preliminary written and oral progress reports on development of the new generation degrees from each of the standing committee chairs.

There was one further meeting of iBUGS in December 2006 and then ten meetings in 2007, four of which were in February, to consider the proposals for the new generation degrees. For 2007, the Vice-Chancellor had appointed the former president of the Academic Board, Professor Loane Skene, as chair of iBUGS. Most of the 2007 meetings were well attended with totals present in the order of 20 to 22 members, including most deans or their nominees. Numbers dropped off somewhat at the meetings held in May, June and July. The final meeting of the iBUGS was held on 13 July 2007.[13] From December 2006 to February 2007, iBUGS worked through a number of issues in the development of the new generation degrees, approved the six course proposals and forwarded them on to the Undergraduate Programs Committee of the Academic Board. Many of the issues raised as concerns in iBUGS were of a policy or procedural nature. For example, iBUGS established a definition of 'breadth' for the Academic Board and formed a working group with academic and student representatives from Arts to explore options relating to Gender Studies.[14] It also clarified a number of topics for the board, including:

- the process for approving breadth subjects
- that an honours program would be available in each of the new generation degrees but not necessarily in every discipline
- that not every discipline would be available for study as a concurrent diploma and a new proposal for the pre-existing diplomas would have to be submitted to iBUGS in accordance with the revised requirements
- a range of processes associated with the concurrent diplomas including eligibility, admissions, progression rules and other matters
- the process for the approval of new subjects offered in the new generation degrees
- who would be responsible for administering the new generation degrees. This was a key topic for discussion in the lead up to and at the June 2007 Planning and Budget Committee Conference.

Course standing committees

Four of the six new generation course standing committees held their first meetings in October 2006 with the remaining two meeting on 1 November 2006. Provisional membership of the six committees had been reported to the Planning and Budget Committee on 13 September 2006, with the stipulation that outstanding matters of membership would be subject to approval by the Deputy Vice-Chancellor (Academic) as BUGS was established after that date.

The standing committees' terms of reference set out their membership, which was to be academics drawn from the disciplines that would be taught in the degree. All members of the standing committees, including the chairs, would be appointed by the Board of Undergraduate Studies once it was established. The categories of members and the members in each group of the first standing committees are set out in Appendix 4b.

The initial terms of reference for the CSCs were comprehensive. The committees' main role was to 'design and develop new course proposals for new generation undergraduate degrees, ensuring the incorporation of the core principles of the Melbourne Model'. The terms of reference also stated that the CSCs would make recommendations to BUGS (or iBUGS) on a range of academic policy matters for the new generation degrees. By early 2007, these policy developments had become the responsibility of the Policy and Procedures Working Group, one of the substreams in the Boston Consulting Group's critical path plan for putting the Melbourne Model in place (this plan will be discussed further in the next chapter).

Each of the standing committees held two to three meetings before the end of 2006 and at least six meetings in 2007. The agendas generally comprised:

- terms of reference and membership
- course developments to date, which incorporated proposals and discussions on which disciplines would be offered as

majors, which subjects would be offered or accepted to satisfy the breadth component if taught by a department not directly involved in the new generation degree, and an extensive range of related matters
• that committee's work plan, critical to ensure the committees were on track to deliver a comprehensive course proposal for each of the new generation degrees for consideration by iBUGS in February 2007, and by the Undergraduate Programs Committee of the Academic Board in March 2007.

Even before the course standing committees were established, most faculties had discussed options for the new generation degrees in their undergraduate studies or equivalent committees, or had established separate working groups to discuss the matters being considered by the Curriculum Commission. For example, the Faculty of Science had a Science Structures and Majors Working Group, which had been working through various issues, including the potential structure of a new generation Bachelor of Science and majors, breadth requirements and opportunities, and the 'plus 2' aspect of the Melbourne Model. The five faculties that were initially to be involved in teaching into the Bachelor of Environments set up an informal inter-faculty working group, as well as a First Year Subjects Working Group, to work through options for the course.

The standing committees had a range of decisions to make and, like the individual faculties in the earlier planning stages, experienced varying degrees of difficulty and complexity throughout the process. Because committee membership was cross-discipline and because the committees needed to design courses that met the requirements of the Melbourne Model, all were operating in a different format from the standard faculty undergraduate studies committee. For some courses, these differences were minimal while for others they were significant – particularly for the five faculties involved in the Bachelor of Environments. Each committee had to determine which disciplines would be eligible to be offered as a major, or core, stream of study in the new generation degree and which would comprise breadth, or non-core, studies. These decisions were reasonably straightforward for most disciplines – but not for all. Difficulties arose partly from the University's practice of designating schools or departments made up of one or more disciplines as part of a faculty for 'budgeting' purposes. For example, Psychology had a long history of being a discipline available as a major field of study in the bachelors of both Science and Arts, and its organisational management subjects were attractive to some students in the Bachelor of Commerce. But Psychology was actually taught by the School of Behavioural Sciences, a budget unit of the Faculty of Medicine, Dentistry and Health Sciences, although it was not available as a major stream of study in undergraduate degrees offered by that faculty. The new generation Bachelor of Arts, Bachelor of Commerce and Bachelor of Science course standing committees each had to determine if Psychology would be offered in the new generation degrees as a major discipline or as a breadth component. Ensuring the numbers of Psychology subjects (or credit points) that would be required or permitted for a 'major' would enable students to meet prerequisites for further study and professional accreditation complicated matters further. The committees considered various permutations, including requiring or permitting X number of points as core and Y number of points as breadth in the relevant disciplines. Course information for the Bachelor of Arts, Bachelor of Commerce and Bachelor of Science available in April 2010 found that students in each of these three degrees who wished to major in Psychology might do so. However, the ways in which students satisfy the requirements for a major study varies among the three degrees. The situation for Economics, a budget discipline of the Faculty of Economics and Commerce (now Business and Economics), was similar. For many years, Economics had been available as a major discipline in the Bachelor of Arts and to accommodate the continuation of this arrangement a structural variation was agreed to, as it had been for Psychology. This enables students to complete the required credit points within the three-year degree.[15]

In addition to their key academic role in developing the new generation degrees, the course standing committees also had to contend with administrative changes to be made as a result of or in parallel with the introduction of the Melbourne Model. For example, faculties were advised that a new subject coding system would be introduced from 2008 as part of the new student system. Because of the alpha-numeric basis of this new schema, it would not accommodate subjects that had been variously referred to as split-level or multi-year subjects. This had a particular impact on the Faculty of Arts, which had offered a substantial number of such subjects through most of its departments. These multi-year subjects were available for second- or third-year level studies, with assessment requirements varying according to the year level being taken. Although the subjects had separate numerical codes, the title was the same. With the new student system, which was expected to be introduced in parallel with the Melbourne Model from 2008 but did not actually go live till 2010, multi-year subjects would not be an option. Some Arts students felt the action reduced their course and subject options, but there were also arguments in favour of the move. Professor Pip Pattison, the president of the Academic Board at the time, argued, too, that there was a pedagogical rationale for designating subjects at only one year level: that studies should be sequential with subjects building on previous ones. This was consistent with the view of the Curriculum Commission and the reviewer of the Faculty of Arts curriculum, Associate Professor D'Agostino, that an undergraduate degree should be coherent and cumulative. Arts was able to work through this massive exercise and largely resolve it by the middle of 2008.

Each of the CSCs also discussed the matter of an honours year or equivalent as a pathway to further studies. Some disciplines definitely wished to have an option for students to proceed to an honours year while others preferred a two-year masters as the pathway to a research degree. There was particular concern that options be kept open for students to be admitted to an honours year after completing a basic three-year degree at another university. It was eventually agreed that each of the six new generation degrees would offer the option of an honours year, but not necessarily in devery discipline.

What is clear from hindsight is both the magnitude of the tasks confronted by the CSCs and the success of their endeavours under the guidance of Professor Loane Skene. While the CSCs all faced and considered common issues, each also had to develop its own path through specific concerns and complexities. Here, we will look into these individual directions.

Science and Biomedicine

The sometimes contentious debates that led to the Melbourne Model including both a Bachelor of Science and a Bachelor of Biomedicine (originally Bioscience; the name was changed in early 2007) among its six degrees were discussed in chapters 4 and 5. The complex ramifications continued after the decision had been made. Some staff argue to this day that having only the Bachelor of Science would have better achieved the objectives of the Melbourne Model. In any case, the situation in 2006 resulted in two course standing committees, one for each of the degrees, being established. A major issue to be resolved by each of these committees was whether some disciplines would be offered as majors through only the Biomedicine degree or through the Science degree as well. To limit majors, many of which had been previously available through the former Bachelor of Science, to only the Biomedicine degree would have closed off opportunities for further study to students in the new generation Bachelor of Science. In particular, the University preferred to avoid a situation where the Biomedicine degree would be seen only as a 'pre-med' course. Consequently, the two degrees have eleven majors in common and students may satisfy the prerequisite requirements for admission to the professional Doctor of Medicine through either the Bachelor of Biomedicine or the Bachelor of Science. Biomedicine also offers a major in 'defence and disease' that is not available through the Science degree, and there are over twenty other majors that may be studied through the Bachelor of Science.

There was considerable overlap in the Science and Biomedicine standing committees' membership and deliberations. It soon became apparent that it was logical to have a single standing committee to govern the two degrees, a decision approved at the 2007 Planning and Budget Committee Conference. The single CSC was established in late 2007 and held its first meeting in February 2008, although the two degrees continued to be separately administered, with separate student centres, until the beginning of 2010 when the student centres were combined (from 2012, administration of the two degrees has again been separated).

Arts

The work of the Arts CSC was complicated by the external review of the faculty that took place during the period the Melbourne Model was being implemented. The Faculty of Arts had determined in 2006 that it would have an external review of its curriculum to be conducted by Associate Professor Fred D'Agostino, director of Studies in Arts at the University of Queensland. The review began in June 2007 with the report expected to be complete by September 2007. The review was related to the faculty's 'school business planning' and budgetary problems, but the terms of reference had from necessity incorporated the characteristics of the Melbourne Model. The report on outcomes of the review was delayed when the then Dean of Arts, Professor Belinda Probert, resigned in September 2007.[16]

This curriculum review had more to do with concerns about the faculty's financial situation over several years rather than with the Melbourne Model. But part of the financial problems were perceived to arise from the faculty offering far too many degree programs and subjects with very low enrolments. In addition to the budgetary issues, there were concerns within the faculty that requirements for the degree had become 'soft' and that too many students who had not completed a major stream of study in an Arts discipline were graduating with a Bachelor of Arts. The review had to be intertwined with the Melbourne Model proposals, although it was recognised that some of its recommendations could not be implemented before 2009 or later. It was also important for the faculty to confidently assure students starting the new generation Bachelor of Arts in 2008 that they would be able to complete their preferred majors and subjects. The Arts CSC worked in parallel with the other CSCs, but it had to delay considering some issues, such as content of majors and the range of subjects to be offered, until late 2007 or early 2008 when the Arts review recommendations had been resolved.

Environments

The Bachelor of Environments course standing committee had a complicated task with five faculties originally scheduled to teach into the degree. When structural changes arose, in part from the introduction of the Melbourne Model, that saw the discipline of Geography moved from being a budget unit within the Faculty of Arts to one within the former Faculty of Land and Food Resources, the number of faculties teaching into the majors in the degree was reduced to four.[17]

The Bachelor of Environments Inter-faculty and First Year working groups, mentioned earlier, had developed a strong base for the standing committee to build on when it was established in October 2006. The First Year Working Group had considered a range of issues to identify what might be the 'best education' for future students in such matters as prerequisites, recognition of prior knowledge, and keeping options open for further study within the parameters of the Melbourne Model objectives. The Inter-faculty Working Group had met on eleven occasions over three months and had identified eleven preliminary fields of study that could be available through the degree. By mid-November 2006, the CSC had developed a discussion paper on issues surrounding the definition of 'breadth' in a degree program encompassing a range of disciplines from several faculties, to present to the BUGS for advice. The standing committee suggested that each degree program should have an 'academic champion' for each of the first year subjects offered. The committee's other main challenge was to ensure that the professional accreditation requirements of several disciplines were considered, and catered for, to guarantee that students would be qualified to proceed to further studies.

Commerce

As mentioned in Chapter 5, the Faculty of Economics and Commerce had argued strongly against students having to meet the full breadth requirement through subjects from outside the faculty. This was in part because of the accreditation requirements for Accounting but it was also a matter of principle for the faculty, which believed it taught a wide range of disciplines that should have been recognised as satisfying the breadth requirements of the new generation degree.[18] There were other aspects of the proposed new generation Bachelor of Commerce that did not meet with full approval of some members of the CSC. This resulted in a high level of tension in some meetings. When the CSC had finalised its Bachelor of Commerce course proposal for forwarding to the iBUGS, one member of the CSC asked that their opposition to the proposed Bachelor of Commerce be noted in the minutes on the basis that they did not consider the proposed course 'to be in the spirit of the Melbourne Model'.

There was also debate over the inclusion of Information Systems as a major discipline within the Bachelor of Commerce. Part of the problem resulted from overlap with subjects taught by the Accounting and Business Information Systems departments and the question of whether there should be exclusions – that is, whether students who did one should be excluded from gaining credit for the other and, if this were done, whether it would be against the basic principles of the Melbourne Model. The chair of iBUGS convened a meeting of representatives of Economics and Commerce and Information Systems/Faculty of Science to discuss the issues. The outcome was an agreement that Information Systems would develop a complementary specialisation from which Commerce students could undertake up to one hundred points of Information Systems subjects drawn from groups B (breadth) and C (core). In addition, Commerce agreed that it would not offer some subjects and would revise others to remove the exclusion problem.

Music

The Curriculum Commission had agreed reasonably early in its deliberations that there would be a Bachelor of Music as one of the six new generation degrees, with a stipulation that the name of the degree be reviewed after the integration of the Victorian College of the Arts and the Faculty of Music. This integration was to occur in 2007 and, in view of the complex situation and the integration agreement, the Deputy Vice-Chancellor (Academic) had recommended that the VCA would have up to five years before it would have to participate in the Melbourne Model. Consequently, the Music CSC designed and developed a new generation Music degree based on the Melbourne Model principles with the Bachelor of Music Performance continuing to be offered through the VCA.[19]

The work continues

After March 2007, in parallel with the work of the academic departments to develop the subjects to be available through the six new generation degrees, the CSCs continued to grapple with numerous other issues. These included further defining the breadth component of their degrees and resolving matters related to majors, discussion of how knowledge transfer would be reflected in the degrees, and issues of policy and procedures. Increasingly, discussions in the CSCs shifted to the degree student centres: where they would be located, how they would operate, and the importance of course advice to the success of the Melbourne

Model. Attention was given to how course changes, including the addition or cancellation of subjects, would be managed. In early 2008, after the first intake of students into the new degrees, the committees reviewed the quality and quantity of the intakes, looking at how the student centres had performed, which subjects had been selected by students for their breadth component and other matters. Although there had been provision for professional staff representation on the CSCs from their inception, the managers of the student centres providing administrative support to the bachelor degree were formally included as members of the relevant standing committee from late 2007. From mid-2007, the standing committees also discussed revisions to the concurrent diplomas, the student cohort experience, development of the student centres, developing pathways to research or professional degrees, and whether these should be via honours or masters degrees.

The primary focus of the standing committees, however, continued to be on the shape of their specific degree, particularly the major areas of study, requirements for satisfying a major study, whether there should be minimum and maximum requirements at each of the three year levels, development of capstone subjects, suitable breadth subject requirements, how or what would be a 'knowledge transfer' component – and the myriad other content matters that are part of a bachelor degree. The committees continued to work with the relevant academic departments to ensure individual subjects for the degrees were developed until July 2007, when final details for the new generation degrees to be offered in 2008 were approved by the Academic Board, on the recommendation of the Undergraduate Programs Committee. The immediate work of the CSCs had been addressed but their tasks were far from over. For some of the degrees, only the first-year subjects had been agreed with later year subjects created from the second half of 2007 into 2008 and 2009. The CSCs were also, and continue to be, involved in other aspects of the degrees such as student cohort experience and the development of centres especially for providing student advice.

That the CSCs successfully developed the new generation degrees within such a short period of time is remarkable, as Professor McPhee recognised when he stated:

> busy academics with wider responsibilities within their faculties made an extraordinary commitment of time and energy in redesigning majors and individual subjects in line with the CC's injunction that the NG courses needed to be fresh and reinvigorated. It is not surprising that there were wrangles over what was to be taught and by whom; what was surprising in fact was how often sensitive issues were worked through with courtesy and good will.[20]

In late 2007, after the position of Provost had been established and Professor McPhee had been appointed to it, the structural changes to the governance and management arrangements that had been approved by the Planning and Budget Committee and University Council in September, including establishment of the Academic Programs Management Committee, were effected. The new Committee of Deans had started its operations in July 2007. The iBUGS was abolished (in any case, the relevant legislative base had never been written) and membership of the course standing committees was revised in line with the new structures. The iBUGS had successfully overseen major design and implementation issues, but ultimately the Planning and Budget Committee had opted for individual faculties to administer the new degrees on behalf of the University.

As iBUGS no longer existed, the CSCs' reporting line was now to the newly established Academic Programs Management Committee (APMC) (which reported to the Committee of Deans). When the restructuring occurred in May and June 2008, the Melbourne Model Committee was established and replaced the APMC. The CSCs then reported to the Senior Executive via this committee. However, the Melbourne Model Committee had a short life and the CSCs were soon given a reporting line to the Academic Board's Academic Programs Committee. The responsibilities and membership of the committees have remained much the same since their initial establishment though reporting lines have changed several times. CSCs continue to oversee the development, delivery and academic management of one or more of the new undergraduate degrees. They are responsible for ensuring the University's policy in relation to the Melbourne Model under-graduate degrees are appropriately translated into practice and that learning outcomes are periodically monitored and evaluated, and for advising the Provost on matters concerning management and delivery of the degrees.

Chairs of standing committees meetings

Many of the structures involved in implementing the Melbourne Model did not have a formal status. One example is the informal meetings of the chairs of the standing committees. These meetings appear to have come about by coincidence in November 2006. Professor McPhee, as Deputy Vice-Chancellor (Academic), had asked the director of Melbourne Model Implementation, Joan Reese, to arrange a meeting of the chairs to discuss a range of matters that had come to his attention from the standing commit-tees. The breadth component of the new generation degrees was of particular interest. One of the emails sent to arrange the meeting included the sentence: 'There will be no formal agenda so please be prepared to raise any issues you want.' At this meeting there appears to have been consensus that further informal meetings of the chairs would be most valuable as a forum to share common problems and consider possible solutions to them. Joan Reese agreed to manage arrangements for the meetings, which continued approximately every three weeks throughout 2007 and 2008 – and which still take place today.

By the end of 2006 and into early 2007, governance and manage-ment structures were put in place that, although not the preference of some, had sufficient stability to allow the issues of designing a new curriculum to be worked through effectively. In parallel with these academic developments, there was considerable activity taking place on the operational aspects of implementing the Melbourne Model. The University community could feel confident about the probity of the new generation courses it would offer in 2008. The events of the launch were an indication of how far the development of the new model had come and an indication of the resistance that greeted some aspects of the change.

The University's ambition to deliver services that were student centred, to have policies and procedures that were consistent across all undergraduate degrees, and to provide course advice of a high standard in a milieu that was quite different from what many were accustomed to, would present unheard-of demands. Creating an organisational structure that would facilitate these new endeavours was equally difficult. These challenges are discussed in the next two chapters.

8

Following a Critical Path

By the end of 2006, the course and degree structures were well on their way to being resolved and, as we have seen, their development had been undertaken by dedicated groups of the academic community who had great experience of teaching within their specific discipline. As mentioned earlier, though, external expertise was called on when necessary and one of the most significant external contributions came from the Boston Consulting Group. Their involvement was crucial in this transitional stage of the Melbourne Model, as they developed a critical path plan for implementing the model, considered the University's change management needs and provided valuable advice about the final version of the student services model. The introduction of the model had provided the necessity and impetus to implement significant improvements in these services which had been long hoped for.

The Boston Consulting Group's relationship with the University of Melbourne in connection with the Melbourne Model began in early 2006.[1] Boston had agreed to partner the University in its bid for funding under programs sponsored by the Australian Government. If the bid were successful, Boston would potentially be involved in three aspects of a project titled 'Transforming the University Administration': academic administration, business metrics and change management.

The critical path plan

The University was notified of its success with the funding bids in October 2006, around the same time the Academic Board approved the final report of the Curriculum Commission.[2] The Senior Vice-Principal, Ian Marshman, then began consultations with Boston over their role in phase one of the Transforming the University Administration project. This was to develop a critical path plan (CPP), to be available for review by the University by mid-October. The CPP was also to be considered at the Senior Managers (Administration) Conference in early November. Boston undertook a three-week scoping exercise, where it conducted interviews with key personnel and reviewed relevant background documents, to help it formulate a critical path to cover the period of implementation from October 2006 to December 2007.

During this time, Boston was also consulted on other aspects of the transition process in which it would be involved. These consultations had to take into account the work on business planning in the faculties that LEK Consulting was doing in conjunction with the University Planning Office. In late October 2006, the head of the MM08 Project Office, Janet Beard, met with the Vice-Chancellor about a number of issues that appeared to require high-level clarification in setting directions and managerial boundaries. The issues included specifying the project teams for the Melbourne Model implementation and business planning work; establishing the processes to ensure LEK's business planning work was included in the critical path plan developed by Boston and that the two projects were aligned; continue the business planning work (and determine its scope); and ensure the administrative and support services needed for the Melbourne Model were planned and implemented.

According to Professor McPhee, this clarification was essential. The Vice-Chancellor, together with Professor McPhee and Ian Marshman, needed to ensure the oversight process provided direction and avoided duplication. Delineating responsibilities clearly helped maximise the sharing of information – vital, as resources were as limited as time.

The outcomes of the discussion were reported to VCAG on 31 October 2006, and may be summarised as follows:

• Relevant work related to the business planning was to be captured in the critical path plan with University staff working with each other and with LEK and Boston.

- The director of the University Planning Office would work with LEK and the faculties and administrative divisions on the business planning,[3] including an activities costing project.[4] Outcomes of this latter exercise were to be available to Boston in March 2007 to inform development of the student service delivery model.
- Boston would finalise the critical path plan, which would incorporate key elements of the business planning. They would also be involved in a workshop to identify elements of the ideal student experience, which would be used to inform development of the student service delivery model in April to June 2007. Finally, Boston would have a limited involvement in change management at a high (senior management) level. This would be through a staff engagement survey tool and advice on interventions in areas identified as being in need of assistance.
- GESO would continue as the coordinating team for overall Growing Esteem priority setting, monitoring progress and communication. The MM08 Taskforce would oversee the Melbourne Model implementation ensuring administrative and academic alignment supported by advice from Boston. The working groups (more or less based on the CPP workstreams described below) that would be reporting to MM08 were: academic transition comprising BUGS, graduate schools, and so on; policy framework; academic administration and student service delivery; Growing Esteem markets; and infrastructure with particular attention on student centres and IT support. Other working groups were likely but the only one that was mentioned was 'change management'.

After these issues had been discussed, a brief report was prepared for the Planning and Budget Committee, the Academic Board and University Council. Boston and LEK representatives attended the annual administration conference in early November 2006 at which the critical path plan, business planning and the overall program of Melbourne Model implementation were explained and discussed.[5]

The critical path plan and, in particular, Boston's involvement in developing the structure for student service delivery, provided an important and overarching framework for the extensive range of work that had to be completed over the coming months if the Melbourne Model courses were to be introduced in 2008.

CPP workstreams and substreams

Boston representatives attended the VCAG retreat on 5 October 2006, held after Academic Board had approved the final report of the Curriculum Commission, but before University Council considered the report on 9 October 2006.[6] The company presented an outline of their project under the agenda item 'Implementing the Melbourne Model post Curriculum Commission'.

Following this, on 13 October 2006, Boston released a slide pack of an 'exposure draft' of the CPP, based on their consultations over the previous three-week period, including the VCAG discussion on 5 October 2006. The draft identified major workstreams; mapped critical activities, processes, decisions, milestones, deadlines and deliverables; compiled an overview of key dependencies and their implications; identified key risks to successful implementation and prioritised activities, based on the above.

The CPP acknowledged that transition to the Melbourne Model had already begun, and that the plan was designed to help resolve three particular matters: to make the work planning more student-centred, to ensure better integration of implementation activities and to provide for high-level design to be urgently followed up by detailed design. Two key risks identified for immediate attention were the need to define postgraduate courses and establish an interim structure to focus on 2008 enrolments. The CPP listed the key dependencies and their implications, identified critical activities, processes and deliverables as well as priorities and timelines for achieving the required outcomes, and noted that implementation had to bridge any divide between curriculum reform and student services reform. It stated that, realistically, there would have to be trade-offs if the 2008 deadline for introducing the Melbourne Model was to be met.

The plan proposed six workstreams, each of which included several substreams.[7] The workstreams were:

- Develop new undergraduate courses
- Refine postgraduate courses
- Develop Melbourne Experience
- Develop management systems
- Develop transition program
- Evaluation of Melbourne Model.[8]

In parallel with the six workstreams, it was proposed that there should be a 'project planning, management and governance' component. This would include the coordination of different workstreams, management of dependencies and timelines and change management.

In December 2006, an updated version of the Boston slide pack was used to brief substream leaders about the CPP. This included a subsection on the role of the MM08 Taskforce and project office, which, in effect, covered the coordination and management responsibilities referred to in the previous paragraph. The presentation emphasised that successful implementation of the Melbourne Model would depend on the MM08 Taskforce and Project Office functioning effectively, and that the work of these two bodies should be regularly reviewed.

The Boston slide pack included the project office's roadmap for the transition and showed that, subject to the agreement of the taskforce, work was ready to be commissioned across the workstreams. The presentation set out responsibilities for tracking progress and the protocol for a 'traffic light' system, where the status of each item could be recorded as green, yellow, red or complete, to assess progress on the tasks to be undertaken by the various workstreams and substreams.

The Deputy Vice-Chancellor (Academic), Professor McPhee, and the Senior Vice-Principal, Ian Marshman, were joint chairs of the taskforce and each was leader for three of the workstreams, split along the lines of academic and administrative tasks, although, as previously reported, Boston had indicated that for the project to be successful there would have to be a bridge joining these two arms. Each of the six workstreams, in turn, had a designated manager and an accountable officer to lead each substream. The managers of the workstreams were members of the project office. For each workstream, the critical path plan described its deliberations, provided an overview of the expected outcomes and details of each of the substreams, outlined critical milestones and established the approval processes and information flows. Various committees and working groups coordinated and supervised by the MM08 Taskforce completed most of the responsibilities outlined in the workstreams and substreams. For example, Workstream 1, for undergraduate courses, operated through the newly established iBUGS and the CSCs, while issues related to postgraduate courses and research higher degrees were considered through the work of a substream in Workstream 2, postgraduate, in liaison with relevant faculty and Academic Board committees, the Research and Research Training Committee and the School of Graduate Studies. GESO and Student Recruitment, Admissions and Access had significant roles in communications aspects of the plan, with the Vice-Principal (Marketing and Communication), Pat Freeland-Small, given the task of recommending an appropriate marketing program for the launch of the Melbourne Model and the introduction of the new generation degrees.

The responsibilities of workstreams 3, 4 and 5 covered the Melbourne Student Experience, the management system for delivering student services and transition to the Melbourne Model. The student experience and delivery of student services would be combined into Boston's Melbourne Student Services Model (MSSM). How this model developed is discussed in detail in the next chapter.

Throughout Boston's involvement in establishing the critical path plan, the company's project leader was in frequent communication, usually through email, with the University Project Leader, Senior Vice-Principal Ian Marshman, and the head of the MM08

Project Office, Janet Beard. Some of the many Boston slides were used for presentations to and briefing of relevant people or groups ranging from the Vice-Chancellor through to the Planning and Budget Committee, to deans and faculty general managers, and others. Their work in preparing the critical path plan in consultation with relevant University staff was crucial for the transition to the Melbourne Model to be carried out effectively. The CPP shaped and steered the activities of the MM08 and related groups.

Melbourne Model 2008 Taskforce (MM08)

The MM08 Taskforce was established as a logical step in the evolution of bodies involved with putting the Melbourne Model in place after the Curriculum Commission had finished its work. It was basically a steering group to oversee implementation of the operational aspects of the model, in parallel with the work on the academic side that was undertaken by the iBUGS and the CSCs.

The MM08 Taskforce had a small membership of Professor McPhee (as Deputy Vice-Chancellor (Academic)), Ian Marshman (Senior Vice Principal), two deans, the president of the Academic Board, one faculty general manager and the appointee to the newly created position of Vice-Principal and Head of Administration. The head of the MM08 Project Office, Janet Beard, and the director, Melbourne Model Implementation, Joan Reese, attended meetings of the MM08 Taskforce on a regular basis as participating observers and in an advisory capacity.[9] Other members of the project office and Boston representatives attended taskforce meetings as necessary.

Council approved the Vice-Principal and Head of Administration position – intended to be the nominated deputy to the Senior Vice-Principal – in November 2006. This was part of the administration's proposed interim arrangements for the Melbourne Model. It also recognised the validity of Boston's conclusion, identified during the scoping exercise, that the longer-term success of the Melbourne Model project depended on strong leadership overseeing the immediate and detailed implementation. The draft critical path plan argued that at least an interim structure for the project management was needed immediately.[10] The initial argument for establishing the new head of administration position was to free the Senior Vice-Principal to undertake the role of project leader for the operational aspects of the Melbourne Model and to oversee the business planning being undertaken by budget divisions. In his role as project leader, Senior Vice-Principal Ian Marshman would work closely with Deputy Vice-Chancellor (Academic) Peter McPhee who continued to have responsibility for academic components of the Melbourne Model.

The broad range of responsibilities of the MM08 was reflected in its terms of reference, which included items ranging from 'develop a plan and program for implementing the Melbourne Model' through to 'manage risks and resolve issues as they arise', to 'advise the Vice-Chancellor and Planning and Budget Committee on resourcing matters'. The purpose of the taskforce was:

> To oversee the implementation of the Melbourne Model and to coordinate the work being undertaken in the University to ensure that the Melbourne Model is implemented effectively for new students commencing in 2008 and to manage continuing students as their courses are phased out.[11]

The MM08 Taskforce held two meetings in 2006 and fourteen meetings in 2007, of which eight were in the first half of the year. In June 2007, the Planning and Budget Committee Conference agreed that the MM08 Taskforce should be revamped and renamed to better reflect its role, in parallel with other changes that were being made to the processes and responsibilities of implementing the Melbourne Model. Consequently, from August 2007 the taskforce's name was changed to Melbourne Model Implementation Taskforce (MMIT). Details of other changes will be covered below. There were six meetings of the MMIT in the second half of 2007, with a further three meetings between

February and May 2008. The new position of Provost would assume responsibility for ongoing work that had been the responsibility of the MM08/MMIT, but although Professor McPhee's redesignation from Deputy Vice-Chancellor (Academic) to Provost had been approved in September 2007, the Office of Provost would not be fully operational before early 2008. In the period before this occurred, the MMIT continued to provide support for a number of developments, some of which are discussed in the next chapter.

Deliberations of the MM08 Taskforce

When the MM08 Taskforce first met in late November 2006, the iBUGS and the CSCs had been appointed and were already beginning their work. The two MM08 Taskforce meetings in 2006 focused on reviewing and finalising its terms of reference, planning a 'vision' workshop which would concentrate on the proposed student-centred services and Melbourne Experience, and finetuning the details of the CPP. In reviewing its terms of reference, the taskforce agreed to amend one of the proposed terms, from 'Identify key policy decisions to be made and presented to relevant committees for approval' to 'Identify key issues and make decisions about how to resolve them, determining timelines and reporting through relevant committees for approval as required.'[12]

The revised statement endorsed the status of the taskforce as a high-level planning group, with the authority to make decisions as appropriate or to refer matters on to other committees or individuals. It also recognised the group's expertise in coordinating, monitoring and managing developments in the workstreams, and ability to operate within tight timelines to ensure the Melbourne Model was implemented smoothly.

The taskforce began with a one-day workshop held off-campus on 1 February 2007 to discuss critical content issues and strategies for implementing the Melbourne Model. The workshop was attended by members of the taskforce, members of the project office and members of the Vice-Chancellor's extended Matins management group, as well as the Boston project leader. The CPP substream accountable officers attended for the morning session. The agenda included:

- a report on progress with the MM08 Project and on identifying remedial action where appropriate
- identifying and discussing key priority issues and agreeing on resolutions where necessary
- setting the final date and approach for the launch of the Melbourne Model (17 April was proposed)
- approving substream work plans
- a brief report on progress of each substream, identifying priority issues for discussion.

The March and April meetings focused on plans for the Melbourne Model launch and issues that needed to be resolved before 17 April. These plans and the resolved issues also contributed to implementation of the Melbourne Model. Boston's traffic light system of monitoring progress of the substreams was used and the monthly tracking reports were very valuable in highlighting critical aspects of developments – both progress and delays.

After the launch, the MM08 Taskforce meetings up to July 2007 concentrated on developing and putting in place the student services component of the new model and identifying the implications of these changes for the University. The associated issue of change management also featured in the taskforce's deliberation over this time, as critical to a student-centred services delivery model and the significant cultural change to the University this would need. At this time, Boston was working to develop what would become the Melbourne Student Services Model, with the aim of having a final proposal prepared for the June Planning and Budget Committee Conference. As the details of this model became more widely known, and aspects of it began to be put in place, the need for change management became even clearer.

Academic concerns

While the critical path plan was largely concerned with the operational aspects of implementing the Melbourne Model, there were two substreams more closely aligned than the others with the academic development of the new generation degrees. The first of these, policies and procedures, was included in the Management Systems Workstream of the critical path plan while the second, academic connectedness, was part of the Melbourne Experience Workstream. The president of the Academic Board, Professor Pip Pattison was the accountable officer for both substreams.

Academic Policy and Procedures Working Group

Recommendation 9 of the PBC Implementing the Melbourne Model Working Group stated that 'new generation courses will operate under a common set of rules and policies which will be applied consistently across the University'. This objective was consistent with providing student-centred advice and services and highly relevant to the policies and procedures substream. The number of policies and procedures that needed review and a determination was extensive. More than 50 items were included in the Policy and Procedures Working Group (PPWG) work plan by mid-2007. They ranged from special consideration and withdrawal from subjects, through leave-of-absence, to advanced standing, grading structures, and many others.

The PPWG had 23 meetings in 2007 on an approximate fortnightly basis from late January, and a further 17 meetings in 2008. Early in 2008, 'Academic' was added to the name of the working group, which continued to meet about fortnightly until November 2008, after which it was wound up.[13] A project officer for the working group started work in May 2007 and assumed responsibility for usual committee secretary tasks, which, up to that time, appear to have been performed by Professor Pattison. This situation indicates the heavy workload and short timelines on which much of the University was operating in 2007 in trying to get the Melbourne Model courses up and running.

Members of the working group included academic and professional staff and students who had been selected by the chair. The initial membership was fairly small but increased and changed over time as the focus of the group changed. The members of the PPWG in early 2007 are listed in Appendix 4c.

The first several meetings covered usual matters such as terms of reference and membership, responsibilities and topics likely to be included for discussion and resolution, and how the PPWG fit into the overall scheme of the critical path plan. As well, attention was given to the group's work plan, which had been drafted by the chair, and the priority to consider policies that required review and or development. Reporting lines were also discussed. The PPWG reported to the MM08 or, as stated in the terms of reference, it was to:

> provide advice to MM08 on the policies and procedures substream of Workstream 4 set out in the BCG Critical Path Plan, including the development and ongoing review of the work plan, a consultation strategy, the review of progress against plan, and in liaison with other relevant workstreams. Where necessary, the Working Group was to ensure recommendations for approval were forwarded to the appropriate bodies.[14]

In a later meeting, the reporting lines for the recommendations of the working group were clarified to be first to iBUGS, after which they would be forwarded to the Undergraduate Programs Committee or the Postgraduate Coursework Programs Committee and finally to the Academic Board.

As the PPWG worked its way through the extensive list of policies and procedures, it developed a protocol for its operations. The first draft of the document setting out the guiding principles and methods of operation of the group was prepared in April and May 2007 and evolved over time.

It was important for this group to liaise closely with the course standing committees about how the new generation degrees were affected by policies and procedures, and vice versa. For most of 2007 and part of 2008, the chair of iBUGS and the director, Melbourne Model Implementation were members of the PPWG and provided the interface between the group and iBUGS and the CSCs. As well, the PPWG consulted the chairs of the CSCs for feedback on the various policies and the chairs were involved in forums organised to discuss the policies.

The development of consistent policies and procedures was a significant achievement through the leadership of Professor Pattison, and was integral to the provision of student centred advice and services under the Melbourne Model. A major outcome of the PPWG was a website, Academic Board Policies and Guidelines, through which the policies and guidelines statements, as well as the academic services policies, are available to the University community.[15] With only one or two exceptions, the many academic services policies as well as the Academic Board policies and guidelines were included in the work plan of the Policy and Procedures Working Group in 2007.

Academic Connectedness Advisory Group

The Academic Connectedness Advisory Group (ACAG) was formed to look at a personalised service approach for students with a focus on academic accessibility and connectedness; a personalised orientation process; the client manager and course adviser role; and the link between online and in-person course advice. Inevitably, the crucial work of this group was closely connected to and informed Boston's work on the development of the Melbourne Student Services Model. Its membership is listed in Appendix 4c.

The group had nine meetings between February and September 2007, when it was dissolved. The responsibilities of the group overlapped with work on student advising undertaken by the Academic Board's Teaching and Learning Quality Assurance Committee (TALQAC), which had been commissioned by the Deputy Vice-Chancellor (Academic), as well as the work of some of the other workstreams and substreams. A critical issue to be resolved was how students would interact with and obtain advice from academic staff under the proposal for student centres or hubs that were linked to degrees rather than to faculties. This was complicated by the introduction of the breadth component in the new generation degrees and because most of the new degrees would have teaching from more than one faculty. The president of the Academic Board, Professor Pattison, wrote a paper on 'The Cohort Experience' as a basis for discussion in the group.

Professor Pattison has summarised the work of the Academic Connectedness Advisory Group as establishing the best way to deal with course advice, particularly to respond to the model for student advising prepared under direction of the chair of the Teaching and Learning Quality Assurance Committee; staff development issues including descriptions for the course advising roles and staff training that would be required; and other aspects of the connections of students to staff.[16] Professor Pattison has indicated that the first two issues continue to be works in progress and that the third item resulted in 'The Cohort Experience' discussion paper. This item also continues to be a work in progress and topic for discussion.

The PPWG and the ACAG were instrumental in bringing about the major cultural shift in the University that has resulted in a shared assumption among professional staff that students in all courses have a right to consistent, high-quality advice and support. The success of the Melbourne Model depends on student centre staff advising all undergraduate students of their graduate options, regardless of their first degree. For this to happen, it is essential course advisers are properly trained and, while this training has been successful, it is also subject to constant review and improvement.

University organisational structure and the 2007 Planning and Budget Committee Conference

As we shall see in the next chapter, there was considerable discussion about how the University would manage the enormous changes involved in transition to the Melbourne Student Services Model. Such concerns appear to have been complicated by the separate, but relevant, discussions within the Vice-Chancellor's Office about the University's organisational structures. These discussions led to proposals for changes to the University's academic and administrative structures that would support and facilitate the Growing Esteem strategy, especially the Melbourne Model.

Consequently, there was a pronounced apprehension and uncertainty about matters to be considered or proposed at the annual Planning and Budget Committee Conference in mid-June, particularly among senior levels of the University's academic and professional staff. Given the significance of this conference in the University's planning and budgeting cycle, it has become fairly common for there be a level of anticipation and anxiety about proposals that may arise. However, 2007 presented a more complex situation than in other years because of the highly significant impact of the Melbourne Model. In addition to Boston's development of the Melbourne Student Services Model proposal and the structural changes that were being discussed at senior executive level, there was a range of other matters to be considered. These included:

- administrative reform consequent to the Melbourne Model and the Melbourne Student Services Model, including the administration costs and containment project and uncertainty about where this would lead
- a new budget model associated with implementation of the Melbourne Model, the proposed Melbourne Student Services Model and structural changes
- new protocols for divisional business plans (resulting in some faculties producing more than 80 pages of documentation) that had been agreed in late 2006 and which had to be prepared for the first time for the forthcoming performance review meetings. The plans had to include student numbers projections, which were complicated by the introduction of the new generation degrees, phasing out of existing degrees, development of the Melbourne Student Services Model, and uncertainty about the impact of the new courses and their requirements, as a number of issues had not yet been resolved

- divisional bids for the Growing Esteem Transition Funds (GETF), which were linked to the business planning.[17] The GETF would operate over the period 2007 to 2012 to provide support for the major transformational activities that would be required of the academic and administrative budget divisions to give effect to the Growing Esteem strategy.

Possible structural changes that were not yet widely known appear to have been of most concern, no doubt because their impact would be far-reaching. A frequent comment made in informal discussions with a number of academic and professional staff about the atmosphere within the University over this period was that 'no one seemed to know who was in charge or making the decisions'.[18] In reality, a great deal of broader consideration was being given to fundamental questions of organisational structure.

The Vice-Chancellor initiated discussions around structural reform. The Boston critical path plan made several references to the need for interim and longer-term structures to manage the Growing Esteem strategy in the broader sense as well as the specific implementation of the Melbourne Model, the Melbourne Student Services Model and related activities. Early in 2007, therefore, the Vice-Chancellor discussed options for organisational structures that would best support the Melbourne Model in the longer term with the Deputy Vice-Chancellor (Academic) and the Senior Vice-Principal. Issues that were canvassed in the discussions as reported in the notes of two meetings (28 February and 28 March) were:

- the number of faculty groupings/faculties
- the number of graduate schools there should be, with a preference for only a few
- whether undergraduate degrees belong to the University
- the desire to have heads of major budget units on the University Executive
- the roles to be carried out across faculties/graduate schools such as quality assurance, performance management of deans,

provision of support services and who would be responsible
for these
- what budget discretion and accountability there should be for
  faculties/graduate schools
- the role of a Provost – with a suggestion that there may be
  two provosts (graduate and undergraduate) as well as a Deputy
  Vice-Chancellor (Academic).[19]

A discussion paper, dated 11 April 2007, was drafted and circulated to the University's senior executives by the Vice-Chancellor.
The paper refers to an earlier, extended version containing multiple options for an academic structure, which drew together three
different models: a North American example of a single undergraduate faculty, one that offered a limited number of new generation faculties and graduate schools and a deregulated model that
made financial viability the only criterion for the establishment of
new graduate schools but which would fragment the University's
then existing faculties. The Vice-Chancellor suggests, in the introduction to the 11 April discussion paper, that this complex
approach would not be the best way to proceed and, instead, sets
out a single model acknowledging that 'any discussion of structures creates anxiety', although budgets are more important
matters. The paper comments on the demands the Melbourne
Model would place on the University's organisational structure,
indicating five key issues:

- the academic structure
- managing new generation degrees
- managing graduate programs
- delivery of student and faculty support services
- the structure of senior management (as in the proposal for a
  provost position).

Three issues yet to be resolved were mentioned, with a note that
their resolution would have to occur in a climate of a difficult
financial outlook. These were organisation of student services

through the work of Boston; budget principles, which were under review by a working group of deans and senior executives; and organisational structure, which was the main subject of the discussion paper. The paper states that key decisions had already been reached on the curriculum, the quality of teaching, and the overall integration of learning, research and knowledge transfer.

In mid-May, following earlier discussions with Professor McPhee, the consultant Peter Acton and the manager of GESO, Pat McLean, were asked by the Vice-Chancellor to draft a structures proposal that took into account and incorporated feedback received on the Vice-Chancellor's April 'principles' paper, with the aim of having a document ready for the Planning and Budget Committee Conference to be held from 14 to 16 June. This further document was circulated to senior academic and professional staff for comment before the conference. An outline for the proposal, drafted by Peter Acton, indicated that the following five critical questions needed to be resolved:

What structures will best support the Melbourne Model?

What does this mean for the role and composition of academic units?

How should management and administrative roles and responsibilities be structured?

What are the implications for the planning and budgeting processes?

How can we best implement change?

By the time a draft structures paper was ready for the June 2007 Planning and Budget Committee Conference, the number of key issues canvassed had been refined to eight and there was greater detail for each one than had been indicated in earlier iterations of the discussion paper. The eight issues were:

- composition of academic units
- role of the Provost
- graduate schools
- management committees
- corporate support structures
- senior academic structure
- research and research training
- the change process

From the list of items, it can be assumed that some of the concerns among those involved in reviewing the structural proposals were linked to particular groups and the power base they were accustomed to holding before the introduction of the Melbourne Model. The inclusion of 'the change process' in the list was new, but the issue was not. Certainly, while the Curriculum Commission was reviewing and revamping the University's undergraduate course structure and proposing to introduce a graduate school model, there had been frequent references to the extent and pace of the changes and the need for more and improved consultation, as well as the question of support, including financial assistance for the changes being proposed. The Boston critical path plan included change management as a substream within the Transition Workstream, recognising that changes to the University's usual operations caused by the Melbourne Student Services Model would be substantial and wide-ranging. The Boston 'pulse' surveys, which surveyed around 700 academic and professional staff over four occasions between November 2006 and December 2007, helped to gauge the impact of the changes.[20]

In the lead-up to the 2007 Planning and Budget Committee Conference and in conjunction with discussions on University structures and concerns about change management, particularly the disquiet being expressed by a number of academic and professional staff, Boston was asked to develop the previously mentioned 'change leadership survey'. About a 170 senior academic and professional leaders and their direct reports participated in this survey.[21] The outcomes were presented at the Planning and Budget

Committee Conference with the following executive summary of the general results for the five areas surveyed:

- a strong commitment to change and a belief that the objectives of the Melbourne Model were achievable
- a perception that strong leadership was critical to the success of implementing the Melbourne Model, but that among the University's senior group leadership effectiveness was variable
- doubts that senior management would make the hard decisions, remove obstacles for achieving the objectives and provide sufficient support
- recognition that increased collaboration was critical to the success of introducing the Melbourne Model but the responses showed that the lack of collaboration was a major issue
- a poor perception of the decision-making processes and forums, which were thought to be in need of improvement.

As previously reported, in addition to the University structures proposal and the report on outcomes of the leadership survey, the conference agenda included reports and/or proposals on the Melbourne Student Services Model, administrative reform (managing corporate services), a new budget model and bids for the GETF. A number of these papers were designated 'for members only', usually a sign of considerable sensitivity within the University community to the subject matter and any associated proposals. As usual, the Planning and Budget Committee Conference ended with a formal meeting of the committee at which the various proposals and recommendations that had been discussed were endorsed, some with amendments, for forwarding to the University Council for its consideration. These recommendations included structural changes, including creation of the position of Provost, to support the Growing Esteem strategy.

The committee also adopted Boston's proposal for the Melbourne Student Services Model and approved allocation of the Growing Esteem Transition funds. The Senior Vice-Principal, Ian Marshman, and the Head of Administration, Liz Bare, were asked to bring forward plans to better align University services to the September Planning and Budget Committee meeting. The University services item, a 'members-only' paper prepared by the Head of Administration, concerned administrative reform and costs of administrative services. The paper arose from the LEK Consulting project on administrative costs that had also been used to inform Boston's development of the Melbourne Student Services Model. The committee also endorsed a statement reporting on the conference outcomes in some detail, which was the content of a Vice-Chancellor's all-staff email on 21 June 2007. On that same day, there was an open forum on outcomes of the conference for staff. Attendance was so high that many who wished to attend had to be turned away. The session was subsequently made available digitally as an i-lecture.

The Vice-Chancellor's report to the Academic Board meeting on 21 June 2007 also included a brief outline of the outcomes of the Planning and Budget Committee Conference. These included that the Planning and Budget Committee had adopted in principle the recommendations from Boston Consulting Group to establish 'hubs' within faculties and graduate schools for each new generation degree, while also noting that the considerable demands being carried by faculties and divisions would make it more likely that the new hubs will be developed sequentially over the following two to three years, and recognising that a different model might be required for smaller campuses. The Planning and Budget Committee Conference also saw within the model opportunities for significant cost containment and resolved to commission a comprehensive review of budget planning at the University.

The Planning and Budget Committee recommendations about University structures were discussed at the July University Council meeting and outlined to staff over July and August 2007 in a series of forums and faculty briefings. There were minor amendments made to the paper taking into account feedback received in the various discussions with subsequent iterations presented to Planning and Budget Committee and the Academic Board and a final draft endorsed by council in September 2007.

The Vice-Chancellor's report to the August Academic Board meeting stated that the mid-year Deans and Heads Conference scheduled for later in August would develop a clear roadmap for navigating the change agenda over the next six months in the lead-up to the introduction of the new generation bachelor degrees in early 2008.

The new organisational structure

It was obvious that the structural changes brought about by the introduction of the Melbourne Model, some of which have already been discussed, would be many and incremental, and would have to continue over several years. The changes were too numerous and too far-reaching to be introduced at once. Most of the structural proposals considered from March to June 2007 have now been implemented, although several have been revamped in light of other changes and developments in the University. Certainly, there has been a lot of compromise on the part of all parties in the changes that have been made. These gradual structural changes, based on compromise and agreement, are assisting the substantive pedagogical and cultural changes that have also been made. More immediate and comprehensive mandated changes would have carried a high risk of failing through lack of support.

The Planning and Budget Committee recommendations that were endorsed by University Council in September 2007 are summarised below. The recommendations were mostly in line with the eight key issues, or some variation of them, that were listed in the University structures paper submitted to council.

Academic units

Academic units would continue to be based on the (then) existing faculties. Each faculty would be led by a dean, six with responsibility for delivering a Melbourne Model undergraduate degree. The faculties would also teach postgraduate programs housed in a faculty-based institute or a school with the designation of Graduate School.

Custodianship for the six new generation degrees would be:

- Arts – Dean of Arts
- Biomedicine – Dean of Medicine Dentistry and Health Sciences
- Commerce – Dean of Commerce
- Environments – Dean of Architecture Building and Planning
- Music – Dean of Music pending outcomes of a review of Music
- Science – Dean of Science[22]

The decision to continue faculty-based academic units was a compromise. It ended the idea of the BUGS and weakened the 'consistency' agenda, although huge steps had been taken towards achieving greater consistency in student policies and practices. The positive side was that a faculty would 'own' and be accountable for an undergraduate degree. It had been hoped that the new generation degrees would align with student service hubs or centres, although it was recognised that this matter would require further consideration (the section on the Melbourne Student Services Model in the next chapter explores these matters further).[23]

Discussion of academic units and faculties in the context of the Melbourne Model led to several other structural anomalies being reviewed. This resulted in changes to the academic location for some departments and units. The discipline of geography was moved from Arts to the Faculty of Land and Food Resources. The Office for Environmental Programs, which had been part of the School of Graduate Studies, was also transferred to Land and Food Resources where it would continue to manage the programs on behalf of all participating faculties. Bio21 became a research institute, reporting to the Dean of Science, and management and reporting for the Developmental Biology and Neurosciences centres in association with Florey Neurosciences became the responsibility of the Faculty of Medicine, Dentistry and Health Sciences. Other discipline areas were reviewed over subsequent months for their most appropriate location. This included Psychology, for which it was agreed that it should continue as a budget unit within the Faculty of Medicine, Dentistry and Health Sciences.

Role of the Provost

The position of Provost was to be created through re-designation of the position of Deputy Vice-Chancellor (Academic). The provost would be the University's senior academic officer and would work closely with deans, faculties and graduate schools in order to realise the vision of the Melbourne Model. He or she would also provide leadership to and work with professional staff in achieving the University's ambitions for an enhanced Melbourne Experience. For Professor McPhee, the position offered a precious opportunity to tie together more closely the academic responsibilities of deans with the work of those responsible for other dimensions of the student experience, such as space planning, student services, the library and sport.

There was considerable sensitivity about the proposed role of the provost, among deans in particular. Any suggestion that the deans would report to a position other than the Vice-Chancellor was seen as a 'demotion' of their status, even though the deans themselves had called for more regular meetings with a senior officer. Consequently, the document recommending creation of the position was carefully worded to indicate that deans would continue to work directly with the Vice-Chancellor on external matters and on faculty strategy through his leadership of the annual divisional review process and his joint (with the provost) involvement in the deans' performance appraisals.

Graduate schools

A number of faculties would become stand-alone graduate schools while continuing to be involved in undergraduate teaching. The names of the graduate schools had yet to be resolved but would include Education; Engineering; Land and Food Resources; Law and Veterinary Science. The School of Graduate Studies would be renamed as the Melbourne School of Graduate Research.

Management committees

The Planning and Budget Committee endorsed a recommendation that a Committee of Deans be established to replace the former interim Board of Undergraduate Studies.[24] This would be a management committee with responsibility for integrating academic and administrative dimensions of the Melbourne Model. The course standing committees would continue but would report to the Committee of Deans through a new Academic Programs Management Committee (see Chapter 7).

A further recommendation proposed a review of the role of other University committees in light of the structural change proposals. The review was to be completed and approved for implementation in early 2008. There was an extensive consultation process on the proposals arising from this review, including a discussion at the Deans and Heads Conference in February 2008.

Corporate support structures and senior academic structure
In relation to senior administrative leadership, the Planning and Budget Committee recommended some modification of the role of the Senior Vice-Principal and continuation of the position of Head of Administration but with a subsequent change of name to Head of University Services. The Senior Vice-Principal would be responsible for providing high-level strategic planning and resourcing advice to the Vice-Chancellor, and for oversight of the University's corporate operations. The Head of Administration would be responsible for day-to-day oversight of key University services, except for those that would report directly to the Provost or to the Senior Vice-Principal.

Boston's proposal for the Melbourne Student Services Model, which would result in the establishment of student centres and student-focused services, was endorsed. However, there was a lack of certainty about how many centres there would be.

The change process
The final version of the structural changes proposal endorsed by University Council included Section 9, 'Supporting staff in a period of change', which included the following affirmation.

PBC affirms that the following principles should govern the University's approach to managing change:

(a) The senior leadership group will communicate a clear vision and understanding of the reasons for change

(b) There will be clear and consistent communication on the nature and expectations of change – internally (to our own staff and students) and externally to our stakeholders

(c) Implementation timeframes will be reasonable and well thought out

(d) The change process will be consistent and clearly understood

(e) There will be a formal process for feedback during implementation, providing ample opportunities for discussion and with clear measures of success.

The paper went on to state:

PBC recommends to Council that all the changes proposed in this paper should be introduced carefully, with the first step being that the Head of University Services bring forward a high level Implementation and Change Management Plan. This change process will be supported by the Director Organisational Development. In addition, an external consultant has also been appointed to work with the Senior Vice-Principal to ensure changes implicit in the introduction of Melbourne Student Services Model are fully supported. Note that PBC noted the considerable workload now being carried out by faculties and divisions and resolves to adopt a project plan that is measured, thorough and manageable.[25]

The significance of the affirmation is not obvious, as it does not appear to have been repeated or widely notified to the University community through any of the usual avenues. The Vice-Chancellor's all-staff email of 21 June 2007 reported that 'PBC will recommend to Council that all these changes (for restructuring) should be introduced carefully, with the first step being the development of a detailed implementation plan by September 2007'. In relation to implementing student services, the email reported that:

> PBC noted the considerable workload now being carried out by faculties and divisions and resolved to adopt a project plan that is measured, thorough and manageable. Consequently, it is likely that new hubs will be developed sequentially over the next 2 to 3 years with recognition that a different model will be required for smaller campuses.[26]

The Implementation and Change Management Plan referred to in the statement seems to have become the People and Change Plan, which included the principles for managing change set out in the Planning and Budget Committee affirmation. However, the statement of affirmation was not included in a summary of the Planning and Budget Committee recommendations presented to council, although it had been included in the main document setting out the case for organisational restructure.

Change management
There is no doubt that change management emerged as a major issue throughout 2007, but University responses to it were far from clear cut. A Change Management Coordination Group had been established by the MM08 in February 2007, largely in response to recommendations from Boston that the University was ill prepared for the changes that would occur with the introduction of the Melbourne Student Services Model. It was intended that this group would anticipate the change management support

that would be needed across the University, and act as an advisory and monitoring body for the Human Resources Division. Liz Bare, the convenor of the group, was the head of University Services, which perhaps explains why she was to develop the Implementation and Change Management Plan referred to in the statement to council above. But there still seemed to be considerable confusion over what this meant or involved. As the final, massive, section of the Melbourne Model, the Melbourne Student Services Model, began to be implemented from April 2007 onwards, this sense of confusion became more apparent.

9

The Melbourne Student Services Model and Managing Change

As has been indicated throughout this book, reforming the delivery of student services at the University was a parallel endeavour to curriculum reform and seen as vital to the success of the Melbourne Model as a whole. Details of what this reform would involve, however, could not be determined until much of the academic side of the model had been developed and endorsed. Boston Consulting Group's development of the Melbourne Student Services Model was informed by outcomes of the December 2006 'vision' workshop, described in detail below, but did not occur until after the basic curriculum and framework for the new generation degrees had been approved by the Academic Board in March 2007. This was to ensure that the model proposed for student services was consistent with the academic structure of the new degrees.

Boston's brief was to advise on the best design for a new student services model that met the objectives of the Melbourne Model. That is, they were to explore how the University could deliver first-rate and equitable student academic, support and enrichment services encompassing writing and language skills, computer facilities and careers advice, which had previously been available through central services as well as locally in several better-resourced faculties. The model Boston arrived at was based on students receiving excellent, integrated services through one-stop student hubs or centres set up for each new generation degree. The model's design was also closely linked to outcomes of the Boston staff 'pulse' surveys of how staff were coping with the significant changes. These surveys were administered on four occasions: in December 2006, February 2007, August 2007 and November 2007.

Developing the Melbourne Student Services Model and putting it in place was only one of a number of major tasks that remained to be completed in the second half of 2007. Many critical decisions about the Melbourne Model had been made between October 2006 and June 2007 and the transition process was well underway. Nevertheless, a considerable amount of work remained to be done and what must have been a very weary group of people had to find the enthusiasm and energy to continue with their tasks in the last six months of 2007. Action was still needed to:

- coordinate and oversee the implementation program by a revamped MM08, now renamed the Melbourne Model Implementation Taskforce (MMIT)
- implement the Melbourne Student Services Model and establish student centres
- develop and refine the role of provost and establish the Office of Provost to encompass the relevant student services units
- establish and convene the new Committee of Deans and the Academic Programs Management Committee (APMC)
- complete the work of the Melbourne Model Marketing Taskforce
- establish and launch the graduate schools with their new curricula.

Melbourne Model Implementation Taskforce (MMIT)

Revamping the MM08 as the body to coordinate and oversee implementation of the Melbourne Model took into account the revised organisational structures of the University, particularly the decision for each undergraduate degree to be the responsibility of a relevant faculty and the creation of the provost position to oversee academic programs and student services. The new name of the taskforce better reflected its responsibilities after these changes. There were also minor changes that allowed a third dean and an additional professional staff member to become members.

The main items discussed in the 2007 MMIT meetings related to the Melbourne Student Services Model, covering everything from where student centres would be located and how centre managers would be appointed, through information technology requirements to various issues raised in reports of the Marketing Taskforce. It is not the purpose of this story to give an in-depth description of the taskforce's discussions, which were extensive. But this group and its deliberations were of great importance and to do justice to it a list of items considered in its meetings between 2006 and 2008 is provided at Appendix 8. Here, it is the taskforce's role in implementing the Melbourne Student Services Model that will be discussed, after the development of the model is outlined in more detail. This requires going back, briefly, to late 2006.

Melbourne Student Services Model: The vision
One of the first initiatives of the MM08 Project Office was to organise a vision workshop, 'Defining the Vision: Next Generation Services for New Generation Students', for early December 2006. This workshop provided a definitive understanding of expectations for student services under the Melbourne Model. Around seventy people participated in the workshop: academic and professional staff including managers of student administrative and support services, associate deans, chairs of course standing committees, academic program managers, faculty general managers and vice-principals.

The vision for the new generation student-centred services developed through the workshop was based on the idea that the Melbourne Model 'aspired to offer a distinctive Melbourne Experience through its support services'. The services needed to:

- be developed from a student perspective to meet diverse student needs
- operate from a consistent set of policies and procedures and are coordinated, seamless and equitable
- be flexible and easily accessible

- enable a well-supported individual experience through a 'client management' approach
- enable a well-supported broad cohort experience in which students forge strong relationships with cohorts, staff, alumni and industry
- provide a campus experience (real and virtual) which will develop a sense of belonging and connectedness through
  - an 'academic village' with a clear geographical blueprint
  - common times and events to support a cohort experience
  - high quality physical and IT infrastructure
- enable students to be guided through their courses, with first-rate advice
- provide opportunities for students through supporting international study, industry placements, community projects
- support the achievement of graduate attributes and graduate outcomes
- continue a Melbourne Experience beyond graduation.

The report on outcomes of the vision workshop also included a statement of the participants' perspective that to make the vision happen would take:

- a clear map of pathways with clear, consistent communication – internally and externally
- a model to ensure processes were managed holistically and that the approach was adequately resourced
- the right people, the right skills – and the necessary training and support to achieve this
- a culture change – commitment to shared values and new ways of doing things to ensure a proactive and enabling approach to customer service delivery

- a shared understanding of expectations – with measurable quality indicators
- first-rate, University-wide facilities and services which meet next generation student expectations.[1]

Apart from the vision workshop, no major work on developing the Melbourne Student Services Model took place until after the Academic Board had approved the new generation degrees in March 2007 and the Melbourne Model had been successfully launched in April.

Melbourne Student Services Model: The design

It is important to recall that the basic premise of the efforts to design and develop a new student services model was that, with the introduction of the Melbourne Model, the University was in a unique position to change to a student-centred model rather than continue the mostly provider-driven service model that had been the pattern. The ambition was for a limited number of 'one-stop shops'; that is, one venue from which students based around a cluster of disciplines would receive the course and related information and advice they required, rather than having to visit a number of offices or faculties, depending on their needs. It was thought that such a structure for the student centres or hubs would encourage strong academic connectedness. The Melbourne Student Services Model final proposal was consistent with the vision outlined above, and ambitious in its scope. In short, the Melbourne Student Services Model was to be student-centred, coordinated, flexible and accessible, and would provide support at the highest level. In parallel with these service principles, the University adopted internal business principles designed to ensure effectiveness and efficiency, such as:

- support for learning and teaching programs
- support for effective and engaged staff
- adaptable and effective management of risk

- cost efficiency
- support for other activities of the University.

Managing the development of the Melbourne Student Services Model was multilayered. The MM08 Taskforce was accountable for delivery of the Melbourne Student Services Model proposal and the MM08 Project Office had responsibility for managing day-to-day issues. Boston provided a core team of six staff to work on the Melbourne Student Services Model with the University's core team.[2] In addition, there were two other groups involved in the development phase: a University extended team with a representative from each faculty and key central student services units who could provide expertise on practices at the time and feedback on the proposed model and a reference group, smaller than the extended team, formed from academic and professional staff members who were expected to contribute advice about possible service delivery models and comment on proposed models.

From late March to the end of May 2007, the project team and Boston representatives had extensive consultations with central administration and faculty units involved in delivering student services, deans, committees and other key personnel to provide information and obtain input and feedback on developments.

A vital aspect of the Melbourne Student Services Model proposal was that it would combine the 'vision' derived from the December 2006 workshop and consequent proposed changes to the student services with an understanding of the impact on, or what would have to happen to, other related policies and processes of the University. For example, there would have to be changes to organisational and budget structures, and the University culture, if the proposed student services model was to be successful. This combination of factors is also what made the annual 2007 Planning and Budget Committee Conference so very important, and why it was vital to have proposals for organisational and budget structures available to be considered in conjunction with the Melbourne Student Services Model proposal (as described in the previous chapter). The complexity of these entwined changes made implementing the Melbourne Student Services Model a particularly difficult task.

The key principles of the Melbourne Student Services Model, as drawn from Boston's report presented to the Planning and Budget Committee Conference in June 2007, were:

- a University-wide approach would be implemented with oversight of the service delivery and to ensure the objectives were met would be through the Office of the Provost
- a centre coordinator would be based in the Provost's Office
- a centre would be established for each faculty/graduate school
- each centre would have a centre manager accountable to the Dean for delivery of services
- the alignment of the accountabilities, budgets and incentives for the services would be as follows:
  - transactional services would be managed and budgeted centrally with a component of the budget provided to each centre for delivery of the face to face services
  - academic enrichment services: centres would be accountable and funded for local service delivery with academic units able to determine their own priorities while adhering to University-wide policies
  - the Central Services would be accountable and funded for well-being services with links to academic units through the centres
- the University will aim to have increased online delivery of transactional and enrichment services to meet student expectations

- the School of Graduate Research will have a centre for research students
- the University is to contact a specialist consumer services firm to assist with the design, development and implementation of a student service scorecard for monitoring quality of the student services.[3]

This was a highly ambitious program to be completed in the six months remaining before the first students would enrol in the new generation degrees. It was recognised that a full rollout of the program would not be possible before March 2008 and that only the essential aspects would be in place at this time, with other elements not being implemented until the end of 2008 or beyond. The essential tasks to be completed in this short period of time included appointing an implementation project team, identifying and preparing a space or location for each of the centres to operate in from March 2008, if not before, identifying the key resources required for minimum operations, and ensuring that staff were appointed to and trained for their new roles.

Melbourne Student Services Model: implementation
The MMIT Project Office, using the Boston critical path approach, developed a plan to implement the Melbourne Student Services Model consisting of five workstreams: faculties (encompassing academic support units or departments); transactional; enrichment; wellbeing; and prospective students. The workstreams were established early in September, with the request they undertake three tasks by the end of that month. The tasks were to prioritise services that needed to be changed in readiness for 2008, identify timelines for implementing all the planned changes over the next two to three years, and contribute to requirements for the core services and differentiated services. A communications plan, including consultation meetings and a summary of key milestones to be achieved by the end of 2007, was also developed.

Those who are not familiar with the University of Melbourne and the processes and practices it followed before the introduction of the Melbourne Model may be surprised at the fuss being made over a student services delivery model that arguably should have been the norm. The problem relates to the previous structure of courses and academic units. As indicated in Chapter 4, courses were 'owned' by a faculty for operational matters, with staff in faculty and department offices providing course advice to 'their' students. Local practices and policies had proliferated, for example, regarding assessment of student work. The quality of services and advice delivered was mixed, ranging from excellent to less than average as measured in University-wide student feedback surveys. Also, the range of services varied significantly, with the better-resourced faculties able to provide enrichment services beyond those generally available from University-wide departments. Even in instances where a student received good advice about his or her course, if they were interested in other courses or the second degree for a combined degree student, they would have to seek advice from the other faculty or department. This was far from satisfactory and left the University in a vulnerable position with its mantra of offering students a quality 'Melbourne Experience'.

The new role of Provost, designated as the senior academic management position to work with deans in implementing the Melbourne Model, would also oversee the work of all student services, including the University Library and Melbourne University Sport, with a view to delivering the vision of a whole-of-university approach to the student experience. That such a position was vitally needed had been recognised in the Melbourne Student Services Model principles included in the Boston report presented to the Planning and Budget Committee Conference.

The Boston proposal for the Melbourne Student Services Model recommended that centres for the graduate schools be established, as well as for the new generation undergraduate degrees. How many centres there would be and where they would be located needed to be resolved, as well as the status and reporting lines for centre managers; the resourcing model; an appropriate staff profile; and training for the staff in the centres. Ensuring that connections were maintained between academic staff and students and the staff in the centres was another problem, which has continued to be difficult to resolve.

The Melbourne Model, with its six undergraduate degrees and graduate schools, and the proposed student centres would be catering for different cohorts of students. Staff in the centres would be required to take on a broader role in terms of their student advice and a number would be assigned to, or have to compete for, new positions and locations once the Melbourne Student Services Model had been implemented. The timelines for getting the right staff appropriately trained and into the right positions were exceptionally tight, and caused considerable anxiety among professional staff about their future options. In light of this complex situation, a staff transition framework was developed and considered by the MMIT in October (this document is considered in more detail later in this chapter). The communication plan for the Melbourne Student Services Model was made available at the same time as the staffing framework. These documents were extremely useful for faculties and set out the processes involved clearly, but they did nothing to alleviate the pressures of the timelines.

Managing change
Once the transition to the Melbourne Student Services Model began in earnest, a major problem arose. For the groups involved in developing the academic and management structures related to the Melbourne Model things seemed to be going reasonably smoothly. Problems and concerns had arisen, of course, but these had been resolved successfully through discussion and compromise. It was about to become apparent that the sense of smooth progress was not universal and that the extent of the changes was causing anxiety among some staff, both academic and professional.[4]

The MM08 had received the results of Boston's second pulse survey at its meeting in late March. The survey showed that staff motivation and morale was down, with the areas of workload and implementing the Melbourne Model in individual work units receiving particularly low scores. Many staff members felt worn down by the pace and scale of change. The Melbourne Student Services Model was of vital importance to the success of implementing the Melbourne Model, and the survey results did not augur well for either. At the MM08 April meeting, change management was flagged as a critical area. The Change Management Coordination Group set up by the MM08 in February had met four times by the end of April and documentation available for that period shows that 'things did not appear to be going well'. Concerns were expressed in a number of quarters about both the proposed Melbourne Student Services Model and the impact that it would have across the University, and the organisational structures being discussed at senior management levels. The MM08 asked Boston to provide strategic advice on change management support for staff. The group also debated whether a workforce-planning group should be established.

Throughout May and June 2007, the MM08 deliberations on the development and delivery of a student services and management system also included how the difficulties of transition would be eased. Change management support to help staff cope with the impact the new model would have on them, particularly the issues raised in the pulse surveys, was considered critical. Boston's advice was that much of the support offered be in the form of 'communication', including information on timeframes, feedback and discussion, integration of change activities with policy, funding and work practices, and that detailed individual change plans be developed for departments and sections. Boston also suggested that staff leading and/or coordinating change be supported by professional advice from staff with expertise in the area, either within the University or from outside, and provided with a mentor. However, there appears to be no record of any staff requesting or receiving such support, and frontline workers had to rely on their supervisors and general communications. Again, it appeared that the speed of change and development of the Melbourne Model took its toll.

Morale was also being affected by the need to have various policies and processes resolved (including legislation for the BUGS and course standing committees, which was as yet still lacking), and concern that the University did not have a sound strategy for teaching out the then existing degree programs. But it appears to have been the Melbourne Student Services Model that was the principal reason behind the MM08 establishing the Change Management Coordination Group. The staffing issues associated with establishing the student centres linked to the model had the potential to provide the most serious obstacle yet in the University's management of the substantial changes taking place. And much of this had to do with the timelines. The policies and processes for staffing the student centres were not agreed until early October 2007 and managers were not appointed until later. Consequently, pressure on staff was compounded as the centres could expect to have significant numbers of prospective students asking questions about their VTAC preferences and options for the new courses from late November into December. Staff appointed to the centres would also need to get up to speed on the courses they would be administering, even though in some cases the course information was skeletal. At the same time, the students enrolled in the existing courses still needed to have their results processed and their options for the next year resolved. Any alternative actions to those taken may have resulted in dire outcomes for the students in the short term as well as for the staff in the longer term.

Staff transition framework

It was in light of this complex situation in staffing the student centres that the MMIT produced its staff transition framework in October. The framework set out the vision and key features of the Melbourne Student Services Model and its implementation, identified the services to be provided in the centres and gave details of the staffing strategy and processes for restructuring. It allowed faculties or administrative departments to do some restructuring in support of the model without the need to consult on individual changes on a case-by-case basis. The basic principles of the framework were:

1. Staff will be treated fairly and equitably.

2. Identified positions in the hub, centre or department/ faculty office created through the implementation of the MSSM will be filled using a merit based selection process.

3. A timetable for service changes and therefore potential staff transitions over the next two to three years will be developed before the end of 2007.

4. Positions relating to student facing services, faculty-based back office support services and teaching support will be filled from within the relevant faculty in the first instance.

5. Positions relating to transactional or enrichment services and staff moves between the centre and faculties will be filled from within the affected areas in the first instance. That is, the relevant central section handling transactional or enrichment services, and the relevant faculties involved in the transition. For transactional services, this will involve all faculties; for enrichment services, this may affect some faculties but not necessarily all.

6. All staff from the affected areas (including those on secondment or on leave) will be eligible to participate in the merit based selection exercise.

7. Staff will be provided with reasonable professional development to support them in undertaking their new roles.

8. Where staff are not placed in positions under consideration in the particular transition phase (within the hub, faculty office, department or central area depending on the transition phase) and their current role will become excess to requirements, the University's placement process for professional staff will apply.

9. Job redesign made necessary through the implementation of the MSSM will be undertaken in consultation with the staff member and their representative on a case-by-case basis.[5]

The framework also set out a 'process' for advertising and appointing staff to positions in the student centres or hubs.

A progress report on the Melbourne Student Services Model, including staff movement as the student centres were established, was prepared in early December 2007 under the aegis of the Change Management Coordination Group. The report was sound. But the transition framework had not been finalised until early October 2007 so again the policy and procedures were being written in parallel with implementation. This was a very difficult situation for staff, most of whom were already stretched and concerned about the security of their positions. But, as shown earlier, there was no alternative.

By early 2008, thirteen student centres were in operation for the new generation degrees of Arts and Music, Environments, Commerce, Science, and Biomedicine; the VCA; and the graduate schools of Education, Law, Architecture, Building and Planning, Land and Food Resources, Medicine, Dentistry and Health Sciences, Engineering and Veterinary Science. Some were in temporary locations or had some temporary staff appointments, but all were up and running, ready for the new intake of students.

Change Management Coordination Group

Change management was not, of course, a problem confined to the Melbourne Student Services Model. As discussed earlier, the MM08 Taskforce had established the Change Management Coordination Group in February 2007 to oversee the Melbourne Model change management strategy, to identify priorities and provide advice on relevant issues. In its first meeting the group considered it own role: was it a 'committee' or a 'group' (the decision was the latter); was the group to 'determine' on matters or act in an advisory capacity (again, the decision favoured the latter); and what would the nature of its relationship with GESO be, given the manager of the GESO had been named the accountable officer for change management support in the Transition Workstream of the CPP?[6] In this final point, it was noted that the GESO would provide administrative support to the coordination group, which would report to the MM08 Taskforce and to the VCAG.

Terms of reference
The terms of reference indicated the group would:

- oversee the management of significant workforce change on the basis of advice from the Division of Human Resources during implementation of the Growing Esteem strategy
- coordinate the management of significant workforce change through the provision of advice to Faculties, Departments and Budget Divisions following consideration of proposals for significant workforce change
- adopt a whole-of-University approach when considering proposals for significant workforce change
- support the management of significant workforce change through the provision of advice on timing, communication, consultation and implementation requirements
- receive and commission reports on feedback provided by staff and their representatives on the implementation of the Growing Esteem strategy.

The group's establishment was reported in the Growing Esteem implementation updates 21 to 23 with further reference to the group's role in the Melbourne Student Services Model and Boston's advice on support for the University's leaders in the July update (24). The March update included reference to 'change and leading change' workshops organised by Human Resources for academic and professional staff, and the May update reported outcomes from the first two pulse surveys. The July update also reported the Planning and Budget Committee statement that all structural changes were to be introduced with care, in the context of the recommendations that would be made to University Council in September and the outcomes of the Leadership and Collaboration Survey.

The coordination group held nine meetings, with the first on 1 March 2007 and the last on 5 December 2007. The minutes of the second meeting report the group's expectation that its existence would be temporary – not more than six months. The group's discussions were informed by the outcomes of the first Boston pulse survey. Membership of the group was also expected to include a 'change management expert' from Boston; however, this person attended only one or two meetings and otherwise provided expertise through the group's chair.

A significant task of the early meetings of the group was to draft two memoranda about support for change management during implementation of the *Growing Esteem: Strategic Plan 2006*. The first of these was intended for all staff and the second for deans, vice-principals and heads of departments. The draft memoranda are informative, as the following extracts show:

> Faculties and the Administration have recently concluded business planning which will guide them in the implementation of the Melbourne Model and the other changes that will be required to realise the vision of Growing Esteem. Ensuring that change is sustained and effective will require support from the University for individuals, Dep]artments and Faculties. This memo outlines how the University will support workforce change management during the implementation of Growing Esteem.
>
> *How will workforce change required to implement Growing Esteem be managed?*
> The University is committed to ensuring that significant workforce changes required to implement the Growing Esteem strategy will be managed:
>
> • with support for staff, managers, Departments and Faculties;

- in a planned and considered manner;
- with relevant and appropriate communication;
- in accordance with fair and transparent processes; and
- in consultation with staff and their representatives.[7]

After the introductory comments, both memoranda went on to describe that support would be provided through various avenues, including the coordination group, enterprise agreement discussions, feedback from the pulse surveys, short courses on change management, and formal and informal consultations between Human Resources personnel and staff in departments and faculties.

By late April, the coordination group had decided that the memoranda were no longer required, although it was still necessary to provide relevant information to staff through some means. The Growing Esteem updates were thought to be the logical medium. It would appear that a combination of factors prompted this change in strategy. Boston agreed to help prioritise items listed in a change management grid, work with designated persons who would be involved in training new student advisers, develop and conduct a change leadership survey, and participate in a session at the June Planning and Budget Committee Conference to ensure that the change management agenda had the backing of senior management. Other entities were also involved in change management: Human Resources established a change management website with links from GESO and the MM08 websites and developed a guide to change management for distribution to faculties, and a workforce planning tool was developed for use by faculties by October. Faculties had recently submitted workforce plans as part of their business plans but, as there was no set template for these plans, their value varied. In this context, it should be noted that the University did apply for funding for a workforce planning project under the federal government's Workplace Productivity Program, but it was not successful.

The coordination group was aware of developments with the Melbourne Student Services Model and discussions around the University's organisational structures and noted that any consequent strategic, cultural and operational changes were likely to cause heightened anxiety within the University community. The group also noted there was a need to build the capacity of the Department of Human Resources to support these changes.

The May meetings of the group considered factors that needed to be taken into account for each of the change programs and how these would be managed. For example, a critical item highlighted in meetings between senior human resources personnel on behalf of the coordination group and the deans was the teaching-out process. That is, with so many courses being phased out, mostly over a period of about five years, faculties would have to manage issues such as the impact on staff, space implications, quality of teaching outcomes – especially in relation to staff with fixed-term appointments – and access to facilities outside normal hours. There was also the range of factors that would occur with the introduction of the student-centred approach to delivery of services.

From May 2007, Professor Liz Sonenberg, then head of the Department of Information Systems, took on responsibility for mapping a path to teach out the then existing degrees to the new generation degrees, an issue of primary concern to existing students and one requiring a significant period of transition. The Vice-Principal and Academic Registrar, Gillian Luck, was responsible for the training provided to staff assigned to offer course advice to students. Boston would design and manage the leadership survey for senior leaders and work with them at the June 2007 Planning and Budget Committee Conference. The major area of concern continued to be the staff most affected by the new student services model. In considering these matters, the coordination group took into account outcomes of the two pulse surveys and the changes likely to result from the proposed shifts in organisational structures. Various proposals were made, including the previously mentioned WPP application for funds to support a workforce planning project, for groups of five to be formed within faculties as a 'faculty planning support team', and, eventually, a new and expanded redeployment policy.

In August and September, the coordination group developed a change management program and strategy known as 'People and Change'. A first draft of this document was submitted to the MMIT in early September 2007. The minutes of the MMIT meeting held on 5 September 2007 report that the plan was endorsed by the Change Management Coordination Group and the Planning and Budget Committee.

Unlike the readily identifiable effects of most of the other working groups and committees operating during transition to the Growing Esteem strategy, it is difficult to gauge the impact of the Change Management Coordination Group. This may be in part because of a discrepancy between the group's term of reference, which indicated that it was to focus on workforce planning, and the incomplete draft memoranda, which implied a wider brief. More confusion results from the apparent absence of any current guidelines in the University's human resources policies resulting from the People and Change paper. But there is no doubt that a number of other groups established during this time had more obvious impact. In retrospect, it is easy to be critical of the institution and its staff at the time (including myself) for not taking a more proactive approach to change management at an earlier stage of the process. But this is not really fair. No one really understood or could foresee the extent of the changes that would take place as a result of the curriculum review. Once the wheel started rolling, it continued to gain momentum and, because of the timelines and the wish to introduce new courses in 2008 rather than later, many of the other changes had to follow, swiftly. Some of the administrative initiatives could have waited another year or two – but there is no certainty that the situation would have been easier or better had they been deferred.

Committee of Deans (July 2007 to May 2008)

The Committee of Deans was established as part of the new organisational structure agreed at the July 2007 Planning and Budget Committee Conference. The decision to continue with faculties as the basic academic unit with responsibility for undergraduate degrees had rendered a Board of Undergraduate Studies or similar body unnecessary. The deans' concern that the position of provost as the University's chief academic leader would undermine and marginalise their own positions was also taken into account.

The new Committee of Deans, to be chaired by the Provost, was an attempt to allay these worries. Its terms of reference stated that it was to be 'a management body, responsible for integrating academic and administrative dimensions of the Melbourne Model through overseeing the Academic Management Committee and the Melbourne Experience Committee – and for overseeing the collective operations of academic units'.[8] The Planning and Budget Committee would continue to be responsible for 'financial and significant management decisions', although many of the issues were likely to be discussed first at the Committee of Deans. The Academic Programs Management Committee assumed some of the responsibilities of the former iBUGS, including coordinating and overseeing the work of the course standing committees.[9] Inevitably, the Committee of Deans took on part of the role of the Planning and Budget Committee and it was agreed that the latter committee would meet less frequently than it had previously.

The Committee of Deans began its meetings in July 2007, facing the extensive range of issues that were being considered and which required resolution before the first round of prospective new students applied for admission to the new generation undergraduate degrees. At its first meeting, the committee discussed:

- the proposed organisational structure arrangements and associated uncertainty about decision-making and authority for various matters

- implementation of the new student services model and the cultural change that would have to be adopted across the University for the proposal to be successful. The Deans indicated that they would prefer student centre managers to be internal appointments rather than that the positions be advertised both internally and externally as was recommended (and was carried out)
- marketing issues identified at the VCAG retreat on 16 July and establishment of the Melbourne Model Marketing Taskforce
- proposals for staff redeployment, including the parallel proposal for cost containment activities.

Each of these matters was substantial and all were at the core of the cultural and structural changes that were occurring with the introduction of the Melbourne Model. They continued to be topics of discussion at the committee's meetings over the following months. The tense atmosphere in these meetings, Professor McPhee has said, made them sometimes 'unpleasant and arduous'. As with students and professional staff, academic staff had a lot of change to deal with, all in a short period of time.

Other issues considered by the committee over the period of its brief existence included:

- the relationship between the Committee of Deans, the PBC, the Melbourne Experience Committee and the Academic Programs Management Committee
- academic/professorial promotions
- a proposal to establish an Information Technology Council that would be a subcommittee of the PBC and would have a focus on IT planning
- nomenclature for graduate schools
- the decentralisation of some aspects of PhD admission and candidature administration from the School of Graduate Research to the faculties.

As time went on, there was increasing overlap and duplication between the business of the Committee of Deans and the Planning and Budget Committee, particularly in budgetary matters. For example, monthly budget reports prepared by Financial Operations were on the agenda for the Committee of Deans as well as for the Planning and Budget Committee. The faculty business plans were scheduled for presentation to the Committee of Deans and it was asked to sign off on proposals for other budget-related matters. The routine matters considered by the committee included composition of the course standing committees; the schedules for conferring ceremonies; reports on faculty performance in meeting student enrolment targets; and flexible use of the academic year.

The Committee of Deans, its subcommittees and various other committees, were dissolved in May 2008 when a new philosophy, subsidiarity, was adopted for the University's administration. Subsidiarity 'is based on the principle that decisions should be taken as close as possible to where services are delivered and people affected. To support more devolved decision-making, services need to be aligned accordingly to provide the support and advice required at the local level.'[10] A Senior Executive Committee and its subordinate Melbourne Model Committee were established in place of the Committee of Deans to be responsible for coordinating the academic and administrative aspects of the University's undergraduate courses. The Senior Executive Committee remains the University's principal management committee and is responsible for overseeing the development of University planning and budgeting and, once approved, for monitoring performance against plans and budgets. It has replaced the former Planning and Budget Committee. The Melbourne Model Committee no longer exists, as the CSCs do the day-to-day work related to courses and subjects and make recommendations to the Academic Programs Committee and faculties as necessary.

Academic Programs Management Committee (May 2007 to November 2008)

The Academic Programs Management Committee's (APMC) role was to coordinate planning and delivery of the University's undergraduate education, including the development, monitoring, academic management, resourcing and continuous improvement of the new generation undergraduate degrees. The faculties responsible for custody of a new generation degree would be accountable to the Committee of Deans and the Provost through the APMC. The committee's membership included the deans or nominees of all faculties and graduate schools, the chairs of the course standing committees and a number of others. The committee met on only six occasions between November 2007 and May 2008, when it was superseded by yet another committee restructure. The business conducted at these meetings was consistent with the terms of reference and the committee's purpose, and included proposals for new or revised courses and the subject content of these as forwarded from the course standing committees. The committee also considered proposals for breadth subjects and concurrent diplomas.

Marketing: June to December 2007

The Markets Working Group had its last four meetings in May and June 2007. In these, it debriefed after the Melbourne Model launch and discussed the post-launch communications for internal, national, international and alumni stakeholders. Preparations for the Open Day in August were also discussed, including staff arrangements and training, and the publications that would be needed for the day.

Marketing summit

Concerns about market research for and the marketing of the Melbourne Model have been constant from 2006 to the present. However, in the lead-up to the June 2007 Planning and Budget Committee Conference, when, as discussed in the previous chapter, so many issues were causing anxiety, there was intense concern about the University's marketing program. It was coming up to the real test – what the demand for the new generation courses would be – and there were no guarantees that students would preference the Melbourne Model courses in their VTAC applications. The Senior Vice-Principal convened a 'marketing summit' in early June 2007, before the Planning and Budget Committee Conference. It appeared that the former Markets Working Group did not have the correct structure and agenda to allay the deans' concerns. The notes from the summit report that the problem arose from a lack of communication between the faculties and the central areas responsible for marketing activities. This has been a recurrent theme over the last fifteen to twenty years, especially from the mid- to late 1990s when competition among universities for the increasing numbers of international and postgraduate coursework students intensified greatly. But, with the introduction of the Melbourne Model new generation degrees, the issues were particularly critical for Melbourne as it was only four months before prospective students would finalise their course preferences for 2008.

The agenda for the summit included a stocktake of faculty and central administration marketing activities, an overview of Open Day planning, market research in general, and the identification of issues for the longer term that would require planning or for which there could be difficulties needing early attention. Representatives of most faculties and central administrative departments who were involved in marketing activities attended the summit. Issues of particular concern included the marketing of new generation degrees that involved teaching by more than one faculty, postgraduate recruitment – including publications for this activity required by the faculties – and web marketing and improvements that would enhance its use for both undergraduate and postgraduate courses. The notes for the summit also refer to market research being undertaken by Beaton Consulting on scoping the market at graduate level. The summit participants were very aware of the opportunities presented by the system for whole-of-university marketing and recruitment, especially at the undergraduate level.

To overcome the lack of communication that had led to the summit, and to ensure that it did not continue into the future, it was proposed that fortnightly meetings be arranged between marketing and recruitment staff in central departments and faculty general managers or their nominees to discuss relevant issues. However, it appears that establishment of the Melbourne Model Marketing Taskforce superseded these proposed meetings. The establishment of this taskforce was supported in the 16 July VCAG retreat, which had marketing as its main theme. The concerns raised in the retreat tended to focus on the upcoming Open Day and many of the issues that had been raised in previous forums. These included faculty or centre coordination of marketing activities, the future of Engineering courses, promotion of the Melbourne Experience, and appropriate communication and promotion of the Bachelor of Science and Bachelor of Environments courses, together with a need to explain the main characteristics of all the new generation undergraduate degrees.

Marketing Taskforce

The Marketing Taskforce was intended to be a short-term group, operating for around six to eight weeks to tackle the immediate marketing challenges associated with the Melbourne Model as identified by 'anecdotal feedback from domestic and international markets'.[11] It was more senior than the previous Markets Working Group, with members including the Deputy Vice-Chancellor (Academic), four deans and Professor Bryan Lukas, Professor of Marketing, and it was chaired by the Senior Vice-Principal. It reported to the MM08/MMIT.

In the end, the taskforce existed for six months and met on thirteen occasions between mid-July and early December 2007. The taskforce's first progress report, delivered at the end of July, reported on considerable activity including a gap analysis of information available on websites and in publications, a meeting of key personnel to consider arrangements for a whole of University approach to marketing the Bachelor of Environments, discussion on how to clarify key marketing messages, preparation of a critical path plan for marketing deadlines, a draft letter to school principals; mythbusting strategies to dismantle misperceptions about the Melbourne Model, and a range of postgraduate issues.

Later meetings of the taskforce considered issues of equal importance: the deans' need to clarify who, between the faculties and the centre, was doing what in relation to marketing and who had responsibility for various activities; clarification of who would be custodial dean for each of the new generation degrees; the key marketing messages for the new generation degrees; resolution of accreditation issues especially for prospective international students; and training staff to become 'Melbourne Model experts' for Open Day. The taskforce discussed approaches to market research, publications and advertising avenues.

The taskforce continued beyond its proposed six to eight weeks because additional issues needing attention kept arising: names and marketing for the graduate schools and promotion of the graduate school launch, a marketing strategy for the 'change of preference' period and marketing of honours courses and research higher degrees among them. Taskforce discussions were informed by Beaton Consulting's market research and survey feedback from Open Day participants and focus groups held in schools. The final report of the taskforce noted that marketing structures, detailing accountabilities for coordination of future marketing activities, were being developed for the Committee of Deans.[12]

A review of the agendas for the key groups that operated in the last four months of 2007 shows the considerable effort that went into finalising and resolving issues associated with the Melbourne Student Services Model in readiness for 2008. As well, a great deal of thought and energy went into considerations around marketing the new generation courses and the selection process for the new degrees. One can only imagine the relief that staff, professional and academic, must have felt when it was time for the end-of-year break. An extract from a progress report to the Change Management Coordination Group, prepared by the head of the MMIT Project Office, Janet Beard, on implementation of the Melbourne Student Services Model summarises the situation at the end of 2007:

> Implementing the MSSM is a major change program and there have been and will continue to be major challenges for everyone involved which the University must manage carefully. For example, the different levels of understanding of how the model could work have created anxieties for academic and professional staff, particularly those in multi-department faculties. The differing states of readiness and capacity of faculties and central areas to make changes, together with the exceptionally tight timelines, has contributed to the pressure of being prepared for 2008. Creating student centres with interim spaces also results in inevitable work-around solutions which differ from faculty to faculty and adds to the pressure for staff. Constant and on-going communication and support is critical to assisting staff involved with this major change program. Notwithstanding these issues, it is a very great tribute to all involved that the MSSM has broadly been embraced with considerable enthusiasm for the concept of the model and student centres and the huge amount which has been achieved across the University in a very short space of time.[13]

And after the break came the first intake of students. While a pivotal – and very exciting – moment, this was not, of course, the end of the story of the Melbourne Model. Throughout 2008 and beyond, matters both operational and academic needed to be fine-tuned, tweaked and finessed. But, as this account shows, March 2008 represented the culmination of massive effort and dedication, on behalf of a great many people within and outside the University, taken in a remarkably short period of time. The Melbourne Model had been built. How it has functioned after its full implementation is another story for another book.

Epilogue 2008–12

This book has charted the extraordinary journey undertaken by a university that agreed on a broad notion of curriculum reform in 2005 and by 2011 had graduated its first cohort of Melbourne Model undergraduates and shifted its professional programs to graduate-level entry. It was a massive transformation of an old and large institution, which ultimately has left no aspect of the University untouched.

A review of the dry minutes of Academic Board and University Council meetings at the end of 2007 and the beginning of 2008 do not reveal the emotions within the University in having made the final steps and decisions in implementing the Melbourne Model and the Melbourne Student Services Model. If there was apprehension about the forthcoming introduction of the Melbourne Model, it is not reflected in the documents. It is possible that many staff were so relieved in reaching the end of 2007 and the scene being set for 2008 that the hubbub of the previous twelve months had become the routine. It was time to move on with what had now become the normal business of the University.

There has been extensive activity and change within the University since the introduction of the Melbourne Model in 2008. The story as told here has not attempted to describe the many budget changes made in association with the adoption of the principle of 'subsidiarity' as the framework for University management and the 'responsible division management' program that resulted, the consequent and continuing organisational and management restructuring, the establishment and development of graduate schools, a revised marketing and recruitment approach, and the introduction of the new professional graduate programs in 2011. Some elements of the Melbourne Model have been subsequently changed, including minor modification to the breadth requirements; the structure and roles of the student centres continue to evolve, and review and revision with the aim of improving student services is ongoing.

New generation degrees

The minutes of the University Council meeting held on 17 March 2008 record this note in the Vice-Chancellor's report:

> 8.5 Student Selection 2008
> Council received a confidential paper detailing the outcomes of the 2008 Student Selection process and noted that overall the University had a very successful selection period, with strong application rates and the highest acceptance rate recorded for at least the past ten years.[1]

This outcome would have provided profound relief to those who had been apprehensive about the change to the Melbourne Model and its six undergraduate degrees, and certainly set a positive scene for the selection of students in future years. While there have been significant changes in the courses offered it is still too early to illustrate the student profile as it will be when the Melbourne Model is fully implemented.[2] Nevertheless, it is worthwhile comparing some aspects of the 2006 and 2010–11 student profiles.

Undergraduate students still apply for admission to the University through Victorian Tertiary Admissions Centre (VTAC) and postgraduates do so direct to the faculties or graduate schools responsible for administering the relevant courses. Between 2006 and 2011, there was little change in the median Australian Tertiary Admission Rank (ATAR) for undergraduates with 94.30 in 2006 and 93.10 in 2011. In 2011, four of the new generation degrees were in the top ten most popular Commonwealth-supported place courses according to VTAC first preferences data. Five of the new generation degrees were in the top ten in 2012.[3]

The worries voiced between 2006 and 2008 about the prospect of 'bright flight' have not been realised. While there was some decrease in numbers of VCE high achievers due to those who opted to study law and medicine at the undergraduate level at other universities, the introduction of the Chancellor's Scholars program in 2012 for very high-achieving students has been successful with more than 90 offers being made to students with an ATAR of 99.9 or above. The University has also been successful in broadening its student representation base with an increase of 16 per cent between 2010 and 2011 and 24 per cent between 2011 and 2012 in the number of applications through the Access Melbourne program for disadvantaged students.[4]

Just over 50 per cent of the students who began a new generation undergraduate degree in 2008 had completed their course by the end of 2010. Of the completing students, 72 per cent applied for further study, mostly in a graduate or honours program, of which 83 per cent were offered a place. This is a very satisfactory outcome for the first Melbourne Model cohort and the rates of both completions and progression to further study are expected to increase over time.[5]

Student services model

As was to be expected, throughout 2008 and 2009 there were further developments in the student centres, their staffing profile and the quality of the services delivered. In June 2009, the Responsible Division Management and Implementation Taskforce made a recommendation to the Senior Executive Committee for a revised student service model that would deliver reduced costs, greater consistency of advice and improved services to students. The aim of the proposal was to reduce the total number of student centres to three for the new generation undergraduate degrees, with names dissociated from the names of degrees or faculties (that is, the names would be Eastern Precinct, West and University

Square). A fourth centre would operate at the Southbank campus in association with the 'West Centre'. The centres would be managed through the Office of the Provost in the longer term, with a management committee reporting to the custodial dean to be set up as an interim measure for 2010. Review of and changes to provision of student services continues, with a recent decision to have a student centre for each of the six new generation degrees from 2013. The provost will continue to exercise an overarching policy and accountability framework for the centres.

The outcomes of the Melbourne Experience Survey (MES) reinforce the successful progress of the Melbourne Model in terms of student satisfaction. The MES was introduced in 2007 to provide baseline data before introduction of the Melbourne Model in 2008. The MES 2011 results showed that students viewed their overall experience at the University of Melbourne very favourably. Nearly 80 per cent of first-year undergraduates, for example, described their experience so far as 'good to excellent' and only around 5 per cent reported they had a poor experience overall. Students also reported a very positive view of the overall quality of their course in the course experience questionnaire. About 80 per cent of undergraduate and around 75 per cent of postgraduate coursework students agreed that they were satisfied. Outcomes were more positive than the previous year and higher still compared to the 2007 results.[6] Coming as they did after the introduction of the Melbourne Model and changes to student centres, the results were reassuring for those closely involved in delivering on the promises of the Curriculum Commission.

Graduate schools

The final component of the Melbourne Model – the transition to professional degrees at graduate level – was launched on 26 October 2007. As for the launch of the Melbourne Model, key stakeholders, media representatives and University staff were invited to attend the Graduate Schools' launch. It was also an opportunity for the University to raise awareness of the benefits of the graduate school model of education and to acknowledge the significant contributions for all involved in creating the graduate schools. The schools launched in 2007 were the Melbourne School of Design, Melbourne Business School, Melbourne Graduate School of Education, Melbourne School of Engineering, Melbourne Law School, Melbourne Graduate School of Science, Melbourne School of Graduate Research, Melbourne Graduate School of Land and Environment and Melbourne School of Veterinary Science. A further eight graduate schools have been established since 2007: Melbourne Medical School, Melbourne Dental School, Melbourne School of Population Health, Melbourne School of Health Science, Melbourne School of Information, Graduate School of Humanities and Social Sciences, Graduate School of Business and Economics and Faculty of Victorian College of the Arts and Music. In all these new graduate schools, as in the library and undergraduate teaching spaces, attention has been paid to imaginative teaching and study spaces in line with broader aspirations to offer a state-of-the art campus. To some extent, the new facilities are the transforming aspect that encourages students to change their study and experience practices and, in turn, expect the University to change as well.

Knowledge transfer/engagement

Although there was cause for satisfaction with the progress of the initial Growing Esteem objectives, a review of the strategic plan was undertaken as part of the University's normal cycle of three-yearly planning. A discussion paper, 'Refining the Strategy', was released to the University community by the Vice-Chancellor's Office for consideration in 2009 as part of an interim review of the overall Growing Esteem strategy.[7] The paper reported on a significant lack of understanding and communication of the third core strand of activity, knowledge transfer. That there was no clear definition of knowledge transfer was identified as a large part of the issue. As a result of consultations on the review paper and further discussion, the Growing Esteem Strategy 2010 reports that a decision had been taken to change the preferred terminology to 'engagement' rather than 'knowledge transfer'. Engagement is defined as 'the final strand', which:

> encompasses interaction between the University and the wider society. It includes knowledge partnerships, public programs, interactions with alumni, advancement activities and international programs.[8]

Senior executive

The Senior Executive Committee established in May 2008 is a different body from the groups that existed in the 1990s and early 2000s. It is described as:

> the University's principal management committee. Its membership comprises the Vice-Chancellor, President of the Academic Board and other senior officers with significant program or budget division accountability and associated authorities. The Committee is responsible for overseeing the development of University planning and budgeting and, once approved, for monitoring performance against plans and budgets. The Committee exercises authorities in relation to matters delegated to it by the Vice-Chancellor. The activities of the Committee are reported, where appropriate, to Council through the Vice-Chancellor and to Academic Board through the President of the Academic Board.[9]

The Planning and Budget Conference continues to be held in mid-year to consider and prepare the annual operational plan and budget in as collegial manner as is possible for such matters.

Research outcomes

The University of Melbourne, like most comprehensive research universities, gives great weight to recognition of its research and research training activities. The University is proud of its long record in achieving the highest place within Australia on measures of overall competitive research funding and research higher degree enrolments. The University has continued to rank highly in research performance (relative to other Australian universities) throughout the seven years of change brought about through the Growing Esteem strategy. In international league ladders such as the 2010–11 *Times Higher Education* rankings, Melbourne was the highest ranked Australian university and the thirty-sixth in the world. In the August 2011 Shanghai Jiao Tong University Academic Rankings of World Universities, Melbourne's standing had improved to the sixtieth position, a jump of 32 places since the rankings began in 2003. Melbourne was confirmed as the top research university in Australia in the Excellence in Research for Australia (ERA) assessment. These results were reassuring for those who had been anxious that the heavy burden of curriculum reform might undermine the attention paid to research. This successful outcome in research is a tribute to the academic staff who maintained the focus on their research during the Melbourne Model activities.

When the University agreed to implement the Melbourne Model from 2008 it knew that this would be a ten-year transition. The first new generation undergraduates would not graduate until the end of 2010; the first graduates from the new programs in medicine and veterinary science would not graduate until the end of 2014; and there would be students completing 'heritage' double degrees until 2016. Changes continue to be made; inevitably, given the evolving nature of higher education and its resourcing. How these changes will alter the face of the University and what their impact at the national and international levels will be in the longer term have yet to be seen.[10] The process of working through the transition to the Melbourne Model and the structural changes associated with it will take several more years, especially as these processes have been complicated by the effect on the University of the global financial crisis and any number of internal and external factors. The impact of the changes will continue to be incremental with more visible outcomes becoming evident over the next several years.

Whatever the case, the implementation of the Growing Esteem strategy, and the Melbourne Model in particular, has been the most profound academic change in the history of the University of Melbourne, and a major new element in debates about higher education in Australia and globally. The scope and pace of developments that occurred from 2006 to 2008 were phenomenal and it is particularly astounding to see how rapidly the new courses and graduate schools have been bedded down. Although other Australian universities have and are copying the Melbourne Model initiatives, no other institution has yet matched the successful differentiation and diversity that Melbourne has achieved. The Melbourne Model has brought a new generation of degrees to a new generation of students and the future for both is looking extremely promising.

Appendices

Appendix 1: Curriculum Commission Terms of Reference

Design dimensions:

- the number and type of undergraduate and postgraduate degrees to be offered
- the core knowledge and skills to be covered by each degree
- development of a significantly stronger student cohort experience
- the number of core and optional subjects to be offered
- pathways from undergraduate into postgraduate programs, including arrangements to facilitate entry to graduate programs for non-Melbourne graduates and under-represented groups (this might include entry exams)
- explicit pathways for RHD programs and mechanisms for transition between research and 'professional' pathways
- exceptions to the typical 3/2/3 structure for Bachelors/Masters/Doctorate in the Melbourne Model, for example Honours years
- whether all degrees should include a humanities and science and technology component and/or a language

Market/access dimensions (in coordination with the Policy and Advocacy Taskforce):

- gaining support from government on student profile, subsidy and pricing issues
- gaining support from students, parents and employers for the Melbourne Model
- revising entry criteria and selection at undergraduate, postgraduate and RHD level

- extending student access and support mechanisms
- ensuring professional accreditation requirements are met
- options for reducing completion time

Delivery dimensions:
- modes of delivery, staffing and facilities requirements for the new programs
- special features (e.g. online subjects, work placements, study abroad)
- economics of course delivery (cost, pricing, revenue, subsidy/ surplus projections)
- staff workloads during the transition from old to new models
- options for enrolled students who may wish to migrate from old to new programs
- maximising federal fundraising for students entering a research training pathway

Appendix 2: Curriculum Commission Coordinating Team 2006

The Curriculum Commission Coordinating Team consisted of Peter McPhee, Mary Emison and Gioconda Di Lorenzo. The following table lists matters discussed at weekly meetings and meetings with other groups and people throughout 2006.

	Matters discussed	Meetings with other groups/people
January	First cut report on faculty perspectives Issues list for CC, ToR, planning	P. McP and MRE with V. Massaro and L. Perry
February	Market research Engineering review Graduate attributes review VCAG follow-up J Wilkinson visit Criteria for 'general' component Grad schools in 2008	P. McP and MRE with RHD Committee P. McP and MRE with ADs (RAGS) and FGMs P. McP, MRE with V. Massaro and L. Perry
March	Report for PBC, JFK reporting templates Schedule of future work Market research CC info for faculty websites or distribution Courses continued/discontinued BBiosciences? General ed. component – R James Draft statement to schools PGCW programs Conditional offers in Law	MRE with M. Bryan, J. Borland, C. Reid re schedule for new courses approval dates/track MRE with 'implementation' group (L. Currie, C. Stewardson, LM) re terminology for course requirements, timetabling, handbook P. McP and MRE with John Vines (APESMA) P. McP and MRE with VPs re DEST profile, WPP Student/Staff Forum (VC, etc) P. McP and MRE with I. Marshman, A. Norton, M. Beaton-Wells and C. Smith re DEST modelling
April	VCAG report, bi-weekly update AVCC Bologna questions and DEST paper GE messages Core principles James Wilkinson arrangements PAT meeting 5 May FGMs retreat Faculty timelines for course proposals	P. McP presentation to c. 90 admin staff VCAG retreat (GE implementation unit; communications strategy, integrated report to PBC/council, GE feedback; College of UG Studies) P. McP and MRE with A. Nelligan re Discovery Week and offshore agents presentation

May	James Wilkinson visit plans Courses to be continued/discontinued Core principles PBC Conference Deferred places General ed. paper (James/Krause) Checklist 150 point masters CC dinner	Ad hoc group of R James, W Bebbington, K-L Krause, J Beard, MRE re proposal for College of UG Studies
June	Issues paper for forthcoming breakfast re Engineering Conditional offers for Law JD Finalise names of new gen degrees for AB discussion Open Day planning	PMcP presentation to parent evenings at Xavier College and elsewhere PMcP participation in PBC Conference
July	Issues with Physiotherapy and Social Work Course 'product sheets' and list of courses for Open Day Graduate school model Wilkinson visit and media conference Issues to raise with VCAG Non-budget department majors (e.g. Psychology)	All staff briefing on the MM Lunch with Prof. Wilkinson Menzies Oration and dinner PMcP presentations (e.g., Melbourne Grammar dinner, VPs/Deans, Trinity College board retreat) and attendance at VC/Principals' breakfast
August	Admin support for proposed course standing committees BAg prerequisites for 2008 Honours year coordination Legislation for new gen degrees	VC's dinner for principals Presentations at Open Day Presentation to interstate careers' advisers Deans/Heads Conference
September	Future agenda items Course standing committees BUGS membership Print run of CC final report Core principles for grad. schools	VC and Deans breakfast VC et al. breakfast meeting re Engineering participation in MM

Appendix 3: Academic Programs Committee

The Academic Programs Committee of the Academic Board (APC) is at the core of the University's committee structure. It is responsible for all academic matters related to courses in the University, including reviewing and recommending on new courses and changes to courses. Its terms of reference and membership can be found at: http://www.unimelb.edu.au/unisec/ acadboard/apc.html.

For many years, the APC dealt with all undergraduate and postgraduate coursework proposals – the Research Higher Degrees Committee and its predecessor and successor committees were or are responsible for vetting the University's research higher degrees. In the mid-1990s, the University stepped up its efforts to take advantage of the federal government's changed rules about institutions charging fees for postgraduate coursework programs. As faculties put forward increasing numbers of coursework program proposals, the APC workload increased significantly, and eventually led to the establishment of a Postgraduate Coursework Programs Sub-Committee. This arrangement lasted until the end of 2006 when, as a result of the recommendations of the Curriculum Commission and the APC, the Academic Board agreed to establish separate committees to consider course proposals during the transition to the Melbourne Model. This resulted in an Undergraduate Programs Committee (UPC) and a Postgraduate Coursework Programs Committee (PGPC), each with new terms of reference, to be established from the beginning of 2007. But even before the APC was split into two committees it was developing new forms, policies, processes and requisite guidelines, drawn from the Curriculum Commission's final report. These were to be used in applications for the Melbourne Model undergraduate degrees that were being considered by the newly established course standing committees and, eventually, the applications that would come forward for professional postgraduate coursework programs.

In early March 2007, the APC met three times in three weeks to consider the six new generation degrees proposals and approve them for forwarding to the Academic Board. The recommendations to the Academic Board noted that there would be a number of new generation course–related matters submitted for approval later in the year: the content and course-specific rules governing the breadth component; the range and content of honours year programs; new compulsory subjects for each course and descriptions of other new subjects. The UPC considered most of these additional details of the new generation degrees over two meetings in July 2007, with its recommendations approved by the Academic Board in late July. These recommendations included details of the University breadth subjects that would be offered in 2008 and the revised arrangements for concurrent diplomas. Most of the developments and recommendations for the new generation degrees covered details only for 2008, with further consideration to be given over time to details of the content and structure of the courses beyond 2008.

The UPC and PGPC had a range of other Melbourne Model–related issues that required attention over the remainder of 2007, many of which were reviewed by both committees and, on occasion, by a joint working group of the two. These included:

- guidelines for phasing out degrees that would be superseded by the new generation bachelors degrees and the introduction of professional graduate degrees. This encompassed the teaching out of these degrees and processes for faculties to follow
- major changes to the Engineering and Agriculture bachelors degrees to fit the Melbourne Model scheme
- implications of the introduction of the Melbourne Model for students wishing to enter a course in 2008 at later year level (that is, with credit)
- consideration of the numerous policy and procedures proposals that were put forward by the Policy and Procedures Working Group through iBUGS
- resolution of the question of authority for approval of minor changes to courses and breadth subjects in the context of

course standing committees, faculty committees and the Academic Programs Management Committee (the committee that replaced iBUGS).

The Academic Board approved the recombination of the UPC and the PGPC back to a single Academic Programs Committee with effect from the beginning of 2009.

Appendix 4: Members of taskforces, committees and working groups integral to the development and implementation of the MM

4a: Curriculum Commission and concurrent groups

Curriculum Commission	Policy & Advocacy Taskforce	MM Taskforce	MM Market Research Steering Committee
DVC (A) (Chair) P. McPhee	VC (Chair) G. Davis	GM, MROn W. Holden	DVC (A) P. McPhee
AVC (T&L) S. Elliott	DVC (A) P. McPhee	GM, MROff	VP (Int. Devel.) B. Bayley
President AB or nom J. Borland	SVP I .Marshman	Admissions x 2 E. Knowles, K. Gould	Dir UPO (Acting) M. Beaton-Wells
Dean (SGS) B. Evans	D. Kemp (VC's Fellow)	Dir., Student Access C. Murphy	VP (Market &Devel) P. Freeland-Small
Director (CSHE) R. James	S. Marginson (CSHE)	Art x 1 J. Jones	Dean of Law M. Crommelin
Faculty AD or equiv: ABP – P. Walker Arts – S. James EcoCom – B. Griffiths Educ – R. Misson Eng – D. Smith LFR – R. Beilin Law – I.Malkin MDHS – S. Harrap Music – C. Falk Sci – M. Livett Vet Sci – B. Parry VCA – J. Stockdale	OVC Policy & Government Relations Advisor – A. Norton	ABP x 1 N. Robinson	Dir. MCP M. Emison
Pres. UMSU J. Giles Pres. UMPA T. Williams	Student Representative P. Donegan	Science G. Slatcher	
VPAR G. Luck	Director OVC D. Speagle	Education N. Staggard	
Director MCP M. Emison	GESO P. McLean	Eco & Com B. Young	
Observers MBS J. George SPC B. Hughes GESO P. McLean		SGS T. Tjia	

Note: The Shared Service Review Implementation Group was: SVP (chair), two to three deans or their nominees (F. Rickards, R. Frampton, C. Stewardson); VPs of relevant areas; VP HR, EO – J. Beard.

GE Markets Working Group	New Generation Course Approvals Working Group	PBC Implementing the MM Working Group
SVP (Chair) I. Marshman	DVC (A) (Chair) P. McPhee	DVC (A) (Chair) P. McPhee
DVC (A) P. McPhee	Chair, APC J. Borland	Pres AB L. Skene
PVC (Uni Rel) W. Bebbington	Chair SPC B. Hughes	Dean Eco & Com M. Abernethy
Dir, OVC D. Speagle	Chair PGCW Com R. Misson	Dean MDHS J. Angus
VP (Internatl Devel) B. Bayley	Pres AB L. Skene	Dean ABP R. Fincher
VP (Marketing & Devel) P. Freeland-Small	Dir Melb Curric Proj M. Emison – Dir MMI (Nov) – J. Reese	Dean Arts B. Probert
Dir., Student Access C. Murphy	Dir., Student Access C. Murphy	Dean Science P. Rathjen
GM, MROn W. Holden	Secretary to APC C. Reid	SVP I. Marshman
GM ABP— GM LFR N. Robinson — T Tjia	VPAR G. Luck	FGM, Science C. Stewardson
GM, Eng N. Robinson	GESO S. Eshuys P. McLean	EO (Dir. Integ. Admin.) – J .Beard
Dir Melb Curric Proj M Emison — Dir MMI – J. Reese		
VPAR G. Luck		
GESO P. McLean		

4b: iBUGS (at February 2007) and Course Standing Committees (members at September–October 2006)

(Interim) BUGS	CSC member categories set by CC	Arts	Biosci/Biomed *
DVC (A) (Chair) or nominee L. Skene	Chair (nominated from among members and appointed by BUGS)	S. James	M. Hargreaves
Pres. AB P. Pattison	Members drawn from discipline areas taught in the course and appointed by the BUGS	M. Campbell – Engl. N. Enright – SAGES J. Fletcher – Linguistics & App. Ling. C. Kovesi – History A. O'Brien – Creative Arts R. Robins – HPS K. McDonald – Soc. H Jackson. – MDHS (Behav Sci) S Howard. – Sci.	G. McColl – Med S. Harrap – Physiology T. Goodwin – Anat. G. Bowes – Paed. H. Jackson – Behav. Sci. G. Webb – Physio. K. Nightingale – Nursing D. Smith – Eng. G. McFadden – Sci. M. Renfree – Sci. N. McBrien – Sci.
10 Deans or noms* ABP – T Kvan Arts – B Probert EcoCom – M Abernethy Educ – F Rickards Eng – I Mareels LFR – R Roush Law – M Crommelin MDHS – J Angus Music – C Falk Sci – P Rathjen	Members drawn from professional staff and appointed by BUGS	C Bird – Arts Fac Office A Hall – Music Degree Program Manager	
VPAR or nom. G. Luck	Student rep. appointed by UMSU#		
VP IS or nom. L. O'Brien	Up to three co-optees – appointed by the standing committee	J. O'Toole – Educ. C. Beaton-Wells – Law S. Baker – VCA	M. Singh – LFR J. Gilkerson – Vet. Sci.
CSC chairs Arts – S. James Com. – B. Griffiths Envs – R. Fincher Biosci. – M. Hargreaves Sci. – M. Livett Music – C. Falk			
Pres. UMSU or nom. B. Ahrens			
2 coopted: Dean VetSc. or nominee – G. Browning Dir. VCA or nom. – J. Stockdale			

* The Science and Biomedicine standing committees were combined to form one committee from the start of 2008 as had been agreed at the PBC 2007 June Conference.

Commerce	Environments	Music	Science*
B. Griffiths	R. Fincher	C. Falk	M. Livett
A. Lillis – ABIS	P. Walker – ABP	Dean of Music	A. Drinnan – Bot.
S. Leech –ABIS	J .Robinson – ABP	D. Grocke – Assoc Dean	T. Guttmann – Maths &
P. Kofman – Finance	C. Bull – ABP	(Research)	Stats
J. Borland – Eco.	P. Christoff – Arts	One rep from each of	J. Hergt – Earth Sci.
D. Dickson – Economics	(SAGES)	these groups:	R. O'Hair – Chem.
(Act St)	I. Bishop – Eng	Performance – I. Holtham	R. Webster – Phys.
B. Lukas – Man. and	(Geomatics)	Composition –	One other from Sci.
Mark.	G. Moore – Eng (Civil	S. Greenbaum	A. Moffat – Eng (Comp.
Dean or nominee	and Environ.)	Musicology – K. Murphy	Sci).
M. Lambiris – Law	R. Keenan – LFR	Music Therapy – vacant	S .Barlow LFR
H Rubinstein – Sci.	R. Beilin – LFR	in 2006	J. Hill – LFR
L Sonenberg – Sci.	A. Gleadow – Sci.		P. Gleeson – MDHS
	M. Keough – Sci.		P. McIntyre – MDHS
			R. Bell – MDHS
FGM – Eco. and Com.	FGM – ABP	One of FGM Music or	Science Faculty Office –
F Pecoraro	FGM – LFR	Music Degree Program	M Eden
		Manager	
G. Lakomski – Educ.		C. Marshall – Arts	K. Stacey – Educ.
D. O'Brien – LFR		N. Jeanneret – Educ.	I. Beveridge – Vet. Sci.
S. James – Arts		J. Stockdale – VCA	R. Robins – Arts

4c: Post Curriculum Commission groups

(PBC) MM08 — MMIT	Policy & Procedures Working Group (at May 2007)	ACAG*	CMCG
DVC (A) (joint Chair) P. McPhee	Pres. AB (Chair) P. Pattison	Pres AB (Chair) P. Pattison	VP & Head of Admin. L. Bare
SVP (joint Chair) I. Marshman	VP & Gen Counsel C Penman	Chair, TALQAC L. Hawthorne	DVC (R) J. McKenzie
President AB L. Skene, then P. Pattison in 2007	Academic, faculty & professional staff with relevant expertise Prev. chair of APC – M. Bryan Chair BUGS – L. Skene Univ. Sec. – L. Currie Dir., SAS – L. Cameron R. Slocombe M. Devlin M. Eden M. Coyle K. Stevenson-McBride	Expert areas reps: HR expert in professional staff appointments – J. McQuillan Student System project – K. Stevenson-McBride Transition Office – C. Rhoden VPAR – G. Luck	AB officer P. Pattison
Dean EcoCom. M. Abernethy	VPAR G. Luck	Faculty reps: EcoCom. – B. Harley Educ. – E C.app Arts – tba Bioscience – tba Architecture – tba	A. Dean R. Roush
Dean, Science P. Rathjen	EO to Group H. Thomas	Director, CSHE R. James	SVP I Marshman
VP & HA L. Bare		Chair of BUGS L. Skene	VP (HR) N. Waugh
FGM, Eng N. Robinson		MM08 Project Office J. Reese	A Faculty GM L. Capp
7 in attendance+			Dep. Client Serv. J. McQuillan
			GM OSVP J. Mann
			GESO P. McLean

* The ACAG had several other members but the meeting notes do not indicate their positions or departments, and they are no longer listed in the University directory. It is assumed that they were faculty representatives.

Marketing TF	Committee of Deans (at March 2008)	APMC (at February 2008)
SVP (Chair) I. Marshman	DVC (A)/Provost (Chair) P. McPhee	Provost or nom. (Chair) S. Elliott
DVC (A) P. McPhee	Pres AB P Pattison	Pres AB or nom. R. Slocombe
Deans of Arts – B. Probert ABP – T. Kvan Sci. – P. Rathjen Eng. – I. Mareels	Deans ABP – T. Kvan Arts – M. Considine EcoCom. – M. Abernethy Educ. – F. Rickards Eng. – I. Mareels LFR – R. Roush Law – J. Hathaway MDHS – J. Angus Music – C. Falk Sci. – P. Rathjen Vet. Sci. – K. Hinchcliff VCA – A. Hull SGR – D. Strugnell	Deans of faculties & grad schools or noms ABP – P. Ashford Arts – M. Considine EcoCom – A Loi Educ – R. Misson Eng – A. Moffat LFR – D. O'Brien Law – S. Evans MDHS – G. McColl Music – C. Falk Sci. – L. Sonenberg Vet. Sci. – B. Parry VCA – S. Baker
Prof. Marketing & Com. – B. Lukas	SVP I. Marshman	VPAR or nom. G. Luck
VP (Mark. & Com.) P. Freeland-Small	Head Uni Serv L Bare	VP (IS) or nom. L O'Brien
Dir., Internatl T. Crook		CSC Chairs Arts – M. Campbell Biom/Sci – M. Livett Com – G. Whitwell Envs – I. Bishop Music – I. Holtham
DP (Natl Markts & Global Schols) C. Murphy		Student Pres or nom UMSU – O. Bishop. UMPA – J. Ruth
Dir. EcoCom. Grad School B. Young		2 chosen for expertise Sci – L. Sonenberg MDHS – M. Hargreaves
GM MROn W. Holden		PVC (T&L) or nom. J. Reese
GESO x 1 P. McLean		
GM, OSVP J Mann		

+ The seven eligible to attend meetings as observers were: executive officer to the taskforce (who was also director, Integrated Administration), director (University Planning Office), general manager (Office of the SVP), manager (GESO), director (Melbourne Model Implementation) and two consultants from the Boston Consulting Group.

Appendix 5: Funding the Melbourne Model

There were two particular funding sources that were critical to the development and implementation of the Melbourne Model: the federal government's Workplace Productivity Program and the Growing Esteem Transition Fund provided by the University Council. Each of these programs has been mentioned in the main body of the book, but the importance of the funds in the transition to the Melbourne Model merits a brief, consolidated description of the key activities that the funds supported. The federal government's Diversity and Structural Adjustment Fund, which was mentioned in Chapter 5, was also critical to the introduction of Melbourne Model changes in the Faculty of Education (now the Graduate School of Education).

Workplace Productivity Program

Anticipating that implementing the Curriculum Commission's recommendations would be costly, the University had begun applying for federal government funding from early 2006. The submissions, 'Curriculum Reform Under the Melbourne Model' and 'Transforming University Programs', were made to the DEST under the Collaboration and Structural Reform (CASR) Program and the Workplace Productivity Program (WPP).[1] The Boston Consulting Group was approached by the University to be a partner in the funding bid as it was understood the chances of success would be enhanced with another organisation or institution as a collaborator. Boston had worked with the University in the mid-1990s, and the Vice-Chancellor was familiar with their work through a number of avenues, including their role in establishing the Australian and New Zealand School of Government.

The WPP application was submitted to DEST in April 2006 while an expression of interest for the CASR funds was submitted at the end of May. The WPP application was premised on a case, made to the 20 April VCAG Retreat by the Senior Vice-Principal, for achieving administrative reform and improvements to support Growing Esteem initiatives. These administrative reform and shared services developments would be a flow-on, or extension, of actions taken as a result of the 2005 Shared Services Reviews, which had aimed to ensure that service areas supported the core activities of the University in an effective and cost-efficient manner.

The Senior Vice-Principal proposed that adopting the Growing Esteem strategy and the many changes it involved gave the University a unique opportunity to set new priorities for business improvements in administrative services. These improvements would be additional to those that were already part of the Shared Services Reviews. A number of improvements across various administrative areas were listed with the proposal for the 'academic administration reform and planning tools' review, to be carried out over 2006 and 2007, being the most immediately relevant to the Growing Esteem initiatives. The proposal was to:

> Review and streamline the policy and regulatory framework for student and course administration and develop a new model of student-centred service delivery made possible by the consolidation of academic programs under the Melbourne Model.

These proposed strategies were endorsed by VCAG, which noted that a detailed plan of action would not be possible for the critical item of academic administration reform until the Curriculum Commission had finalised the structure it would recommend for courses under the Melbourne Model.

The WPP application was for funding of $1.8 million to support the project, and to appoint consultants to work with the University on business modelling and service reform and design. There was a proviso that if the WPP application was not successful, the University would need to approach the project in other ways to meet the needs of the 'student of the future'.

In the July 2006 VCAG retreat, the Senior Vice-Principal provided timelines for the administrative reforms to be funded if the WPP application was successful. This included preliminary mapping of processes and costing data about the student services as they were at the time, to form a baseline for future investigations. This costing project was completed in 2007 in time to inform the Boston proposals for the Melbourne Student Services Model and later changes to the University's budget principles.

The University was notified in early October 2006 that the WPP application, 'Transforming University Programs', had been successful. The University's expression of interest for funding for the 'Curriculum Reform under the Melbourne Model' project, was also successful, with DEST providing funds under the WPP.

The University received $2.25 million for the curriculum reform project, split equally over the three years from 2006 to 2008. Most of the funds were used for work associated with the design and development of the new generation degrees; that is, salary costs of staff involved in developing the curriculum including teaching buy-out, and the cost of induction programs for sessional staff. Around 15 per cent of the grant was a contribution to the Boston and LEK consultancies for their work on the critical path plan and the business planning for the new generation degrees.

Of the $1.8 million received over the 2006 to 2008 period for 'Transforming University Programs', about 70 per cent was paid to Boston, LEK and various other consultants for their work on business metrics and modelling, and for developing the critical path plan and the Melbourne Student Services Model. Around a third of the funds supported a range of change management activities in several faculties and the Office of the Provost.

In 2007, the University applied for further funding under the WPP for a 'Strategy-Driven Workplace Reform: The Next Phase' project which would have had three components, but the application was not successful.

Growing Esteem Transition Fund (GETF)

The availability of the WPP funds in 2006 was seen as a great opportunity for the University by its leaders and resulted in the two successful applications reported above. Although the $4 million received was useful in kick-starting the implementation and transition to the Growing Esteem program with particular attention on the Melbourne Model, it was barely the tip of the iceberg in relation to the cost of the changes the University would experience over 2006 to 2015. Fortunately, again the University's leaders were able to foresee the complexity of the situation. The Growing Esteem Transition Fund proposal was first floated at the Planning and Budget Committee Conference in June 2006. The fund was to provide 'targeted assistance to faculties with the courseware development and structural adjustment costs associated with the implementation of business plans to give effect to Growing Esteem and the Melbourne Model'. The proposal recognised the work that faculties would have to do to design and develop new generation undergraduate degrees and professional degrees at the graduate level, in teaching out the superseded programs, and in establishing graduate schools.

The Planning and Budget Committee Conference agreed to recommend to the Finance Committee that it seek council approval for a Growing Esteem transition fund of $85 million on a ratio of $3 University to $1 faculty basis to operate over the period from 2007 to 2012. Council agreed to the proposal at its meeting in July 2006, indicating that the funds were to support the transition to the Melbourne Model and strengthen research and research training capability. The Finance Committee would release funds only after a faculty had demonstrated appropriate business planning. Reports on the use of any GETF funds allocated would be required on a quarterly basis. The business plans developed to facilitate the bids for GETF are briefly referred to in Chapter 8. LEK Consulting provided the template for use by faculties in developing their plans and one for the plans for the new generation degrees.

The categories of uses to which the GETF was allocated included:

• subject and course development and curriculum design at undergraduate and postgraduate levels

- teach-out and academic transition issues
- course marketing and recruitment
- change management and infrastructure
- staff training for student centres
- faculty learning support programs
- scholarships
- business planning systems improvement.

By the end of 2010, all GET funds had been allocated. The range of activities the funds supported is extensive, with about $40 million allocated directly to faculties, $12.5 million to scholarships and activities associated with these, $12.5 million for infrastructure and the remainder of $14 million to administrative units. All faculties benefited from the GETF, which supported these activities:

- development of subjects for new generation degrees and for graduate programs
- workforce planning and change management
- teaching out of courses
- teaching spaces and computer labs upgrades
- marketing and communication
- development of breadth subjects.

The administrative units used their allocations for activities that would support the faculties and the students:

- Kwong Lee Dow and other scholarships, and support for administration of scholarships
- renovation of locations to be developed into student centres
- change management, corporate restructuring and business planning
- branding, marketing and recruitment, the Melbourne Model launch activities and open days.

Particular note is to be taken of the importance of the GET and the Teaching and Learning Performance funds for the major roll-out of new teaching and learning spaces, starting with the Old Engineering Building and the student centres. The Education Resource Centre (ERC) of the University Library was also significantly improved.

Appendix 6: Final recommendations
6a: Recommendations of the Curriculum Commission[2]
(Note: appendices are not included)

G. Summary of recommendations
The following recommendations are proposed by the University of Melbourne Curriculum Commission to facilitate transition to the Melbourne Model.
The Curriculum Commission recommends:

1. Approval by the Academic Board of this report on the core principles of the undergraduate, postgraduate coursework and research higher degree elements of the Melbourne Model, and the pathways between them.
2. That the educational needs of undergraduates not enrolled in 'new generation' degrees be the focus of special attention in faculty learning and teaching plans and Teaching and Learning Quality Assurance Committee (TALQAC) course reviews.
3. That the revised statement of graduate attributes (as set out in Appendix 3) be adopted and that, in the further development and implementation of the Melbourne Model, particular attention be paid to the other recommendations of the AWiL report.
4. That the Melbourne Experience Committee pay particular attention to ways in which statements of graduate attributes, the 'Melbourne Experience', and the Student Expectations and Responsibilities Policy may best be highlighted to the University community.
5. That particular attention be paid to the core characteristics identified for the 'new generation' undergraduate courses, and specifically that the 'new generation' courses:

   • are characterised by academic development across the three years;
   • focus on first- and final-year cohort experiences;

- ensure that all students undertake at least one 'major' or equivalent;
- ensure that multiple postgraduate options are kept open through all three years of the course wherever possible;
- have an exposure to an appropriate research experience;
- are characterised by a 'knowledge transfer' component, and draw on the advice of an external advisory board;
- pay explicit attention to e-learning experiences and development; and
- are available as sequential degrees with reciprocal recognition of 100 points of credit.

6. That the core principle of the breadth component is that it will allow students to be exposed to and to learn about alternative domains of knowledge, different methods of enquiry and different 'ways of knowing'.

7. That students undertake the minimum of 75 points (or one-quarter of the degree) of breadth subjects in disciplines which are not available within their core programs.

8. That the breadth subjects normally be completed in each of the three years of a course. The Commission recommends that breadth subjects and sequences be structured so that it is possible for at least one 37.5-point cluster and for a 300 level breadth subject to be taken.

9. That breadth subjects be a mixture of 'custom-designed', existing and revised subjects and clusters identified and approved as strengthening the core program.

10. That the proposed Board of Undergraduate Studies endorse breadth subjects that involve multi-disciplinary approaches to foundational knowledge from across the humanities, social sciences and sciences as 'University subjects' to be available to students in all undergraduate degrees.

11. That the breadth component of the 'new generation' degrees be recommended by course standing committees and endorsed by the proposed Board of Undergraduate Studies in line with

the criteria outlined in *The Proposal and Endorsement of Breadth Subjects* (Appendix 5) before being submitted to the Academic Programs Committee for approval.

12. That each faculty review its postgraduate coursework offerings to ensure that they pay attention to entry criteria, coherence, viability, and pathways from and into other programs.

13. That, in recognition of the increased focus on the importance and quality of postgraduate coursework programs, the Academic Board consider making the Postgraduate Coursework Programs Sub-Committee a full committee of the Board rather than a subcommittee of Academic Programs Committee.

14. That the seven recommendations outlined in the policy documents on the proposed principal pathways to research higher degrees in the Melbourne Model and on the characteristics of the distinctive 'Melbourne PhD Experience' be endorsed:

   a. That the University endorses two principal pathways to enter research higher degrees – the honours pathway and a two-year masters pathway – on the understanding that normal entry requirements for the research higher degrees must be met and that CSPs will be available.

   b. That the six standing committees for the new generation degrees would outline an honours program (which is an undergraduate year) attached to their degree, while a masters degree pathway would be the responsibility of graduate schools or faculties. Each would need to provide for the entry requirements into the research higher degrees as determined by the Research Higher Degrees Committee.

   c. That faculties with current undergraduate programs continuing in 2008 or beyond will determine their position with relation to the two principal pathways for entry to RHDs.

   d. That there will be clear points of articulation into research higher degrees (research masters and doctorates) from other programs according to criteria based on a student's academic background and experience, and clear points of early exit with an appropriate (and desirable) qualification.

e. That the University should more overtly promote the fact that all PhD students of the University are strongly encouraged to gain international experience during their candidature and are provided with some financial support to achieve this.

f. That the University endorses in principle the development of a 'Melbourne Advanced Studies Award' (MASA) as a recognised award program, not compulsory and for doctoral students only. This award should be compatible with the new Commercialisation Training Scheme (CTS) and NICTA certificate programs.

g. That the University continues to investigate, as a matter of urgency, the level of funds that can be made available for both the delivery of the MASA program and for additional stipend funding that would be required for participating students.

15. That further consideration be given to issues identified in Section E of the Commission's final report to the Academic Board and that these issues should be considered as deemed appropriate by the Academic Board and faculties in consultation with the proposed Board of Undergraduate Studies.

16. That, whatever the structure for the administration and curriculum development of the new generation undergraduate courses, expert course advice and course planning, both in person and online, be readily available to all students.

17. That through the Academic Programs Committee and TALQAC, the Academic Board continue to have the central role in approving and monitoring the characteristics, quality and coherence of the new degrees.

6b: Recommendations of the PBC implementing the Melbourne Model Working Group[3]
(Note: appendices are not included)

7. Summary of Recommendations
Recommendation 1
That a University-wide framework is required for planning, designing, implementing and managing the new generation undergraduate degrees and that this should be achieved through the establishment of:

(i) Course Standing Committees for each new generation undergraduate degree with responsibility for designing and developing the courses, with membership and terms of reference as described in Appendix 2.

(ii) A Board of Undergraduate Studies (BUGS), which is the primary mechanism for the faculties to act in concert to ensure the recommendations from the course Standing Committees adhere to the new generation degree core principles and University policies, and makes recommendations on the courses to the Academic Board via its subcommittees (terms of reference described in Appendix 3).

Recommendation 2
That BUGS be chaired by a nominee of the Vice-Chancellor and have membership comprising Deans or their nominees and the Chairs of the course Standing Committees.

Recommendation 3
That the remit of BUGS be the new generation courses, including a role in making recommendations to the Academic Board on policies and practices applicable to the delivery of undergraduate courses generally.

Recommendation 4
That in order to carry forward the detailed development of the new undergraduate degrees:

(i)   The course Standing Committees be established immediately on an interim basis with membership approved by the Deputy Vice-Chancellor on advice from Deans, until they are formally constituted as Standing Committees from the beginning of 2007;

(ii) The Chair of the Standing Committees be appointed until the end of 2007 and that the normal term of office be for two years;

(iii) The Board of Undergraduate Studies be established on an interim basis when the Curriculum Commission disbands from September 2006 until formally established from the beginning of 2007.

Recommendation 5
That the Chairs of the Standing Committees and the Chair of BUGS be provided with appropriate resourcing to ensure the smooth development, implementation and on-going management of the new generation undergraduate courses through:

(i)   Central funding of 0.3 to 0.5 EFT for each Standing Committee Chair, depending on the course, until the end of 2007 during the period of designing and preparing for implementation of the courses, reducing to a smaller fraction to be determined at the time.

(ii) Central funding of approximately 0.3 to 0.5 EFT professional staff support for each Standing Committee, depending on the course, until the end of 2007 when the level of support should be reviewed to identify the on-going requirements.

(iii) Centrally provided resourcing for the Chair of BUGS including a full-time professional staff member to support BUGS and its Chair and to work closely with the secretariat for the course Standing Committees, the Standing Committees and other groups involved in implementing and overseeing the Melbourne Model.

Recommendation 6

That all course advisers for new generation undergraduate degree students undergo a University training program to ensure that student-centred and high-quality, expert course advice across all degrees is available to students.

Recommendation 7

That all postgraduate coursework courses, including Graduate Certificates and Diplomas, will be offered through Graduate Schools created in accordance with the criteria (i) to (vii) for Graduate Schools outlined in Section 5.2.1 of this report noting that these criteria will be fleshed out in the second quarter of 2007 following the submission of faculty business plans to the Planning and Budget Committee about implementing Growing Esteem.

Recommendation 8

That faculties are strongly encouraged to develop and refine proposals for Graduate Schools which are responsive to cross-disciplinary programs, financial sustainability, postgraduate student experience, and market expectations, and that these matters are canvassed in faculty business plans so that the Planning and Budget Committee can consider the appropriate framework for Graduate Schools in the second quarter of 2007 after the first round of faculty planning.

Recommendation 9
That the new generation courses will operate under a common set of rules and policies that will be applied consistently across the University.

Recommendation 10
That the Planning and Budget Committee establish a steering group which:

(i)   Oversees the work required to support the Melbourne Model on defining course rules and procedures for consistent application of the rules, mechanisms for the optimal provision of course advice, and the management and location of appropriate student academic and administrative support services;

(ii)   Has the capacity to establish further working groups as required and to receive reports from other groups in the University working on related issues;

(iii) Has membership recommended by the Deputy Vice-Chancellor (Academic), the incoming President of the Academic Board and the Senior Vice-Principal but includes the Vice-Principal and Academic Registrar, the Vice-Principal (Information Services), the Director (Student Administration and Systems) or nominee as well as Academic Board and faculty representation.

Appendix 7: Critical path plan: workstreams and substreams

The six workstreams and the substreams established in late 2006, as well as the leaders, managers and the accountable officers for each one, are shown in the following table, which also gives an idea of the magnitude of the tasks.[4]

Workstream	1 Undergraduate	2 Postgraduate	3 Melbourne Exp	4 Management System	5 Transition	6 Evaluation
Leader	P. McPhee	P. McPhee	P. McPhee	I .Marshman	I. Marshman	I. Marshman
Manager	J. Reese	J. Reese	J. Beard	J. Beard	J. Mann	J. Mann
Substreams Accountable Officers	1.1 Curriculum & subject design) Chair, BUGS	2.1 Curriculum & subject design) AB officer – R. Slocombe	3.1 Recruitment, admissions & access VP (ID)	4.1 Student services SVP	5.1 Communication & advocacy) VP (M&C)	6.1 Overall project evaluation Director, Planning
	1.2 Positioning & marketing VP (ID) & SVP as Leader	2.2 Positioning & marketing VP (ID) & SVP as Leader	3.2 Personalised support services VPAR	4.2 Marketing & recruitment VP (ID)	5.2 Change management support Manager, GESO	6.2 Workstream & substream evaluation Director, Planning
		2.3 Research HDs PVC (Res. Training)	3.3 Personalised academic enrichment L. Skene	4.3 fundraising, external relations PVC (Uni Rels)	5.3 Set up interim management systems SVP	
	1.3 Course management DVC (Acad.)	2.4 Course management DVC (Acad.)	3.4 Personalised academic connectedness Pres AB	4.4 Support functions VP & Head (Admin.)	5.4 Develop interim solutions VPAR	
	1.4 Resourcing and delivery PVC (TLE)	2.5 Resourcing & delivery PVC (TLE)	3.5 Cohort support services VP & Head (Admin)	4.5 Policies & procedures Pres AB	5.5 Manage new & continuing cohorts Dean of Law	
			3.6 Transition out PVC (University Relations)	4.6 Resourcing SVP		

Appendix 8: Matters considered by the MM08/MMIT 2006–08

The following list is in chronological order of when the issues appeared on meeting agendas, which is not necessarily the order in which they were resolved.

Boston Critical Path Plan
Vision Workshop
Pulse survey
MM launch date and marketing
Student load strategies
Student access and equity
Workplace Productivity Program grants
Course Standing Committees – financial support
Reviews of CPP substreams progress
Marketing plan (Dreamlarge)
Change management
Student centres developments
Undergraduate and postgraduate courses issues
Knowledge transfer
MSSM/delivery of student services
BUGS/CSC legislation
GETF bids
Recruitment marketing post MM Launch
Academic policies and procedures
Cohorts Working Group
Open Day and marketing
Teach-out issues
Role and name of taskforce
Communication plan
Committees' structures
Budgeting for MSSM

Appendix 9: Vice-Chancellor's Report to the Academic Board, 21 June 2007

This report provides an outline of the outcomes of the June 2007 Planning and Budget Committee Conference.[5]

This year's Planning and Budget Conference was held at the Mt Eliza campus of the Melbourne Business School from 14–17 June 2007. Important issues were discussed in a constructive and collegial manner leading to a number of landmark decisions as the University continues to develop the detail of the Melbourne Model and to implement the Growing Esteem strategy.

PBC adopted in principle the recommendations from Boston Consulting Group to establish hubs within faculties and graduate schools for each new generation degree bringing together transactional, well-being and enhancement services for students, including research students. However, PBC also noted the considerable demands now being carried by faculties and divisions and resolved to adopt a project plan that is measured, thorough and manageable. Consequently, it is likely that the new hubs will be developed sequentially over the next 2 to 3 years, with recognition that a different model may be required for smaller campuses.

In adopting the BCG recommendations, PBC noted that there would be opportunities for significant cost containment, especially for the delivery of transactional services. PBC agreed that, while savings would in the medium term be required for new investments in systems improvement, it would be vital that efficiencies were clearly identified from the outset.

PBC acknowledged that a budget methodology that has worked well for a long period of growth may lack appropriate rigour and analysis for the more difficult period ahead. The volatility of domestic and international markets, coupled with the continued absence of funding indexation, means the University must be better positioned to manage a fluctuating income. Consequently, PBC resolved to commission a comprehensive review of budget planning and methodology and machinery at the University, including articulating a rigorous and integrated business planning process and budget proposal cost-benefit analysis.

Despite some good news in the Commonwealth budget, financial pressures remain acute. A number of faculties are struggling to cover costs given modest CSP payments and falling income from fee-paying students. While money is provided in the 2008 budget to help faculties return to surplus by 2010, cost containment will be required to keep the overall University within the parameters set by Finance Committee.

A paper recommending to Council modest structural changes to support the University's Growing Esteem strategy will be tabled at the meeting.[6]

Notes

Introduction: Transforming Academic Structures in the University of Melbourne

1   The term 'Growing Esteem' derives from the University's motto: 'We shall grow in the esteem of future generations'.
2   Triple helix is also the name of a student organisation founded in the United States in 2005, with an affiliate at the University of Melbourne.
3   The appendices in this volume give an indication of the range and level of participation in the activities leading to the introduction of the Melbourne Model.
4   The University of Melbourne, Annual Report 2011 (UM USO)
5   As director, I was chief administrator for the Curriculum Commission, responsible for ensuring that its procedures ran smoothly and its tasks were performed.
6   Although many in the first cohort of undergraduates completed a Melbourne Model undergraduate degree in 2010, the many who proceed to a professional or other graduate program will not complete before 2013 or 2014, depending on the course studied.

1   The Birth of the Melbourne Model

1   Minutes of University Council meeting 6/03. Item 6.1 (UM USO).
2   Email from Professor Davis to Mary Emison on 1 April 2009.
3   Minutes of University Council meeting 1/04. Item 2 (UM USO).
4   Minutes of University Council meeting 6/04, held on 10 May 2004, in which the Chancellor is reported as advising that 'stocktakes' would be conducted in the third quarter of 2004 on the University's research, teaching and learning, administration and finance (UM USO).
5   Council Planning Conference 2005, (Summary) Report on Due Diligence Reviews: Issues (UM USO).
6   Ibid.
7   An equivalent full-time student unit (EFTSL) is a measure of the workload for students undertaking a full year of study in a particular year. It is used by the Federal Government to determine student workload by discipline in the universities. In the University of Melbourne, a full year of study is equivalent to 100 credit points with individual subjects contributing 0.125 EFTSL each in most instances.
8   In 2005, around 150 people were invited to attend the Deans and Heads Conference. These included the Vice-Chancellor and deputy vice-chancellors, Academic Board officers, deans of faculties, heads of academic departments

and schools, vice-principals (now executive directors), faculty general managers and heads of key administrative departments.

9   The conference is now held in the nearby town of Torquay.

10 Email correspondence between Professor Davis and Mary Emison on 1 April 2009.

11 Email from Professor Davis to Mary Emison on 1 April 2009.

12 The 'Melbourne Experience' concept was introduced as part of the Melbourne Agenda. It aimed to provide a superior campus-based experience for students in all their interactions with the University, from before applying for admission to after completion, that encompassed all student services.

13 The Melbourne Agenda – Messages from Deans and Heads Conference 2005. Copy of a PowerPoint presentation by Professor Davis to the Deans and Heads Conference that was tabled at the Council Planning Conference 2005 (UM USO).

14 Personal communication from Professor McPhee to Mary Emison on 1 March 2011.

15 The membership of the University Council is the Chancellor, Vice-Chancellor, president of the Academic Board, six members appointed by the Governor-in-Council, six members appointed by the council, two academic staff members and one professional staff member elected by the staff, two students elected by students and one person appointed by the minister responsible for higher education. The number of external members is fourteen including the Chancellor. The deputy vice-chancellors and senior professional officers also attend meetings of council as observers.

16 Council conferences are normally attended only by its members, the deputy vice-chancellors and the Senior Vice-Principal. Others may be invited to attend for specific sessions or to give presentations on matters relevant to the conference agenda.

17 Council Planning Conference 2005, Learning and Teaching Due Diligence Review: Confidential Report to Council Members (October 2004), page ii (UM USO).

18 Minutes of University Council meeting 3/05, held on 11 April 2005, and the paper circulated as Item A.3a Chancellor's Matters (UM USO).

19 Also known as the 'sandstone' universities: Melbourne, Sydney, ANU, Queensland, Adelaide, Western Australia, UNSW and Monash.

20 The course experience questionnaire (CEQ) and the postgraduate research experience questionnaire (PREQ) are major parts of the Australian Graduate Survey, which seeks the views of new graduates on various aspects of the course just completed. The questionnaires are sent together with the graduate destination survey to graduates four months after they have completed their course of study. In accordance with the requirements of the Commonwealth Government, all Australian higher education institutions administer the survey to their own graduates consistent with a common standard

methodology and coding protocol co-ordinated by Graduate Careers Australia.

21 This Senior Executive should not be confused with the Senior Executive Committee that was established in May 2008.

22 Planning and Budget Committee, Minutes of meeting 3/05, held on 13 April 2005 (UM USO).

23 The initial Matins group consisted of the Vice-Chancellor, the deputy vice-chancellors and the Senior Vice-Principal. Its membership has increased and varied over the years in line with structural changes to the senior executive cohort.

24 Council Planning Conference 2005. Due Diligence Review – Administration and Finance: Confidential Report to Council Members (October 2004), page 39 (UM USO).

25 Draft 2.2 at 15 June 2005; PBC 2005 Conference papers (UM USO).

26 Professor McKenzie on 30 April 2009 and Professor McPhee on 1 May 2009.

27 The Bologna Model (now referred to as the Bologna Process) was named after the Bologna Declaration, which was agreed in June 1999 by 29 European countries. It refers to 'easily readable and comparable degrees organised in a three-cycle structure (that is, bachelor-master-doctorate)'. The official Bologna Process website July 2007 – June 2010, http://www.ehea. info/.

28 *Uninews*, vol. 14, no. 11. The name and format of *UniNews* was changed to the *University of Melbourne Voice* in mid-March 2007.

29 G. Sharrock and G. Davis, *Growing Esteem: Choices for the University: A Discussion Paper that Invites Involvement and Response*, Melbourne: University of Melbourne, July 2005, p. 32, n. 1.

30 Jane-Frances Kelly's role is discussed further in a later chapter. She worked as a consultant to Vice-Chancellor Davis from time to time from late 2005 and had previously worked in the office of British prime minister Tony Blair as well as in the Office of the Premier of Victoria. From 2010, she holds an appointment in the Grattan Institute, an independent public policy think tank, of which the University of Melbourne was a founding member.

31 J. Cain and J. Hewitt, *Off Course: From Public Place to Marketplace at Melbourne University*, Melbourne: Scribe, 2004.

32 Information provided by G. Sharrock in a telephone conversation with Mary Emison on 10 June 2009.

33 The discussion paper may be found at this website: http://growingesteem. unimelb.edu.au/ under the subheading 'Publications'.

34 Sharrock and Davis, *Growing Esteem: Choices*, pp. 27–8.

2   Consultations and Outcomes

1   As advised by Michael Beaton-Wells in an email exchange on 3 March 2010.

2   In the United States, most professional courses (that is, law, medicine, veterinary science and so on) are available only at the graduate level and are undertaken after completion of a four-year undergraduate liberal arts degree. Graduate schools also offer research degrees and other non-professional graduate courses.

3   A description of the workshop is provided in Appendix 1 to the *Growing Esteem: Consultation Report*, Melbourne: University of Melbourne, 11 October 2005.

Those who attended the workshop and their positions in 2005 were: Professor James Angus, Dean of Medicine, Dentistry and Health Sciences; Mr Michael Beaton-Wells, Acting Director, University Planning Office; Mr Sean Cooney, Faculty of Law and Staff Association Representative; Professor Glyn Davis, Vice-Chancellor; Professor David Kemp, Professorial Fellow, Australian and New Zealand School of Government; Dr Kerri-Lee Krause, Centre for the Study of Higher Education; Professor Simon Marginson, Professorial Fellow, Monash University; Ms Linda O'Brien, Vice-Principal (Information); Professor Field Rickards, Dean of Education; Mr Geoff Sharrock, Office of the Vice-Chancellor; Professor Ross Williams, Professorial Fellow, Melbourne Institute for Applied Economic and Social Research and former Dean of Economics and Commerce; Ms Brooke Young, Manager, Marketing and Development, Faculty of Economics and Commerce.

4   *Growing Esteem: Consultation Report*, p. 46.

5   Ibid., p. 43.

6   The definition of knowledge transfer used in the final report of the Curriculum Commission (September 2006) was:

Melbourne's knowledge transfer develops intellectual capital through a two-way mutually beneficial interaction between the university and non-academic sectors with direct links to teaching and learning and research, and informed by social and global issues. The University of Melbourne's knowledge transfer is anchored in its intellectual capital, history and tradition, and a reputation for world-class expertise. The 'new generation' undergraduate degrees will have a new emphasis on knowledge transfer with students being provided with opportunities for international experience and greater engagement with industry and the community.

7   FEE-HELP is an Australian Government loan scheme that was introduced to help domestic students undertaking fee-based postgraduate courses at approved institutions meet the tuition costs of their course. There is a limit on the loan available over the life of the student. The total limit for the loan is dependent on the course studied. Courses are broadly split into medicine and veterinary science (the 2012 limit is around $112,000) and all others (the

2012 limit is about $90,000). The total limit is indexed at the start of each year. Eligibility for the loan is not means-tested but it is repaid through the tax system when an individual's income reaches the compulsory repayment threshold for all HELP loans a student may have had for their studies. In 2012, this threshold is about $47,000.

8   Growing Esteem – a paper provided to Academic Board meeting 10/05 on 24 November 2005 as Appendix A to the Vice-Chancellor's Report, p. 4 (UM USO).

9   Ibid., pp. 12–13.

10 Further comments on attendances at Academic Board meetings are made in Chapter 3.

11 Although it is tempting to suggest this statement was the source of the University's 'Dreamlarge' advertising campaign for the Melbourne Model, I suspect it was not.

12 Because the 12 December draft of this report is not readily available, I have used the November version for footnotes. This can be accessed through Academic Board papers (UM USO).

13 Minutes of Council meeting 11/05, held on 12 December 2005, item 9.1 Growing Esteem (UM USO).

14 Telephone conversation between Professor Davis and Mary Emison on 10 June 2009.

15 'Melbourne Shapes Up to Face the Future as a Rubik's Cube', *Campus Review*, 27 July 2005.

16 *Australian*, 16 November 2005; *Canberra Times*, 23 November 2005.

17 Email exchange between Jane-Frances Kelly and Mary Emison on 2 July 2009.

18 The Melbourne Experience Survey (MES) for first-year students was developed and piloted in 2007. The survey is conducted annually. Initial planning for the Eastern Precinct Student Centre began in late 2006, and the first phase opened in 2008. Renovation of the centre was completed early in 2010.

19 Telephone conversation between Professor Davis and Mary Emison on 10 June 2009.

3   The Curriculum Commission

1   The distinction made between academic and operational aspects is based on my own interpretation, rather than on universally defined categories. Others may have different assessments of the events, but I find the distinction allows a clearer understanding of the sequence in which decisions were made and the priorities of the various groups involved.

2   The full terms of references can be found in Appendix 1.

3   For further details of some of the matters discussed by the coordinating team and people or groups with whom they met, see Appendix 2.

4   When there was a change of government at the November 2007 federal
     election, the proposed research quality framework did not go ahead, and was
     replaced by the federal government's Excellence in Research for Australia
     (ERA) initiative in 2009.

5   The Melbourne Model Issues Paper Lorne 2005 was listed as agenda item
     2.2 of Curriculum Commission meeting 1/06, held on 10 February 2006
     (UM USO).

6   A definition of the Melbourne Experience is provided in Chapter 1, note 12.

7   In addition to her incredible workload as secretary to the Curriculum
     Commission, Gioconda also completed writing her PhD thesis and submitted
     it for examination in July. The result was available in October and the degree
     was conferred in December 2006.

8   Email correspondence between Professor Borland and Mary Emison on
     18 February 2010.

9   It would be of considerable value for the history of the University if at
     least some faculties wrote stories of their participation in the Curriculum
     Commission and in subsequent actions in implementation of the Melbourne
     Model.

10 The presidents of the Melbourne Undergraduate Student Union and the
     University of Melbourne Postgraduate Association.

11 Further communications activities associated with the *Growing Esteem:
     Strategic Plan 2006* will be covered in a later section.

12 Professor McPhee had suggested this change to Professor Davis as a more
     realistic objective and one that would help the academic community to focus
     on the serious policy decisions to be made.

13 These questions included: what were the pedagogical and practical
     reasons for moving to the Melbourne Model? Would there be required or
     recommended subjects to be completed at bachelor's level for entry to any
     professional graduate degree offered by the faculty? Were there accreditation
     issues? What were the faculty's expectations for a major in the bachelor's
     degree?

14 Professor Michael Bryan was the previous chair while Professor Jeff Borland
     was the current chair.

15 Until 1978, the prime academic body was the Professorial Board. The
     name was changed to take account of changes in the University's statutes
     that provided for members of academic staff, other than the professors,
     to become heads of departments and, consequently, to be members of the
     academic governing body – now called the Academic Board. *Keys of the Past*,
     Melbourne: University of Melbourne Archives, http://www.lib.unimelb.edu.
     au/collections/archives/exhibitions/keys/web/022.html#51.

16 Academic Board membership is the chancellor, the vice-chancellor, the
     deputy chancellors, the deputy vice-chancellors, the pro-vice-chancellors,
     the senior vice-principal, the vice-principal (information), the vice-principal

and academic registrar, the professors, the full-time salaried professorial fellows, the deans of faculties, the heads of academic departments, the heads of schools, the president and education officer of the Melbourne University Student Union, the president of the University of Melbourne Postgraduate Association, two members elected by and from the general staff, any other persons whom the board determines.

17 Further details of the role of the APC over the 2006 to 2008 period of implementing the Melbourne Model are provided in Appendix 3.

4 Pathways to Key Decisions

1 Email from Ian Marshman to Mary Emison on 20 July 2012.

2 Further details of the GETF and other funding sources can be found in Appendix 5.

3 The Headstart professional development program provided an opportunity for senior academic leaders in teaching and research to develop an understanding of the role of head of department.

4 *The Melbourne Model: Report of the Curriculum Commission*, Melbourne: University of Melbourne, 2005, p. 19 (UM USO).

5 Curriculum Commission meeting 10/06, held on 12 May 2006, agenda item 3.2 Revised draft of the Core Principles for Undergraduate Courses. The conditions associated with the proposed names of the degrees were: * a decision is to be made on a proposed 'PPE' degree: Bachelor of Philosophy, Politics and Economics; ** a decision is to be made on a proposed Bachelor of Human Biosciences degree pending decision on the move to graduate entry into the Faculty of MDHS; *** decision necessary on name; *** name of degree to be reviewed pending the move of courses at the VCA to the Melbourne Model (UM USO).

6 Minutes of Academic Board meeting 4/06, held on 25 May 2006, item 8.3 Implementation of Growing Esteem – Report from the Curriculum Commission.

7 Minutes of Academic Board meeting 6/06, held on 27 July 2006, item 5 Minutes (item 8.1) (UM USO).

8 Minutes of Academic Board meeting 7/06, held on 24 August 2006, item 8.3 Minutes of Academic Board meeting 5/06 (UM USO).

9 Minutes of Academic Board meeting 6/06, held on 27 July 2006, item 11.2 Entry Prerequisites for New Generation Undergraduate Degrees (UM USO).

10 *Growing Esteem: The University of Melbourne Strategic Plan 2006.* Melbourne: University of Melbourne, 2006, Appendix 4 Terms of Reference for major review bodies (UM USO).

11 Minutes of Academic Board meeting 8/06, held on 21 September 2006, item 11.2 PBC Working Group on Implementing the Melbourne Model (UM USO).

5 The Faculties

1 Quote provided by Professor McPhee to Mary Emison.

2 See Chapter 6 for details.

3 The first concurrent diploma was introduced in the 1990s in Modern Languages and was followed by Music and Mathematical Sciences. The diploma allows students to undertake additional studies in a designated area of study and hence expand their options for employment or further study in coursework, professional or research higher degrees. The diplomas require the equivalent of 100 points or one year of full-time study. Under the Melbourne Model, 50 of the 100 points may be achieved through cross-crediting of subjects.

4 See also later section on the Victorian College of the Arts in this chapter.

5 The Biomedical Sciences degree had been introduced in 1999 and was taught jointly by the Science and MDHS faculties. The course was administered through the Faculty of Science.

6 See Chapter 1 for a description of the VCAG.

6 The Curriculum Commission and Operational Matters

1 VICTER is published by the Victorian Tertiary Admissions Centre (VTAC) on behalf of the institutions that participate in its activities.

2 Membership of the Melbourne Model Taskforce was: general manager, Marketing and Recruitment Onshore, general manager, Marketing and Recruitment Offshore, two staff from the Admissions Office, the director, Student Access, and one representative from each of these faculties: Arts, Architecture Building and Planning, Science, Education, Economics and Commerce and the School of Graduate Studies.

3 Email exchange on 22 February 2006 between director of Student Access, Carmel Murphy, and Senior Vice-Principal Ian Marshman, and between Ian Marshman, Professor McPhee and Vice-Chancellor Professor Davis.

4 Minutes of Melbourne Model Taskforce meeting 2/06, held on 8 March 2006 (UM USO).

5 Email exchange between Mary Emison and Jane-Frances Kelly in June and July 2009.

6 Role of the Growing Esteem Strategy Office as given in *Growing Esteem Implementation Update* #19, 29 January to 9 February 2007, and published on the GESO website, although this is no longer accessible (UM GESOF).

7 As advised by Dr P. McLean on 21 May 2010, these meetings involved the Vice-Chancellor, the director of the Vice-Chancellor's Office, the Policy and Government Relations adviser, the Manager Corporate Affairs Unit (in the Marketing and Communications Division) and the Vice-Chancellor's speechwriter.

8 Email communication from Dr P. McLean on 21 May 2010.

9　Matins is one of the 'management' groups established by Vice-Chancellor Professor Davis.

10　The Teaching and Learning Performance Fund was a federal government initiative that operated from 2006 to 2009 to reward universities for excellence in teaching and learning for undergraduates.

11　Various names were used for this group with Melbourne Model Market Research Steering Committee being the most common.

12　Personal communication from Professor Peter McPhee to Mary Emison on 1 March 2011.

13　The Vice-Chancellor announced to the Academic Board in its meeting in March 2007, at which details of the six new generation degrees were approved, that he had received advice from DEST of its approval of the University's request to transfer Commonwealth-supported places from undergraduate to postgraduate.

14　For a number of years, the Academic Board's Academic Programs Committee had a reference guide, known as the Blue Book, which set out policy and procedural matters for the approval of new courses and major changes to courses. This book has been replaced by the Course Approval and Management Procedures (CAMP): see http://www.unimelb.edu.au/abp/camp/index.html.

15　Planning and Budget Committee Conference June 2006, Revised Index of Reports: A Discussion Paper for Implementing the Melbourne Model Part A and Part B (UM USO).

16　Final Report of the Working Group on Implementing the Melbourne Model in the Planning and Budget Committee Report to Academic Board meeting 8/06, held on 21 September 2006, item A.7(b), Appendix 2 (UM USO).

17　From a legislative basis, all courses are 'degrees of the University'. In this instance, the probable concern for the faculties was that a non-faculty body, the iBUGS, would *control* the undergraduate courses.

18　Final Report of the Working Group on Implementing the Melbourne Model in the Planning and Budget Committee Report to Academic Board meeting 8/06, held on 21 September 2006, item a.7(b), Appendix 2 (UM USO).

19　*Growing Esteem: The University of Melbourne Strategic Plan 2006*, p. 51 (UM GESOF).

20　Minutes of Shared Services Review Implementation Group meeting 9/06, held on 13 October 2006, item 4 Academic Administration (UM MMF).

21　Ibid., item 2.2 Action Sheet (UM MMF).

22　The VCAG action sheet refers to a 'Biomed Science' degree but, as indicated elsewhere, initial approval by the Curriculum Commission and the Academic Board was for the degree to be named Bioscience. The name was changed in early 2007, after a January meeting involving the deans of Science and MDHS agreed to 'Biomedicine', to avoid confusion with the Science degree (UM VCO).

23 This appointment seems not to have eventuated as alternative arrangements were made for the Deputy Vice-Chancellor (Academic) and the Senior Vice-Principal to have joint responsibility for overall management of implementing the Melbourne Model project.

7   Launching the Melbourne Model

1 Further details on the University's scholarship support for the Melbourne Model can be found in Appendix 5.
2 This decision had been taken in 2006 by the Faculty of Arts, partly for financial reasons to do with low student numbers. The faculty was reducing the numbers of subjects and majors it offered to deal with its budgeting problems as well the change to the Melbourne Model.
3 The KLD young scholars program is designed for secondary school students, who are nominated by their school and selected for the three-year program when they are in Year 10. Over the three years, the University organises activities that include visits to the campus to encourage and support a network and community of high-achieving students. It is hoped that a wider cross-section of students will be encouraged to apply for a Melbourne University course. Other scholarship programs were revamped with increased benefits at this time, including Melbourne Access Scholarships and Melbourne National Scholarships.
4 http://archive.uninews.unimelb.edu.au/news/4505/index.html.
5 *Growing Esteem Implementation Update* #22, May 2007 (UM GESOF).
6 Certainly, the advertisements continue to be used on television and in the print media, indicating that it has been a successful branding campaign.
7 University House is a staff club that provides dining facilities for its members.
8 A decision to close the Department of Creative Arts had been made some years earlier.
9 Chris Peterson, 'Students Disrupt Launch of "Melbourne Model"', *GreenLeft Weekly*, 21 April 2007, http://www.greenleft.org.au/node/37437.
10 From June 2007, the group was replaced by a marketing taskforce, which reported to the MM08. Further details of both these taskforces are provided in Chapter 8.
11 Final Report of the Working Group on Implementing the Melbourne Model in the Planning and Budget Committee Report to Academic Board meeting 8/06, held on 21 September 2006, item A.7(b) Appendix 2 (UM GESOF). Note that the appendices mentioned in this extract are not included here. The full set of recommendations is provided in Appendix 6b of this book.
12 Minutes of iBUGS 1.06, held on 29 September 2006 (UM GESOF).
13 By this time the future of iBUGS was caught up in the discussions, led by the Vice-Chancellor, on identifying the best organisational structures to support implementation of the *Growing Esteem: Strategic Plan 2006* and the

Melbourne Model, in particular, in the longer term. See Chapter 7 for further details.

14 This was a specific response to the student representatives on the Academic Board voting against the six proposed new generation degrees at the board meeting in March 2007. The main aim of the group was to explore options for Gender Studies, which the faculty had previously decided to discontinue as a major stream of study, and to advise the Bachelor of Arts standing committee on these in time for 2008. The working group met twice but its role was superseded by the Faculty of Arts curriculum review.

15 In August 2010, the University announced a change to the breadth requirement in the new generation degrees to take effect from 2011.

16 As reported in the minutes of the Bachelor of Arts CSC meeting 7/07 (held on 17 September 2007) (Joan Reese).

17 The discipline of Geography, which had been within a department of the Faculty of Arts, became a budget unit within the former Faculty of Land and Food Resources (now Land and Environment).

18 Other faculties could have made similar arguments.

19 Further details about changes at the VCA are provided in Chapter 5.

20 Personal communication from Peter McPhee to Mary Emison on 1 March 2011.

8 Following a Critical Path

1 Boston Consulting Group had previously worked with the University during the Penington era.

2 More information about this funding is given in Appendix 5.

3 The need to develop business plans was linked to the Growing Esteem Transition Funds for which Finance Committee had stated that allocations would be released only on condition that viable business plans were available (see Appendix 5).

4 Various terms were used to refer to the activities costing project but, in effect, the exercise was to ascertain faculty and central administrative expenditure on the delivery of services to students. This information would inform Boston's development of the MSSM and proposals for the cultural change to a student-centred services delivery model and, eventually, changes to the budgeting process.

5 The annual Administration Conference is led by the Senior Vice-Principal. Usual attendees were the vice-principals (now known as executive directors), their direct reports, most of whom are the heads of central administrative units, and faculty general managers or equivalents. Around 50 people attend.

6 This was the third such retreat held in 2006. See Chapter 6 for reference to other VCAG retreats.

7 These are listed in full in Appendix 7.

8   A table featuring the six workstreams, their substreams and the people in charge of them appears in Appendix 7.

9   Members of the MM08 Project Office listed in the initial MM08 Taskforce Terms of Reference were: Director of Integrated Administration, Director Melbourne Model Implementation, Manager GES Office, General Manager Administration and Director University Planning Office.

10 Although the intention was for the Head of Administration position to be short-term, from 20 November 2006 to 30 June 2007, the initial occupant, Liz Bare, held the post until her retirement from the University at the end of 2009. The University Council approved conversion of the position to continuing, with changes to the name and responsibilities in September 2007 as part of the structural changes. The rationale for continuing the position in its modified form may have been a result of the ever-expanding activities occurring in the University and, in 2007, the yet-to-be-completed implementation of the Melbourne Model.

11 Terms of Reference for the MM08, agenda item 2 in the MM08 meeting 1/06, held 21 November 2006 (UM MMF).

12 Minutes of MM08 meeting 1/06, held on 21 November 2006, item 2 Draft Terms of Reference for the MM08 Taskforce (UM MMF).

13 Professor Pattison, who was chair of the working group, advises that by early 2008 everyone was doing policy, hence the need to add 'academic' to the name of the working group.

14 Notes of the Policy and Procedures Working Group meeting 1/07, held on 24 January 2007, Terms of Reference. Notes as included as part of Workstream 4 reports to MM08 meeting 1/07, held on 1 February 2007 (UM MMF).

15 See http://www.unimelb.edu.au/abp/policies/index.html. The academic services policies may be accessed through the Academic Board website but are the responsibility of the Executive Director and Academic Registrar in the Provost's Office. To have a consistent set of the policies and guidelines accessible through one central website is a tremendous achievement. It is doubtful that this comprehensive listing would have been possible had it not been for the original recommendation of the Curriculum Commission for the University to have consistent policies and procedures for the degrees of the Melbourne Model.

16 Email exchange in August 2010 between Mary Emison and Professor Pattison, president of the Academic Board in 2007 and 2008.

17 See Appendix 5: Funding for the Melbourne Model for information about the GETF.

18 The members of the MM08 Taskforce and the Project Office would have been aware of, and probably directly involved in, discussions on the structural changes and the administrative reform proposals that were underway in the

lead up to the Planning and Budget Committee Conference. Consequently, the situation is interactive and/or circular: planning for the Planning and Budget Committee Conference feeds into the work of most standing committees and these committees know that forthcoming proposals are likely to impact on their operations and maybe also their structures. The uncertainty associated with these 'unknown' proposals tends to result in a level of unease for those involved.

19 Notes of confidential discussions on 28 February 2007 and 28 March 2007. I understand that these discussions involved the Vice-Chancellor, the Deputy Vice-Chancellor (Academic), the Senior Vice-Principal and the Director of the Vice-Chancellor's Office (UM GESOF).

20 Results of the first three of these surveys are covered in other sections. The outcomes of the fourth survey have not been located.

21 Those who participated in the survey were the Vice-Chancellor, deputy vice-chancellors, deans, senior vice-principals, vice-principals and their direct reports.

22 Recommendation A.1 Structural Change to support the Growing Esteem Strategy, Appendix 1 to the Report of Planning and Budget Committee meeting 5/07, held on 8 August 2007, to Council meeting 9/07, held on 10 September 2007 (UM USO).

23 Early terminology proposed for the physical venue from which student services would be delivered was 'hub'. However, this name proved not to be popular with students, who preferred 'centres'.

24 Although the Planning and Budget Committee's recommendations were not endorsed by the University Council until September 2007, the new Committee of Deans began to operate in July 2007.

25 Recommendation A.1 Structural Change to support the Growing Esteem Strategy, Appendix 1 to the Report of Planning and Budget Committee meeting 5/07, held on 8 August 2007, to Council meeting 9/07, held on 10 September 2007 (UM USO).

26 All-staff email, 21 June 2006 (Glyn Davis).

9 The Melbourne Student Services Model and Managing Change

1 MM08 meeting 2/06, held on 15 December 2006, agenda item 4.1. A vision for how student-centred services will contribute to the Melbourne Experience with the Melbourne Model: Outcomes from the Vision workshop (UM MMF).

2 Members of the University core team were: the Senior Vice-Principal; head of the MM08 Project Office; director of Student Administrative Services and three faculty representatives – one from each of MDHS (0.8 basis), Education (0.7 basis), and Arts (1.0).

3 Planning and Budget Committee meeting 5/07, held on 8 August 2007,

Report to Council meeting 9/07, held on 10 September 2007, Item A.1 Structural change to support the Growing Esteem Strategy August 2007, Appendix 1, Attachment 6 (UM USO).

4   The Senior Vice-Principal, Ian Marshman, has commented that the change management issue was made more complicated because of the recognition that the University's revenue would flatten due to the Melbourne Model, at least over the ten-year period of implementation. This resulted in a focus on cost containment and administration budget reductions of some $45 million over a three-year period. Comment on text received in an email on 7 July 2012.

5   Melbourne Model Implementation Taskforce meeting 12/07, held on 19 October 2007, agenda item 3.13 Implementing the Melbourne Student Services Model: Staff Transition Framework (revised 9 October) (UM MMF).

6   Membership of this group is listed in Appendix 4c.

7   Change Management Coordination Group meeting 3/07, held on 11 April 2007, agenda item 5 Memo to all staff and memo to Deans: Supporting Growing Esteem (UM MMF).

8   The name of the Academic Management Committee was subsequently changed to Academic Programs Management Committee. The Melbourne Experience Committee was a by-product of discussions about the 'Melbourne Agenda' held early in 2005 and questions about what defined the Melbourne Experience. A Melbourne Experience Working Group was established and converted to committee status in 2006. Its predominant role was to advise the Vice-Chancellor on meanings of the Melbourne Experience in light of research and student expectations and how the University might achieve these expectations. As the Melbourne Model and the Melbourne Student Services Model were developed, the Melbourne Experience Committee reviewed relevant documents and proposals and provided comment on them to the relevant bodies.

9   Membership of the new committees is listed in Appendix 4c.

10 Adoption of this philosophy resulted in the ongoing program of responsible divisional management (RDM) being initiated in the second half of 2008.

11 Melbourne Model Implementation Taskforce meeting 9/07, held on 3 August 2007, agenda item 6.1 Marketing Taskforce Progress Report, 31 July 2007 (UM MMF).

12 A proposal for marketing arrangements was approved by the newly established Senior Executive Committee in May 2008 (UM USO).

13 Change Management Coordination Group meeting 9/07, held on 5 December 2007, agenda item 7, Progress Report on change management associated with implementing the Melbourne Student Services Model (UM MMF).

Epilogue 2008–12

1 Minutes of Council meeting 2/08, item 8.5 (UM USO).
2 It is important to remember that a small number of the previous undergraduate degrees continued to have new student intakes between 2008 and 2010.
3 The University of Melbourne, Annual Report 2011 (UM USO).
4 The University of Melbourne Annual Report 2011 (UM USO) and Vice-Chancellor's all-staff email on 2010 VTAC offers dated 16 January 2012.
5 Statistical data provided by way of email attachments to Mary Emison by the University Budgets and Divisional Planning department of the University of Melbourne Finance and Planning Group (Mary Emison).
6 The University of Melbourne Annual Report 2011 (UM USO).
7 http://growingesteem.unimelb.edu.au/about/refining_our_strategy.
8 http://growingesteem.unimelb.edu.au/triple_helix/engagement.
9 See http://www.unimelb.edu.au/seniorexecutive/.
10 The Growing Esteem strategy proposed a ten-year time frame from 2006 to 2015 to develop and introduce the full range of changes associated with the Melbourne Model. Although the first cohort of undergraduates completed a new generation degree in 2010, many who proceed to a professional or other graduate program will not complete before 2013 or 2014, depending on the course they are studying.

Appendices

1 The objective of the Collaboration and Structural Reform Fund was to achieve better outcomes in teaching, learning, research and innovation by promoting structural reform and collaboration in the higher education sector. The structural reform was to involve large-scale change aimed at improving performance and the achievement of outcomes at individual institution level or across the sector as a whole. This program commenced in 2005 and was funded for three years.

The objective of the Workplace Productivity Programme, a competitive grants program that was announced as part of the government's *Our Universities: Backing Australia's Future* reform package in 2003, and commenced in 2006, was to encourage higher education providers to progress workplace reform that strengthens their capability to manage and implement workplace change. The WPP was intended to encourage flexible working arrangements, direct relationships between employers and employees and improved productivity and performance.

The details of these two programs are published in the Higher Education Report 2007, Australian Government, Department of Education, Employment and Workplace Relations (deewr.gov.au/HigherEducation/Publications/HEReports/Documents/HEReport07.pdf)

2   Extract from the Report of the Curriculum Commission to the Academic Board, 21 September 2006 (UM USO).

3   Extract from the Report to the Academic Board, 21 September 2006 (UM USO).

4   This is a revised version (at 25 January 2007) of a slide that had been included in the Boston slide pack sent with the 20 December 2006 commissioning letter to CPP substream accountable officers (UM MMF).

5   Vice-Chancellor's Report to the Academic Board, June 2007 (UM USO).

6   A number of staff would have argued that the consequences of the structural changes were far more than 'modest'.

Abbreviations

AB	Academic Board
ABP	Architecture Building and Planning
ACAG	Academic Connectedness Advisory Group
AD	Associate Dean
APC	Academic Programs Committee
APMC	Academic Programs Management Committee
AVC	Assistant Vice-Chancellor
AVC (T&L)	Assistant Vice-Chancellor (Teaching and Learning)
AVC (UR)	Assistant Vice-Chancellor (University Relations)
AWIL	Academic Women in Leadership
BCG	Boston Consulting Group
BUGS/iBUGS	Board of Undergraduate Studies/Interim Board of Undergraduate Studies
CC	Curriculum Commission
CEQ	Course Experience Questionnaire
CMCG	Change Management Coordination Group
CPP	Critical Path Plan
CS/CSP	Commonwealth Supported/Commonwealth Supported Place
CSC	Course Standing Committee
CSHE	Centre for the Study of Higher Education
DP	Deputy Principal
DVC	Deputy Vice-Chancellor
DVC (A)	Deputy Vice-Chancellor (Academic)
DVC (I)	Deputy Vice-Chancellor (International)
DVC (ID)	Deputy Vice-Chancellor (Innovation and Development)
DVC (R)	Deputy Vice-Chancellor (Research)
FGM or GM	Faculty General Manager or General Manager

GDS	Graduate Destinations Survey
GE/GES	Growing Esteem/Growing Esteem Strategy
GEMWG	Growing Esteem Markets Working Group
GESO	Growing Esteem Strategy Office
GETF	Growing Esteem Transition Fund
IMM	Implementing the Melbourne Model
KPI	Key Performance Indicator
KT	Knowledge Transfer
LFR	Land and Food Resources
MDHS	Medicine Dentistry and Health Sciences
MEC	Melbourne Experience Committee
MES	Melbourne Experience Survey
MM	Melbourne Model
MM08	Melbourne Model Towards 2008 Taskforce
MMIT	Melbourne Model Implementation Taskforce
MROff	Marketing and Recruitment Offshore
MROn	Marketing and Recruitment Onshore
MSSM	Melbourne Student Services Model
NG	New Generation
NGCAWG	New Generation Course Approval Working Group
OSVP	Office of the Senior Vice-Principal
OVC	Office of the Vice-Chancellor
PAT	Policy and Advocacy Taskforce
PBC	Planning and Budget Committee
PGCWC	Postgraduate Coursework Programs Committee
PGCWSC	Postgraduate Coursework Sub-Committee
PPE	(Bachelor of) Philosophy, Politics and Economics
PPWG	Policy and Procedures Working Group

RHD	Research Higher Degree
SEPSC	Student Entry Pathways Sub-Committee
SGS/SGR	School of Graduate Studies/School of Graduate Research
SPC	Selection Procedures Committee
SSRIG	Shared Services Review Implementation Group
SVP	Senior Vice-Principal
ToR	Terms of Reference
UMPA	University of Melbourne Postgraduate Association
UMSU/MUSU	University of Melbourne Student Union/Melbourne University Student Union
VCA/VCAM	Victorian College of the Arts/Victorian College of Arts and Music
VCAG	Vice-Chancellor's Advisory Group
VCE	Victorian Certificate of Education
VICTER	Victorian Tertiary Entrance Requirements
VP	Vice-Principal
VPAR	Vice-Principal and Academic Registrar
VP HA/US	Vice-Principal and Head of Administration/Head of University Services
VP (ID)	Vice-Principal (International Development)
VP (IS)	Vice-Principal (Information Services)
VTAC	Victorian Tertiary Admission Centre
WPP	Workplace Productivity Program

Acknowledgments

As mentioned in the introduction, the invitation to write this book came as a great surprise to me – but it also presented a challenge that was difficult to resist. The project has been even more challenging than I anticipated and it has provided insights into operations of the University beyond those I might have thought about as a full-time employee. I appreciate the confidence that Peter McPhee had in nominating me to undertake the project, for reading the draft manuscript at least twice, for providing context and for many suggestions that have enhanced the story.

There are many who have helped or given support to me in writing this story. Several of these are named in the text but some others also deserve mention: the Vice-Chancellor's Office for providing financial support for the project; Rosa Brezac (former staff member in the Provost's Office) and Julie Ciccone for assisting with office set-up; Peter McPhee and Joan Reese for giving me access to their emails related to Melbourne Model developments over 2006 and 2007; Leanne Dyson and Fiona McRostie (University Secretary's Office) for arranging access to various documents; Gioconda Di Lorenzo for appearing to be the one person in the University to have kept various documents related to development and implementation of the Melbourne Model; Marcus Robson (Infrastructure Services) for his knowledge of and ability to provide access to myriad electronic records (after the 'owner' had given his/her approval for such access); Sandra Whitty for reading early versions of the first three chapters and making invaluable suggestions about style and content; Ian Marshman for reading the manuscript while on annual leave and for providing valuable suggestions; and a wide range of academic and professional staff who provided informal comments about their experiences as well as words of encouragement that the project was important. I hope the story merits the support given. Special thanks to Ann Standish for taking on board the task of editor and for asking astute and pointed questions that have resulted in greater clarity in many sections of the book and for making the text more congenial reading.

Sources

Curriculum Commission papers, original meeting papers and related documents such as correspondence, media clippings and others (provided by Gioconda Di Lorenzo).

Davis, Glyn, Vice-Chancellor's 'all-staff' emails for selected dates (provided by Gioconda Di Lorenzo); personal communication with the author.

Deans and Heads conferences, some papers were available through various electronic sources or as hardcopy documents. Other reports/presentations were found as part of the documentation for various committees that would have received the items for information and/or consideration.

Emison, Mary, personal notes made by the author in 2006 of discussions in meetings of the Curriculum Commission or with faculty representatives or other groups; personal records for the Melbourne Model Taskforce (March 2006), the Melbourne Model Market Research Steering Committee and the Growing Esteem Markets Working Group; emails received and sent as director, Melbourne Curriculum Project

GETF reports, provided by Rebecca Riebeling (Finance and Planning Department).

Growing Esteem, Growing Esteem discussion papers, consultation report, strategic plan and the Curriculum Commission), currently available at http://growingesteem.unimelb.edu.au/ (this avenue of access is not consistent, because there are frequent changes in web page locations).

Master of Teaching funding, details provided by Elizabeth Capp (then Graduate School of Education, now Office of the Provost).

McPhee, Peter, emails relevant to the Melbourne Model developments and implementation, 2006–07; University calendar, 2005–07

Melbourne Experience Committee documents (MEC), loaned by Ronald Baird (Academic Enrichment Services Department).

Reese, Joan, emails relevant to the Melbourne Model developments and implementation 2006–07, particularly relating to course standing committees, and the Academic Programs Management Committee.

University of Melbourne, Growing Esteem Strategy Office electronic folder 2006–07 (UM GESOF) (accessed through the Vice-Chancellor's server) provided documents on the following:

- GE communications
- GE correspondence (from the GE Query Inbox and others)
- events (including open days and a 2006 events summary)
- Growing Esteem reports (monthly updates, reports to PBC and to council, on University structures, and others)
- GESO (media clippings, GESO structure, managing changes, and others)
- GE presentations
- GE review bodies (Boston, including pulse survey outcomes for March and August 2007; Committee of Deans; iBUGS meeting papers; Markets groups; New Generation Course Approvals Working Group; Policy and Advocacy Taskforce meeting papers)
- Vice-Chancellor's Growing Esteem consultations 2005 (submissions, emails, etc)

University of Melbourne, Melbourne Model folder (UM MMF) (accessed through the server of the Senior Vice-Principal) provided documents for the following:

- Change Management Coordination Group
- GETF bids/reports
- Markets Working Group
- MM08/MMIT
- MSSM implementation (more than 20 folders)
- MSSM Operating Model Project (Boston) (21 folders)
- PBC Implementing the Melbourne Model Working Group

- Reports to PBC, CoD, VCAG, etc
- Talks and presentations (33 folders)
- University structures
- Workplace Productivity Program

University of Melbourne, Records of formal committees, namely the University Council and the Academic Board and their committees, made available through the University Secretary's Office (UM USO).

UniNews, The Voice (formerly UniNews) Archive, http://voice. unimelb.edu.au/ and http://archive.uninews.unimelb.edu.au/ uninewsarchive.html.

University of Melbourne, Vice-Chancellor's Office (UM VCO): electronic copies of agendas and action sheets for management committees 2005–08, including VCAG, Matins, VC and Deans and others.

Index